THE HUMAN PARSON

THE
HUMAN PARSON

BY H. R. L. SHEPPARD
VICAR OF ST. MARTIN-IN-THE-FIELDS. HON. CHAPLAIN
TO H.M. THE KING

LONDON
JOHN MURRAY, ALBEMARLE STREET

First Edition	.	.	May 1924
Reprinted	.	.	. May 1924
Reprinted	.	.	October 1924
Reprinted	.	.	November 1924
Reprinted	.	.	October 1925
Reprinted	.	.	November 1926
Reprinted	.	.	November 1927
Reprinted	.	.	. May 1929
Reprinted	.	.	. July 1935

Made and Printed in Great Britain by
Butler & Tanner Ltd., Frome and London

PREFACE

THIS book will doubtless appear rather desultory and in many respects incomplete.

I have no wish for it to escape criticism, but I should like to say here that I am only too conscious of the gaps and unfinished statements that will be obvious to all who read it.

It represents the substance of lectures on Pastoral Theology delivered at Cambridge. I had hoped to re-write and add chapters on such subjects as Public Worship, Parish Work, Doctrine and Practice, but the circumstances of a busy parochial life have prevented me fulfilling my purpose. I send this little book out in the hopes that it may possibly help one or two who are thinking of being ordained to a fresh idea of what a parson's job may be.

CONTENTS

THE HUMAN PARSON

CHAPTER I

THE OPPORTUNITY

THERE are two incidents that often come into my mind because of their vividness. The first, in 1909, was on the top of a 'bus. On the afternoon of the day on which I was ordained a deacon I was travelling to my work in East London. There were two drunken working men as my near neighbours—the one had reached a stage that rendered him ferocious, the other was well disposed to a degree that was almost maudlin.

On catching sight of me the former remarked: "There's a —— parson!" but the other, full of genial intention, stopped him. "Now, George, don't blame him—it's not 'is fault. It's 'ard luck, that's what I says."

And the second was in September, 1914, in a hospital in France. I had gone to see a wounded officer who was dying of tetanus. As he turned and saw me, he exclaimed: "What the devil are you parsons doing out here?"

Of all the episodes that have happened to me since I was ordained I do not think any two have caused me to think more furiously.

After nineteen hundred years of Christian and Church history, the ordinary man (it is equally true of women) has no real conception of what a parson stands for or what our function is.

We are tolerated in the same way as a venerable institution is always tolerated in this country; for an innate reverence for what is quaint and old is one of its characteristics.

A procession of clergy on its way to a cathedral is to the crowd like the Lord Mayor's Show, entertaining but out-of-date and unreal; though, mark this, the one thing in the procession that is real to them—the carried Cross or Crucifix—they salute. In the heart of that crowd how much love or even awe is there? How much understanding is there of the things for which those clergy care most? If there is no contempt, there is at least profound indifference. They are not worth a cheer; far less are they worth molesting. Some would say they are even welcome as a caste, for how else could funerals or weddings or baptisms be done? Besides, have they not proved themselves admirably useful as official propaganda for the established order of things?

Here or there in the crowd is a man or woman who knows what we really want to be—but how few there are!

Surely Abraham Lincoln was right when he said that God liked " ordinary people " best because He made so many of them: yet how is it that to-day it is just these ordinary people who can think it " 'ard luck " that there should have to be members of my profession ? How is it that an officer dying in agony can wonder " what the devil a parson is doing in the midst of that hell " ?

Blame the ordinary people a little if you like —they may deserve it—but do not think of them as men and women who are hardening their hearts against God or goodness, or as people who have no respect or love for Jesus Christ. They are not saints nor would they wish to be thought of as such. But, on the whole, ordinary people are extraordinarily good folk with hearts of gold. No man who has lived with them these last nine years at home and abroad can doubt it. They have their faults and they have their virtues, and they are more ashamed of their virtues than their faults. They are lovable, humorous and kindly hearted. I do not think they are far from the Kingdom of God, but they do not know what on earth a parson stands for. Now and then they guess, and their guesses, which generally have to do with Sunday services, non-swearing, teetotalism and personal salvation, are very wide of the mark. On the whole they would suggest that we exist to try and make them unnatural now with a view to doing them good hereafter.

These are not clever guesses, but these ordinary people do not care for the clergy, and in proportion as they are uninterested they remain uninformed.

In whatever proportion we may decide to allot the blame as between clergy and laity, this fact is beyond dispute—the ordinary layman has but the crudest idea of the reason for our existence.

To make the true reason obvious by clearing away the débris of irrelevancies that makes it so hard now for men to know and choose the paths of righteousness, to know what are and what are not the essentials of Christianity in international, national, personal and parochial life and to get them known—these are among the high tasks that await a new generation of clergy.

Here is no plea for so-called popular clergy or popular religion ; the reverse will probably be the case. To those who give their lives to these and other tasks there will come from men no mild indifference, no complacent patronage. They will not court unpopularity, but it may often be their lot : now ecclesiastical authority, now Capital, now Labour, will be fearful and angry.

There will be, at any rate, an end to men's indifference, and with some hatred and fear will come, I think, much gratitude and love. That will be very much to the good.

My endeavour in this book is to show of what spirit the parson must be if he desire to interpret his profession in any compelling way to his own generation, and to suggest how that spirit may be applied in the affairs that claim so much of his time.

All this will be the more difficult because we are considering a calling more exacting than any other. There is something to be said for men nowadays not lightly deciding to be ordained. Bishops are wont to bemoan the fact that the Headmasters of our schools say that very few of their boys are looking forward to ordination. I am not at all sure that this is entirely to be regretted. No doubt, if the concern of the Church is still to plant some sort of a vicar and some sort of a curate in every parish in England, then, from the official point of view, the shortage of ordination candidates is appalling.

But I cannot help hoping that the new concern of the Church will be the careful selection of its ministers and their better training, not in efficiency so much as in morale ; that it will, in fact, be concerned with quality rather than with quantity, and that the time will come when the official mind will recognise that it is better for the souls of the people to shut up a church than to keep it open under the control of a man about whom even his best friends might say that he ought never to have been ordained.

I have sometimes wondered whether the people of England are not grossly spoilt in the facilities for religious services that are offered to them. I am certain it is so in large centres of population where nearly everyone can choose the kind of service, the kind of hour and the kind of parson that suits the exact condition of his religious leanings—perhaps we might read prejudice for leanings. It is different, of course, in the country, but even there one wonders whether it would not be immensely to the good—in spite of the alienation of present churchwardens—to serve and visit small villages from large centres, rather than to carry on the present system, which is certainly to the good in some places, but woefully to the bad in many more. If we could rid our minds of our English idea that, in order to keep religion alive, full Mattins and full Evensong must of necessity be said every Sunday morning and evening in every parish church, we should be more ready to face the problem of the staffing of churches.

I am well aware that the taking of services (with the exception of the Eucharist) is, or ought to be, one of the lightest tasks to which the clergy are called, but, subconsciously in the official mind and consciously in the mind of the ordinary layman, the prejudice against closing a church is the objection to not having Mattins and Evensong said every Sunday. Added to this there is a very prevalent idea that the Eucharist on a week-day or in the evening is not of the same value as on a Sunday or in the early morning. This makes it appear impossible to feed the souls of the people unless the parson can celebrate the Holy Mysteries at 8.0 or at 12.30 on at least alternate Sundays.

Why is it that so many clergy who are perfectly content to celebrate the Holy Communion in the afternoon (that is at 12.30, when the atmosphere of the church is at its worst and church-people tired after Mattins) raise hands of horror at the suggestion of an evening celebration at an hour distinct from the evening service and yet one most suited to probably sixty per cent of the parishioners ?

I have digressed in trying to make my point, which is that there seems to me to be a good deal to be said for the fact that men are not lightly offering themselves for the hardest life-task that anyone can undertake—the task that begins with ordination.

One does not have to be despondent about the future of the Christian religion to realise that there is a very real religious reconstruction taking place in the minds of many thoughtful people—this is not limited to the young. They have a larger conception of the things that Jesus Christ cared about and came to teach. He is as real to them—perhaps more so than He ever was—but they are less anxious to define Him. I should be inclined to say that He has become so real, so great, and so many-sided that they feel, however great the necessity, the total inadequacy of attempting to say in a document, long or short, just what He is, for man has no celestial language. They are glad to retain the capital H, and to leave their definition at that. They fear that the official demand for any definition, which of necessity must be but partial, will tend to deny such light as is breaking in on men who see Him from other sides.

The conception of the Jesus of history as being so much larger than his Church is making many a thoughtful parson and layman profoundly uninterested in some of the questions which seem of fundamental interest to the ecclesiastically minded.

It is possible to love one's Church passionately, and with an equal passion to believe in it, not perhaps exactly as it is but as it might be, and yet to feel that a great deal of its energy is at the moment being spent on work to which its Founder would attach little, if any, importance, and on the emphasising of matters which He might totally and even indignantly disregard.

What those matters are I shall endeavour to say later ; it is sufficient now to suggest that one result of the religious reconstruction to which we have alluded is to remind men, who desire whole-heartedly to serve God and their fellow-men, that there are other channels besides ordination through which they might give effective and unfettered service. This was not so twenty-five years ago.

Yet I am convinced that, provided only a man can capture for himself the spirit that is needful, there is no more glorious career and no greater channel of service than that which he may offer to God and his fellow-men through the Ministry of the Church.

To the man who has sought ordination primarily because of a desire to know God the Father through a greater intimacy with Jesus Christ so that more of His spirit may be released for the world's need, there will never come, without grave moral deterioration, any lasting regret for his decision, but rather, I believe, a growing sense of gladness that he chose the happiest, if the most difficult, of all professions. There will, of course, be hours of depression and painful realisation of but the poorest achievement ; occasions when the light that once seemed so illuminating is denied ; times of intellectual doubt and difficulty for all who insist on remaining in the true sense free thinkers ; periods of wondering whether the work is worth while and whether the Church itself is worth preserving. Yet beneath all these passing storms of doubt and thought, there will grow a steady, persistent and ever-deepening belief that, given the right spirit, it is all abundantly worth while.

When the numerous critics of the Church have had their say, there is much to be said on the other side. With all its faults the Church has always stood for Jesus Christ : sometimes falteringly, sometimes fearlessly, it has held up before the eyes of men the historical figure of Jesus Christ. The world knows of Him because of the Church ; His name and His life story are more widely known than those of any other man. Men and women do find God through and in the Sacraments of the Society that claims to be of Him.

The Church has constantly supplied, and is still supplying, the leaders, the ideals and the impulses in all movements for the betterment of life and for freedom.

It does with all its weakness stand for the value of each human life and the significance of the individual—it could not do otherwise when its Founder died for him. In short, in the words of Dr. Glover, words which I think might cover our branch of the Church :—

" With all its failures, confusions and omissions, it has been the Church of Christ, and one proof of it is that the Church has achieved new forms from time to time at incalculable cost, and has been glad to do so for the sake of making clearer the mind of its Master. Jesus was right in His comparison of the Kingdom of God with leaven. The life within has never left the Church in what it might call peace and He would call death ; there have been disturbances, upheavals, divisions ; Church history is not pretty reading, but the leaven keeps working. There has been, and is, a terrific dead weight of dough for it to quicken, but a little fresh warmth from the sunshine of God in the face of Christ, and the whole mass heaves together with the pulse of life ; the great ideas revive and Jesus triumphs."

I have seen it for myself when the Church in any particular place or parish has laid all its emphasis on Jesus Christ. It can satisfy ; its Bread and Wine do nourish, its fellowship does unite ; I know no alternative for offering Jesus Christ to ordinary folk. I know no society which has within it a larger spirit of Resurrection.

I have listened to all that its critics have to say and I agree with half of their criticism, and yet I am more and more convinced that the Church of Jesus Christ does possess the field in which the treasure lies, but alas ! the field is to ordinary people as a field of professional ecclesiasticism in which they are very unlikely to wander.

The Church because it is a living thing has unsuspected powers of readjustment without losing its life ; its death is not prophesied so easily now as it used to be, at least not by thoughtful people.

Many have tried to kill it ; it has looked easy, yet it has been found impossible.

" Sire," said Theodore Beza to the King of Navarre, " it belongs in truth to the Church of God, in the name of which I speak, to receive blows and to give them, but it will please your Majesty to take notice that it is an anvil that has worn out many hammers." That is a profound and, I believe, a spiritual truth, and although in my weakest moments I (possibly like you) have despaired of my Church, yet it is my most passionate belief, when I think and when I read history, that there are no heights to which it might not rise—if only it dared.

For myself I am prouder of nothing than that I am permitted to be a humble official of a Society that might save the soul of the world and bring endless joy to the hearts of mankind.

I know that to some the official actions of clergy who think as I do appear from time to time as disloyal to the letter of the Church's law, while others find it hard to understand how, holding the views we do, we are still content to use official forms which we earnestly desire altered and perform official ceremonies which have very little but good intention to be said for them. For myself I can only say that

B

wherever possible, in and sometimes out of season, I urge the most radical reform of many of the Church's ceremonies and formularies, and beyond that I dare to believe my Master will understand and pardon what seems insincere if He knows that the real purpose of my ministry be to make Him known and loved of men, and to do what I humbly can from within His Society to make it more worthy of His Presence.

This that I claim for myself, trusting in His understanding, I believe would help many a man to be ordained if he can feel as I do and claim the same understanding for himself.

Again, the most exhilarating experience to men in my profession is the ever-increasing proof that what they dared to hope on the eve of their ordination is actually and gloriously true, namely, that Jesus, the Master of the art of life, is indeed the satisfaction of a world of men and women—at heart incurably religious. Year by year this certainty increases. If one may so express it, He never misses fire ; He baffles often ; He eludes often ; He goes on ahead ; yet for those who ask and seek, He is not only the Way, but He is with them on the way ; we cannot fail to see this if we watch and pray as we must.

It is the lot of men in my profession to be used in the great planning of God. I believe we are allowed to help a little, to encourage a little, to love a great deal. I believe that we can by the very nature of our commission and communion feed the souls and bodies and minds of men to their Lord's satisfaction. I believe that we can enlist men for active service against all that is contrary to the mind of Jesus and hold them faithful in that service.

Finally, I believe that the function of the clergy in this great day is not to dogmatise, but to become themselves pilgrims with all thoughtful men on the road that leads to truth, walking themselves in such light as comes to them from the Cross on which their Master died for truth—and asking for further truth themselves.

Ours is a great life—rather, it may be a great life, but its strength and power depend not on an automatic authority laid upon our heads by episcopal hands, but in our own persistent attempt to know God as men's Father and to capture the spirit of Jesus Christ to this end and for the world's need.

If that spirit can be ours, then we shall be able to make plain to ordinary men and women why we are what we are, and what are the essentials of Christianity. Our profession is unique alike in its opportunities as in the Cross it offers and the joy it brings.

CHAPTER II

INTIMACY WITH JESUS

WE come now to our most difficult task —the endeavour to describe the one gift essential—that subtle quality which I have called the Spirit of Jesus. It is easier to recognise than to define.

It must be acknowledged that our weakest spot lies in the region of morale. If that was improving as quickly as our machinery, all would be well, but as a matter of fact it is not. It is unquestionably weaker. While it remains so, there can be no general progress. There are to-day, within the Church, a series of groups of men and women and a number of Churches, where the spirit of reverent experiment and progress in thought and action is not lacking, but there is little sign of advance along the whole front.

The authorities are alive to the need—they are indeed, as a whole, unusually progressive so far as men can go who have decided that, as a general rule, Statesmanship rather than Leadership should be their primary function I am not quarrelling with that decision, only recording it. Now and then, the Bishops, as a

whole, give a lead to their followers. Certainly,
we were told that after a great spiritual experience at Lambeth in 1921, the Bishops of the
Anglican Communion were led of God to great
decisions. We believed that absolutely, and
we rejoiced in the noble summons which they
issued to all Christian people. One may,
however, be permitted to ask why, when they
met organised opposition within their Diocesan
Conferences, not a few Bishops failed to stand
firm for the things that had seemed to them in
Council to be the direct leading of God. But,
as a rule, little Leadership can be expected
from Authority beyond suggesting a skirmish
here and there to people who are willing to
mistake a skirmish for a battle. After all, it is
immensely difficult to be a leader, and it is not
much good calling an advance if your followers
are likely to hold back.

It has been said, and I fear with a good deal
of truth, that religion which once went before
the human race as a torch showing it the way
in its march through history is fast becoming
an ambulance in the rear of progress concerned
mainly with picking up the stragglers who have
fallen by the way. This, indeed, is a useful
and a Christ-like work, but it is not merely for
this that the Church exists.

One test of morale is the spirit within the
Churches themselves. " If things are well with
the Churches," says Dr. Cairns, " they will be
full of the spirit of life and adventure, of experiment and adaptability." These things are, as
a general rule, conspicuously absent, as, too,

are others that are equally necessary, fellow-ship, reality, simplicity and, above all, perhaps the application of consecrated common sense to the Church's services. Men and women have some right to expect in their parish church what can only be described by that hard-worked word " atmosphere." They do not find there an atmosphere as if some great business was on hand. They do not catch hold of what they need to sustain them in the difficult and complicated art of Christian living. They find no real song of praise, no summons to high thinking and adventure.

I am afraid it is not far from the truth to say that all too often the most virile are finding what they have of passion for goodness and humanity more readily satisfied at League of Nations and Labour Meetings, or in the numerous Temples of new thought and theos-ophy, that would never have been raised had the Church's morale been higher. There is borne in on me the uncomfortable conviction that these people are not leaving the Churches because of what is worst in them, but because of what is best, because they cannot believe that a Society so cold, so lifeless, so faint-hearted, can ever be as a torch going before the human race to light it in its march through history. They have little use just now for an ambulance. I remember, as if it was yesterday, Father Stanton—of blessed memory—(and those who are likely to follow him in his Catholicism will do well to follow him also in his Evangelical love for souls) almost leaping into his pulpit at S. Alban's, Holborn, and shouting at a vast congregation, "Fire, Fire, Fire !" and then just when a panic was about to begin, he went on, "Everywhere, everywhere except in the Church of England as by law established."

I am well aware that I am giving a rather gloomy view of my beloved Church, but without facing the situation as it actually is, it is impossible to realise the great gulf which, please God, some of us may help to bridge between what might be and what actually is. But at the same time there is another side to the picture. Here and there in cathedral and town and village one stumbles upon the real thing as upon an oasis in the desert. Here you see how wonderful a thing the Church of Christ can be : a neighbourhood sweetened by the influence of the Church—a people whose hearts are aflame with the love of God, whose minds are stimulated to larger thought and Christian achievement. Life is actually nobler and cleaner under the shadow of those spires and the men and women who have come to love their Church and its Altar are actually putting a little more into the common stock of life than they are taking out of it. There is a definite religion at work there, though it may not be of the kind the word denotes to Church ears, for it is not limited to one complexion of churchmanship. It is as likely to happen in an Anglo-Catholic Church as it is in an Evangelical (I do not like these words of contrast, which never seem to me fair to either side, but I know no other way of expressing my meaning). It is still more likely to be found where the vicar would rather not be called either High or Low, he has a profound dislike for ecclesiastic labels, so people who don't know what is going forward call him vague, yet there the truths that are strongest and most beautiful on either side are welded into one irresistible appeal.

I have happened, too, on this reality in country villages whose vicars are engaged mostly in kindliness outside the Church. With all the will in the world they do not find it easy to talk naturally about the Master Who inspires them, with the result that they would be called unspiritual by that type of person, all too often earnest communicants, who find it easy to say who is spiritual and who is not.

What is the secret of this Wind of God which comes so often one knows not whence, and goes one knows not whither? It is easy to recognise it, but it is as hard to define it as it is to calculate its power. It is indeed inscrutable, incalculable.

What is the secret? I believe it is progressively revealed, and its power is progressively available, to those who are learning to lay more and more emphasis on Jesus Christ. That to Dr. Glover is the most striking and outstanding fact in history. " For those," he says, " who believe, as we all do at heart, that the World is rational, and that real effects follow real causes, and conversely that behind great movements lie great forces, the fact must

weigh enormously that wherever the Christian
Church, or a section of it, or a single Christian
has put upon Jesus Christ a higher emphasis,
above all, where everything has been centred
in Jesus Christ, there has been an increase of
power for Church, or community or man.
Where new value has been found in Jesus
Christ, the Church has risen in power, in energy,
in appeal, in victory. . . . On the other hand,
where, through a nebulous philosophy, men
have minimised Jesus, or where, through some
weakness of the human mind, they have sought
the aid of others and relegated Jesus Christ to
a more distant, even if a higher sphere—where,
in short, Christ is not the living centre of
everything, the value of the Church has de-
clined, its life has waned."

In my judgment, no truer words were ever
written. For us who desire a greater intimacy
with Christ that we may capture more of His
spirit for the World's needs, these words are of
the supremest importance. The secret of a
life that can be used of God will be sensitiveness to Jesus Christ. An attempted intimacy
with Him must precede every other consideration. He will be the centre—all else the
circumference. Without Him our belief that
God is love is by no means axiomatic. With
Him there can come that massive faith in God
and His goodness upon which His whole life
and death were staked.

In these tolerant days there is too great a
tendency to sentimentalise the life story of
Jesus. He is often presented as one whose

especial claim to our consideration lies in a nature that was extraordinarily kind-hearted. It would appear that His tenderness to prostitutes and outcasts was the basis of His claim on the world's attention. We all love that tender, understanding side of the Lord's human nature. What Jesus really did was to change the thought of mankind about God. Since Jesus lived, God has become another Being, and one nearer to man. He has become lovable. All through the centuries Jesus has been interpreting God to man—making the human heart larger, more human and more apt to get hold of God. He is our God. It is a measure of that Spirit we desire, and of that massive faith in the purpose of God to draw all men who are willing to Himself that we desire to capture for the world's need.

This is the reason for our attempted intimacy with Jesus Christ. That intimacy is first of all humanising—it allows us to understand human nature as we never did before. There comes with it a growing respect for every man and woman such as He had. We begin really to believe in men. As we see our function now it is not always to be teaching, upbraiding, admonishing, but rather listening and learning as the servants of men on their pilgrim way.

There will also come that amazing sensitiveness to man's every need that belonged to the love of Jesus. And we shall get from Him something of His genius for friendship and the instinct for what was essential. We shall know whom our poor human love can help, and what to stress and what need not be stressed, as we stammer out the message that we would give. Ours, too, will be that natural compelling love for the world's failures which made men and women happy in our Master's company even while they most feared His white-hot purity. And there may come to us some of that easy grace and spontaneity of spirit that can come to those who, like Him, have earned the right to speak in a Gethsemane of prayer—hidden from the sight of man.

We shall not discount humour in the Service of God—we shall not use jargon, nor many technical terms, nor tricks of oratory, nor flights of rhetoric, but we shall speak as He did in the dialect of the human heart. And yet at times there will be an echo in our speech of that passionate withering anger that burst from His lips, not when He Himself was insulted, but when the least of these little ones was offended or treated with less than mercy and justice. Only from a heart aflame with human love could such awful anger proceed.

Jesus will have become to us not the conclusion of an argument or a dogma or a legend, but a living abiding Personality nearer than hands or feet. He will be a Man, too—a carpenter—not a being playing at being a carpenter, but an actual carpenter—an expert in the art of actual living.

And all beautiful things will speak of Him as He speaks of God. Birds, trees and flowers, red sunsets. We shall not come to our fullest faith by " the grinding of general laws out of observed instances." Poetry and art and music will supplement our reasoning—instinct will sometimes carry us safely where intelligence is afraid to tread. William de Morgan describes, in a wonderful passage, the effect of a sonata of Beethoven on a man without special musical gifts or knowledge, in an hour of desolation and despair. It convinced him in its own way. It conveyed to him assurance which nothing else could convey, " I have ever since regarded the latter (Beethoven) not so much as a composer as a Revelation." How often have I said to myself after some perfectly convincing phrase of Beethoven, " Of course, if that is so, there can be no occasion to worry." It could not be translated, of course, into vulgar grammar or syntax, but it left no doubt on the point for all that.

If the mystical intuitions that come from art and poetry and music give more power to life, they must be welcomed as being among the things that lead to God. And any new light that comes into the world and is proved to be true, will be of Him, I believe. Again and again, it has been proved that the new science or the new knowledge or the new psychology that made the timid fearful because it seemed " dangerous " to the Gospel of Christ has nothing in it that was not implicit in the spirit of the Jesus of history.

But most easily will He be found in simple people and simple surroundings and homely things, and especially in ordinary bread and

ordinary wine, when two or three are gathered
together in His name.

And no one can be hopeless, for none was
hopeless to Him, and no one can be outside the
scope of His tenderest attention. (It is for
this reason that I would rather resign my orders
than ever refuse the Communion to anyone
who was willing and able to say, " Lord, I
believe, help Thou mine unbelief.")

We shall not be too interested in high specu-
lations and the arguments of contending schools.
Luther has something to say about this.
" Whenever thou art occupied in the matter of
thy salvation, setting aside all curious specula-
tions of God's unsearchable majesty, all cogitations of works of traditions, of philosophy, yea,
and of God's law, too, run straight to the
manger and embrace this infant and the
Virgin's little babe in thine arms and behold
Him as He was born, growing up conversant
among men, teaching, dying, rising again,
ascending up above all the heavens and having
power above all things. By this means shalt
thou be able to shake off all terrors and errors
like as the sun driveth away the clouds." Or,
again :

" Begin thou to seek God there where Christ
Himself began. He that without danger will
know God and will speculate of Him, let him
look first into the manger—that is, let him
begin below. . . . Afterwards he will finely learn
to know who God is. As then the same knowledge will not affright but it will be most
sweet, loving and comfortable. But take good

heed (I say) in any case of high-climbing cogitations to clamber up to Heaven without this ladder—namely the Lord Christ in His humanity."

If there be an intimacy maintained between Jesus Christ and us, Religion will become so much simpler than it used to be—so much bigger, but so much more real and universal. Yet all the while the Cross is there, but a Cross inseparable from joy, for as there is no real conflict between Jesus, the Man of Sorrows, and Jesus, the Man of Joy, so there need be none for us between our hours of sorrow and our hours of gladness, for " He who lives more lives than one, more deaths than one, must die." You cannot have the joy without the sorrow. So men who look to Jesus shall find, I believe,

> That one face far from vanish, rather grows
> Or decomposes but to recompose,
> Becomes my universe that feels and knows.

I will never believe that all this is mere sentiment and emotion. It is asking for all that is best and most strenuous in man. Nor can I for one instant accept the criticism that a religion completely grounded on the Person of Jesus, and on Him alone, can be vague or mystically unreal or disloyal to the Society which was instituted solely, so far as I can understand, to maintain a relationship of friendship and service between men and their Lord and Master.

I have tried here, all inadequately, to describe

that essential gift which I call the Spirit of Christ, which, if a man capture for himself and the world's needs, is as a joy and an offering beyond compare.

If this at heart be their real endeavour, that special urging that sometimes drives men even against their will towards ordination, then there are no barriers, intellectual or otherwise, that need hold them back, and there is no limit to what God might not choose to do through them.

If that be so, as it must be, so long as we can maintain by constant and disciplined thought and prayer and careful study an intimacy with Jesus which issues in the doing of His will, men will take note of us that we have been with Jesus and they will have no doubt as to why we are what we are, and what are the essentials for Christian living.

CHAPTER III

HIS VALUES AND OUR VALUES

LAYMEN expect the clergy to be almost perfect, and they are often bitterly disappointed. They are apt to forget that clergy can only be recruited from laymen.

The most careless layman looks for a very high standard in his parson, partly because he is still labouring under the superstition that the act of ordination removes a man, as if by magic, from temptations which are the lot of ordinary mortals, and partly because he does still believe (consciously or unconsciously) that Christianity can and should ennoble the lives of those who profess it. This latter is, of course, a tribute to our profession. The parson is watched and discussed with the closest attention, much more than he realises, and often by people whom he least suspects of being interested, since they do not attend church.

If intellectual doubt has slain the faith of hundreds, the moral failure of the clergy to live up to the standard which the layman expects has slain its thousands. The greatest religious difficulty of to-day is, of course, the unsatisfactory lives of professing Christians. We may well protest that it is little short of monstrous that the cause we stand for should be discounted because of our imperfections. We may point out—with a good deal of truth—how often men use our failings as an excuse for their own continued lethargy. Yet when all is said, it is well to remember the situation as it actually is, and to recognise that the vast majority of those who desire to investigate the claims of Jesus Christ will, as a matter of fact, begin with a very searching investigation of the lives of those whose main business it is to expound those claims. After all, it is not surprising that men who so frequently hear us declaring that Christianity does work quite extraordinarily well in the affairs of daily life, should look to us for a pretty vigorous practical demonstration. Every day there are those who are being led to or from Jesus Christ by what they discover in the workaday life of His followers and especially of the clergy. In one sense we can never be off duty. We cannot expect to plant the Kingdom of God anywhere unless it has first taken root very firmly in our own individual heart. This is, of course, a platitude, but we must beware of coming to think that what we lack in nobility of character can be atoned for by bustling activity or eloquent speech, or the correctness of our Church views.

" Lord, is it I ? " is about the most wholesome enquiry that we can make as we go to break bread with our Lord. It is beyond dispute the business of every parson to trans-

c

form his own life until—all unconsciously—it is capable of giving out the same kind of music that Jesus made in Galilee and Jerusalem. It is that music which still allures the world even while it fails to understand it. It is because it is so seldom heard that the world remains perplexed and dazed and life goes on songless and unsanctified. In passing, it is a strange thing to reflect that with all our shibboleths and professional jargon—with all the sickly and grotesque portrayal of our Master in so much of our modern speech and art and song—we have never yet succeeded in making Him ridiculous. The bitterest opponent of the Church has neither the inclination nor the opportunity of ridiculing Jesus Christ. We are never abused or laughed at for being like Him. We are discounted because we are so unlike Him.

Jesus, by universal consent, stands alone —unique, in history. Someone has truly said it would be a fault of taste rather than a blasphemy to bracket Him with the other great men of history. Dr. Glover has put it finely : " There is no figure in human history that signifies more. Men may love Him or hate Him, but they do it intensely. If He was only what some say, He ought to be a mere figure of antiquity by now. But He is more than that. Jesus is not a dead issue ; He has to be reckoned with still, and men who are to treat mankind seriously must make the intellectual effort to understand the Man on Whom has been centred more of the interest and the passion of the most serious and the best of

mankind than on any other. The real secret
is, that human nature is deeply and intensely
spiritual, and that Jesus satisfies it at its most
spiritual point."

That is our Master.

It is beyond dispute the business of any
parson to attempt to obtain something of the
Master's certain touch on life, and to practise
the art of living under His direction. The
world will be at the feet of those who are themselves at the feet of Jesus Christ—that is the
surest thing I know.

I do not think this will remain as un-
practical and mystic as it sounds now if you
will bear with me a little longer.

To me, the one thing of supreme importance
for men of our profession is, that we should
catch the spirit of Jesus Christ. It will be well
or ill with the Church of Christ in proportion
as we succeed or fail. That spirit moves upon
the world—it is available, but not in its fulness
without the most careful and disciplined thought
and prayer.

It is rather a dangerous thing to believe in
God—incredibly wicked and stupid things have
been done by men who thought themselves
inspired of God. What really matters is the
kind of God we believe in. When Mr. Studdert
Kennedy was asked what God was like, he
pointed to a Crucifix. He could do no better—
that is the Christian's answer. The Christian
God is like Jesus Christ. There are very many
professing Christians who have yet to learn
this. Their God, so it at least appears, is more

like Thor, or some Eastern potentate, than Jesus
Christ. Alas! many of the services of the Book
of Common Prayer contain passages which are
untrue in their representation of the character
of God, and are definitely un-Christian.

I doubt if anything like half the members
of the Church of England, or of any other
Christian Church, attempt to think of God and
His outlook on men and affairs in terms of
Jesus Christ. Our faith says, Jesus=God and
God=Jesus, but we have repeated that so often
that we have lost sight of its tremendous impli-
cations. The Church does not attempt to base
its life now on that fundamental of the Christian
revelation. Were it to do so, it would shed
many of its members, as well as its establishment, but it would conquer the world as easily
as that first little company of red-hot Christians conquered the might of Rome. Mr.
Chesterton is true—" Christianity has not been
tried and found wanting, it has been found
difficult and not tried."

The fact that God=Jesus Christ is the great
contribution of Christendom to man's age-long
search into the character of God. That is the
belief we must dare to stake all on—that and
no less is Christianity. It is this that is meant
to give the Christian his new scale of values,
his new outlook on men and affairs.

Yet it is hard beyond words to know God as
we would wish, for Jesus Christ is hard to know;
He is not to be known—in the sense that we
need to know Him—by a mere familiarity with
all that the Gospels tell us. They make us

eager, but they do not satisfy. They ask us questions as well as answer them.

It is not only by His spoken Word that men come to special intimacy with the Will of God. The " Come to Jesus " of the mission preacher is all too often but an invitation to a partial intimacy. He is not fully known in a mere comfortable reclining on His promises of comfort and consolation in adverse circumstances. Men, too, have brought their own prejudices with them as they sought to know Him, and have only found in Him what they were looking for—a revolutionary, a social reformer, a miracle worker, a physician, a kind-hearted philanthropist, an Oriental potentate, an upholder of the established order, and sometimes, apparently, even the first Anglican clergyman.

We have so often looked to Jesus to see what He was going to do for us, what miracle of mercy or fortune He was about to bestow, and so looking we have not seen. In our search for God as He is known in Jesus Christ, we remain blind until we have forgotten our own needs and hopes and wishes. Mr. Clutton Brock has pointed out in this connexion, that if a man goes to listen to Beethoven so that the great composer may do him good—cure his toothache, for instance—he will not hear Beethoven at all. This truth is supremely true about our Lord. We shall not be on the high road to any effective intimacy with Him until we seek Him for Himself. The story of the Syro-Phœnician woman has much to teach us. She brought her sorrow to our Lord, but, so

the story runs, " He answered her not a word."
Then she did the one thing possible, " Behold
she worshipped." She pressed through His
silence into His presence. Later she knew.
This is not easy—for most of us it is a big task.
It needs all that we have of disinterested and
disciplined thought and prayer, and even then,
in the evening of life, we shall still know how
little we know.

But curiously enough, all the effort is abundantly worth while, and we know it on the day
we begin.

Already there is enough light to move by—
enough faith to trade with. But it is the whole
of Jesus Christ that we seek intimacy with.
We want to know Him as He was on the road
to Emmaus, as well as in Galilee: as He has
been in history and in the experience of men
in all ages: as He is to-day still revealing the
mind of God on the sorrows and sins of a world
bankrupt through following its own will.

There is one thing, I believe, we shall soon
discover—His values are really our values, too.
The men He blesses are those we bless, too.
His desire for our world and for us are what
we—at our best moments—also desire.

He is not, as men so often think, interested
in laying down the laws of an arbitrary god
who has strange fancies and curious ideas of
morality. He wishes to make men natural—
not unnatural. He offers an overflowing
vitality. More and more, I believe, we shall
marvel as we come to see how practical was the
teaching of Jesus Christ. We shall find it to

be the amazing answer to man's most persistent and practical problem, " How can I, being what I am, become what I know I ought to be ? How can I live true to my own deepest and noblest aspirations ? "

The Church that is most faithful to its Lord will be mainly concerned in giving with power its Lord's answer ; it will be as practical as He was.   In such terms it will explain the Third Person of the Trinity—its sacraments and its dogmas.   But this discovery presupposes a " coming to Jesus " without any thought of personal advantage.   That is the one condition imposed upon those who would create and maintain an intimacy with Him.   It is the pure in heart (i.e. the disinterested) who shall see God.   It is our main business to see God through Jesus Christ and for His own sake. To me there is a certain quality of life that should issue naturally, spontaneously, through such adventures and through our profession.

In a sentence it will be a life of cross-bearing, but a life also shot through with human interests and the gaiety of a Franciscan joy. It is the part of a great artist to produce his talent without any apparent effort. . As one listens to the finished lecturer, or hears the great musician, one's instinct is to think how easy it is.   There seems to be no straining— surely anyone could do it !   We forget the hours of work and weariness, the periods of ceaseless work and practice that have achieved that finished and effortless perfection.   Artists do not speak of the Cross—they call it drudgery.

We are proud to call it the Cross. To us it is much greater than drudgery, and equally hard, but much more effective. When we talk of the Cross and cross-bearing and remind ourselves of the place it must always have in our lives, we surely mean a cross that once accepted and embraced, ennobles and creates—not a cross that restricts, cramps and represses. We mean that the Cross, which in one sense is disciplined drudgery, is far more powerful even than the midnight oil of the embryo artist, and its purpose the creation of artists in Christianity—among whom it is our business to be numbered. The Cross, like the Truth, makes us free—free to make the song of our Lord heard in the land. That song will be infinitely human, attractive, compelling and effortless because of its background which men call drudgery, but we call the Cross of man's radiance. If then the disciple can maintain a constant conversation with his Lord, the greatest of all gifts will be inevitably his. It will be as natural to him to love as to breathe.

There is nothing so distressing to watch, or indeed, to receive, as that kind of official love which is sometimes bestowed by the clergy, and more often still by church-workers, on their people—and especially on the poor. They seem to have determined that it is part of their professional duty to love, and so they love because they must.

They seem like those who are keeping a resolution, made that morning, that, whether they feel like it or not, the people shall be loved that day, say from half-past two to a quarter past five, and that resolution is being kept against all comers. May we for ever be preserved from loving officially. I wonder whether this attitude is responsible for the fact that " dearly beloved brethren " which ought to be very real is so often made a butt, for human official love deceives no one. It wins no answering response—how could it ? It is altogether unlovely. It has its own set smile, its own unctuous greeting, its own familiar phrases, it is turned on and off conventionally It leaves no impression of real love—it rings false.

But love in its highest manifestation is the richest, most persuasive, loveliest, nicest thing that God has to offer—it is the only weapon we need.

It is full of understanding—it knows how easy it is to sin, how difficult to live nobly. It sees with the eyes of those it loves. It never makes quick, harsh judgments. It gets to the heart of a situation as nothing else. It thinks in terms of men and women and children, and never in terms of " hands " or statistics. It prefers to give itself to the individual. It shuns expression on public platforms. It has no ulterior object except to serve. It would gladly lead if it could—it would never drive. It asks nothing for itself, but it is human enough to long for love in return. It knows when to speak and when to be silent, when to be patient and when to be impatient. It is at home with all sorts and conditions of men and

women and children, and it makes them laugh,
for it has a real vein of humour. It gives and
gets a joy in loving. It believes in all men and
women. There is no such word as " hopeless "
within its vocabulary. It feels ; it is sensitive
to the moods of all to whom it is given. It is
never clumsy, and yet it often steps in where
angels fear to tread. Perhaps its greatest
characteristic is its power to understand. It
anticipates man's needs ; it can see a situation
sometimes before it occurs ; it has an almost
superhuman instinct for what ought to be done
and how to do it. It knows what is in the heart
of man. It is not always declaring itself. Like
all creative forces, its best work is done in
quietness. It prefers action to speech, it would
prefer to visit someone in want to making any
oration on fellowship. It likes best to do small
things that no one else has seen need doing. It
sees sorrow where sorrow is thought to be
hidden, and virtue and grandeur where it is
least expected. It is for ever on the watch for
those who need it. It runs to give itself as the
father ran to the prodigal child, not because
he pitied, but because he couldn't do without
his son. It washes the disciples' feet as He
did because it wants to—not because there is
a lesson in humility to be taught. It is like a
window through which can be heard all the
cries of the market-place without. It knows
no barrier of rank or class, of creed or colour.
It overflows the boundary of its own denomina-
tion—no official channels can hold it entirely.
It flows, perhaps, most tenderly to those who

never enter church, and care little for the love
of God. It sees the crown of their need on
their foreheads and longs to be of service.

It is always courteous, especially to women.
It knows that He Who is Love had a Mother ;
it recognises that, save for the faith and moral
courage of women, it would indeed have gone
hard with His Cause. It suffers no slighting
things to be said of them. It respects them too
much. It grieves and is silent when they fail.
It is courteous—this Love—to older people
and quite young people, too. It likes them to
say what they feel. It enters a slum dwelling
with as much respect as it enters the lordly
mansion. It could not patronise if it tried—it
understands too much. It is generous, yet
strong in controversy. It seeks to win without
wounding—it never descends to personal
abuse, or bitter speech. It is sometimes angry,
for there is nothing sickly or sentimental about
it. It is never shocked. When it is angry it is
because another is hurt—in soul, or mind, or
body. It knows nothing of jealousy—it rejoices
in another's success. It is never petty or mean.
It has all things in their right proportion. It
is ever seeking to disentangle itself from
irrelevancies.

It learns more in listening than in speech.
It is never sarcastic, for it knows that by such
means no soul was ever won. It is the property
of no clique—it wears no ecclesiastical badge.

It cares nothing for its own status—there is
nothing professional about it. It is not always
trying to buy up the opportunity, to point the

lesson, and draw the moral. Above all, its faith in God is massive. It is confident always that in the end darkness must flee before the light.

This love which comes of God through Jesus Christ is the one weapon we need. If we who are to serve in the Society of Christ could possess it from a constant conversation with our Lord, we shall not have lived in vain.

Men who see it will know from whence it comes, and they will give praise to God Who can do such great things. They will also know why we are what we are and what are the essentials of Christianity.

CHAPTER IV

WORKING IT OUT IN DAILY LIFE

WE come now to the parson's actual work which we have seen demands a certain spirit. Our work is many-sided—there is no boundary to it. That makes it very interesting and very difficult. It is not what it is commonly supposed to be. It is thought by most people that we are busy at Christmas and Easter and on Sundays, and then pretty free for the rest of the year. Sunday is spoken of as our " busy day," and people who make polite conversation to us around the Festivals usually suggest that " of course, this is your busy time." As a matter of fact, for the parson who is trying to do his job, the Sundays are easier than the week-days. Week-days make larger demands, and they count more. Every day in the week there is the same need of a high morale. We must be as fit as we can for the work in hand. We must make the right sort of beginning to the day. For us, it consists in a contemplation of our Lord. When we were children we were told to let our first and last thoughts each day be about our Lord. We seldom did it, except sometimes in the evening when we were frightened of the dark.

It will be well if we can begin now to make that recommendation a practice. We shall make it more definite, so that it has psychological as well as devout significance, by attempting to fill our minds with the thought of God's power and of our power through Him to know His Will and to do it. We shall think how that could affect the tasks that we have to do, and what difference it ought to make to our own personal life and our relationship with the people who touch our life. We shall determine with God's help not to live that day below our maximum; not to tire when we need not tire; not to fail when we need not fail; not to be fearful where no fear is. It will sometimes help very much to choose some passage from the life of our Lord, like, for instance, the story of the blind man appealing to Him for succour, and to let the whole scene get hold of our mind. Quietly and without strain we shall build up the picture in our mind's eye. There is our Lord passing by, and there is humanity coming to Him, only half-believing, yet hopeful. Then with equal simplicity we shall become the blind man and Jesus the same Jesus yet God, and we shall tell how we wish to be altered and healed, and then we shall *know* that He is able, and later we shall find how true it is. And then the world of men we know will become in our thoughts as the blind man, and Jesus will do with them as with us, and so we shall begin our day with a sense of the power and love of God pressing upon the world, Jesus of Nazareth still passing by.

And then there will be our prayers. No one
can tell another exactly how he ought to pray,
but there will be the lifting up of ourselves and
our friends to God. Prayer for us will not be
a series of acts finished and completed each
day at certain times. There must be, of course,
times of disciplined prayer, but we shall
endeavour to deepen the whole idea of prayer
until it becomes a constant attitude—independent of prayer-desk or bedside—of being sensitive to God. It will become natural to talk
reverently to God through Jesus Christ about
every single thing that our sense of fitness tells
us is worthy of His attention. And often we
shall speak to Him about Himself, thanking
Him for what He is, and for the hope and
gladness that He has given. I think that when
possible it is best to make our regular prayer
in church, or at least, in some room where
quiet is guaranteed and there is some picture
of our Lord, or a Crucifix. It tends to help us
in control and concentration. The danger of
the new and, I believe, the true conception of
prayer is that we are more likely to star-gaze
than to agonise. We love to think that our
prayers are at their best under the blue sky,
or on a 'bus, or in our own home. There are
rare souls about whom, no doubt, this is true ;
but for most of us who are human, it is not.
" Blue domers," as a rule, are too much distracted by the blue sky to pray, and those
people who say they do not hold with church,
they prefer to worship in their own home, are
usually too much distracted by the noise and

cares around them to worship at all. The ideal is, I think, that we should grow to be independent of our surroundings, but most of us have not reached that stage. St. Augustine, in a rather delicious confession, tells us how his prayers may be disturbed if he catches sight of a lizard snapping up flies on the wall of his room—certainly mine would be. I am sure it is best to say the bulk of what I would call our organised prayer in some place like the church, or in some corner of a room that is arranged specially for the purpose.

When we do go to church, either for public or private prayer, it is entirely essential that we should arrive at the time we decided overnight. I think it is unpardonable for us to make a habit of being late when we either conduct, or are present at, a church service. One of the most dangerous temptations attached to our profession comes from the fact that we are, to a great extent, our own master—the keeper of our own time-table. We badly need supervision when we are young. It is of the utmost importance that we should expect from ourselves the same punctuality as the most exacting business man would expect from his junior clerks. Inertia, laziness, over-indulgence in sleep and slacking are simply soul-destroying to any parson. I am sure it is well that we should make the most stringent rule to be in church at least five minutes before any service, at which we are to officiate or at which we are to be present, is timed to begin; and this rule, especially with regard to the Holy Eucharist, ought, if possible, never to be broken. If it is positively indecent, as I think it is, to arrive panting, breathless and late for public worship, it is equally indecent, to my thinking, to arrive untidy and (in the early morning) unshaved. We are not expected to be smart, but at least we can be clean, and it seems to be monstrous that we should be less tidy at the Altar than we should be in a friend's house; but I am afraid it is not unknown for a man—who might think it very wrong to indulge in an early morning cup of tea—to be celebrating the Holy Mysteries within ten minutes of being called. When this happens, morale is at its weakest. These things count more than we realise. Decency and order are not to be confined to the performance of ritual—untidiness and slackness mean something is wrong.

It is thought nowadays rather out of date for the clergy to read (unless at public services) their morning and evening office. For myself, I only know this, that I am more alert for the tasks in hand, more responsive (I think) to the leadings of the Spirit when I am constant and regular in the performance of this disciplined control. But let me frankly add that I often make alterations in the office—changing, for instance, the first lesson and refusing to read those psalms that express a perfectly heathen delight in a god who—so far as I can see—has no relation to Jesus Christ. I never will repeat in public or in private such a sentence as " Blessed is the man who taketh the children and dasheth them against the stones." Such

D

words represent so primitive a form of morality as to appear to express perfectly immoral sentiments : it seems unutterable humbug and nonsense that we should be advised to give it " a spiritual interpretation." But having said all this, let me make an old-fashioned plea that the clergy should read every morning and evening, unless prevented by some work of mercy and charity, the amended offices of morning and evening prayer. I cannot, however, recommend the practice of a friend of mine whom I caught one night reading in succession the offices for the four preceding evenings which he had neglected.

It is impossible to overstress the importance of intelligent study. We must read and not merely live in the neighbourhood of books We must be intelligent as well as zealous. We are constantly giving out, and our givings will become painfully thin and weak unless we are constantly refreshing our minds at the best sources of knowledge. Sidney Smith once said that he would rather meet a roaring lion in a narrow path than a well-intentioned man who was ignorant. We must at least be as well informed as the average intelligent layman, and no parochial activities can excuse a mind barren of thought and a study table which holds nothing heavier than a book of " Little Sermons for every Sunday in the Christian Year."

If we could aim at knowing the text of the Bible as well as, say, our forefathers knew it— the New Testament well enough to quote, the

Gospels well enough to catch the whole spirit of Him who pervades it—we shall do well enough to go on with.

We have to know the faith we hold, constantly to reconstruct it in the light of new and approved knowledge, and we have to lay it before our hearers in a form both intelligent and recognisable as the result of much fair thinking.

There are words of Bishop Gore in the first volume of his book, "Belief in God," which we might do well to lay to heart. He is talking of the revision of religious belief that is now going on in men's minds. "There is no class for whom this process of fundamental reconstruction of their beliefs is so necessary as for those who are, or are preparing to become, ministers of the Christian Church. They are often enthusiasts for religion, who have no personal doubts, but are eagerly interested in a great many questions, doctrinal and ceremonial and social ; and their temptation is to take up the questions that interest them, which are secondary and derivative, and not really to study and test their foundations. Very likely they will themselves experience reactions and fall into fundamental doubts later in life. Certainly, if they are to be true to their high vocation, they will be constantly occupied in helping others who are in doubt. In either case they will find themselves paralysed if they have never explored their foundations. It is only those who know, from the ground upwards, what they believe and why they believe, who can help either themselves or others in the time of stress. It is only those who are felt to have a real ground for their beliefs and a real sympathy with free enquiry whose help will be sought by those who need it, and it is pitiful to see how many there are among the professed ministers of Christ who, in an hour of popular discussion of some vital truth, are proved, by their perplexity and dismay, or by their uninstructed denunciations, never to have thought at all seriously or deeply about the most momentous questions."

This is not merely a process to be undertaken by those who are about to be ordained—it is to be continued throughout life.

It is essential that we should endeavour to know the thought of the most stimulating minds, and not only those who are, or have been, orthodox in their religious views. All exclusive preoccupation with one kind of mental activity, whatever it be, is a specialising of the mind, which tends to narrowness. We shall be debtors to the Greeks and Barbarians. We shall not think it a waste of time to read one novel a month, and it may even strengthen our sanity to have a Jane Austen or a John Buchan by our bedside. We shall read as much as we can on social matters, for the problems of poverty and unemployment and bad housing will be permanently on our consciences, and we shall realise that knowledge in these matters is as necessary as zeal. We shall beg, borrow or buy all that is written by Inge and Gore and Studdert Kennedy. They make a hotchpotch which is quite digestible and most exhilarating. For papers and magazines : if we can afford " The Times " we will supplement it with " The Daily Herald," if not we will read " The Manchester Guardian," which is surely the penny daily with the highest tone, and which needs least supplementing.) The old colonel who comes to church will let us read his " Spectator," and the young artist who does not can be persuaded to send us " The New Statesman," or " The Nation " a day or so late, and I suppose we ought to read one Church paper to know what is going on. There is a difficulty here, for the one that is most " newsy " is not very Christian, and the one that is most Christian is not very "newsy."

If we keep abreast—so far as we can—of new thought and new knowledge, we shall, I think, marvel to discover that when new light comes into the world which at first seems "dangerous" to the gospel of Christ, it is soon to be discovered that there is nothing in it alien to the Spirit of the Jesus of history, and often, as is the new science of psychology, we shall find what is now new was implied in the teaching of our Lord.

But a caution is necessary—not every new and popular cry, nor every new scientific statement is of God ; while it is certainly our business to cross-question with great frankness traditional religious belief, it is equally our duty to do the same to the current dogmas of contemporary intellectual thought.

There are many who reject what is old simply

because it is old, and accept what is new simply because it is new. Neither the oracles of yesterday nor of to-day are necessarily of God. In the sphere of religion that means that we have no more right to impart verbal inspiration to Dr. Streeter than we have to St. Paul.

But above all, in our reading, we shall endeavour, I hope, to steep our minds in books such as come notably from Dr. Glover, that bring before us so vividly and with such intellectual force the Jesus of history and the Jesus in the experience of men. Why is it that we have no Anglican writers who compare with him in presenting us with the things that really matter? Our most intelligent authors are most concerned in proving the case for the Church, or attempting to reconcile different points of view. These things are secondary.

We shall not, I think, be very much interested in books of so-called Christian apologetics (I wish the word " apologetic " in connexion with Christianity could be abandoned once and for all). I used to read them very carefully before going to speak in the Park. They very nearly undermined my faith. On discovering that not a single question which they professed to answer was ever asked at question time in the Park, I was happily released from any further obligation to read them.

The man who writes Christian evidence seems, as someone has said, to be like the ladies in " Cranford," who put newspapers on the carpet to keep the sun out, and then had to move the newspaper in half an hour's time.

We shall also, I hope, burn and banish from our library those little *vade mecums* of the " full faith " that profess to explain the whole of God and His every purpose in fifty pages which include a preface by a Church dignitary. I am as fearful of those books getting into the hands of the ordinary intelligent layman as I am of his seeing the ordinary parish magazine. The preface to these little books generally pronounces them as eminently suitable for those about to be confirmed. To my thinking they are eminently unsuitable. I am afraid that the book suitable for those about to be confirmed has yet to be written, at least, I have not discovered it, though I have searched diligently for the last ten years.

While I am on the subject of literature, allow me to make a suggestion to those who are wont to publish their sermons. The sermons of some people (Dr. Temple, for instance) are well worth a large public, only there is no large public now willing to read sermons. If only those same sermons could be published without their opening text and under some title, like Essays in Christianity, there are many who would read them who are now prejudiced against reading them in the form of sermons.

So much, then, on the general subject of our reading. It is of the greatest possible importance. We must be able to hold our own in the pulpit, or in the smoking-room. To boast, as many clergy do, that they have no time to read is tantamount to confessing that they have their whole life's work in wrong proportion, and are neglecting one of the primary duties attached to our profession.

I am not speaking in ignorance of the overwhelming cares and duties that crush parochial clergy. I have had my full share of those for nearly fifteen years, but I am convinced that we must find time somehow for our reading. There are days, of course, when the reading has to go by the board in answer to some human need that arises, but it should go with the greatest reluctance. In the years in which we cease to continue our education, we shall have very little to offer to anyone, and that of the thinnest description.

I hope our sense of what is fitting will also persuade us to use our study table for a task at which the clergy are not always at their best. There is no reason for our being careless in dealing with our correspondence. To leave letters unanswered day after day is indefensible. I am afraid it would be true to say that if a Rural Dean were good enough to send an invitation to breakfast to the clergy of his deanery, quite a considerable number would be guilty of the discourtesy of not even sending him a reply This extremely bad habit comes, I fear, from want of business training and proper business supervision at the beginning of our career. One is sometimes tempted to wish that the Bishops would insist on every ordination candidate spending at least a year in some secular work. And the carelessness is not limited to correspondence. It is often very conspicuous in the way we handle the finance entrusted to us. Men who have never had a dishonest thought in their minds have dealt with money with what can only be called criminal carelessness. I am afraid there is something amiss—some symptom of decay in the character of people who are casual and careless in dealing with their letters and other people's money, and surely we ought to be above reproach in these matters.

I do not think it is realised, either, how much help and encouragement can sometimes be sent through the medium of the postman. If you look into your own memory you will probably find that the encouragement, or the comfort, that some letter once brought is amongst your most cherished possessions. A letter to some-one going through rough times, or far away or starting a new work, or a birthday or an anni-versary remembered, are amongst those signs of human interest and affection which I think should come from the love of God—no one is too busy to think out acts like this, so simple and yet so grateful to those who receive them. It is generally the busy people who write them.

Very many hours in your working life will be spent in seeing, or what is called interviewing, people. There is no work which more needs the grace of God. There are four things essential :

1. That you should pray before the interview ;
2. That whoever comes should feel they are
   coming to someone who is human ;

3. That you should listen more than you talk ; and,

4. As important as (1), that you should genuinely expect that whoever is coming has got something to offer you.

Let me say a word on this fourth condition. If we are going to regard everybody who comes to see us as someone who is coming to be benefited by us, we shall not only be incapable of assisting, but we shall soon lose any human freshness we possess. Unless and until we can really feel that God is as likely to send that man or that woman to us for our sakes as well as theirs, we are not in a fitting condition to be of service. Let that prayer that is said before they come be a request that you may be able to learn your lesson and help as well. When people become " cases," or " patients," we cease to be in touch with them ; when they come as messengers we can get our message and sometimes give one in reply.

One so often hears the clergy saying, " So-and-so, who is in hospital, wants to see me," or " So-and-so, who is out of work, needs me." How seldom is there any idea of the lesson that may be learnt from the man in hospital, or the courage and patience that the man out of work may have to teach.

Above everything else, do let us remain humble and genuine. We are not infallible, not even the youngest of us. Our advice may often be wrong, therefore we will not give it easily, but we will, as fellow-pilgrims with other men who seek the light, welcome all who come to us, pray for them, listen to them, learn of them, and, please God, give them something of ourselves besides. We must be very careful that we do not lose the art of listening as all men who talk much and easily are tempted to do.

The great men in Church and State are commonly supposed to be the men who do most of the talking. The few really great men whom I have met are distinguished chiefly by their power of listening. We are not likely to fail in our desire to be of service if we can cultivate the much-neglected art of listening.

At all times, and especially at times of controversy, the gift of listening must go hand-in-hand with that of the open mind. I hope we shall never be guilty of the sin of Caiaphas, which was that of the closed mind. Caiaphas was chiefly reprehensible because he would not listen. When truth came before him, he shut his ears and refused to listen. This is a terrible state of mind, but one that is not altogether uncommon. There is not lacking a certain type of clergy belonging to different schools who are united in nothing except in shouting " blasphemy " when something that men say is the truth comes before them for judgment It is not necessarily our business to accept what others say as true, but it is our business to give it attention and the respect that is due to any opinion to which men passionately cling.

May the Lord preserve us from the sin of the closed mind.

A great deal of our time will be spent in

visiting those who live in the parish or district to which we are attached. It is a delicate business and needs all the grace we can summon to our aid. One generally returns from an afternoon's visiting in a more cheerful state than on starting out. Our welcome is uncertain. As in interviewing so in visiting. If we go ready to confer benefit, we had almost better remain at home for all the good we shall do. If we go with a genuine desire to enter into the cares and experience of those who live under the shadow of the church we shall not go in vain.

The object of visiting is not to make the docile more docile, but to become acquainted with everyone who is willing to know us, so that, in any hour of need, they may care instinctively to turn to us for spiritual assistance, or indeed, assistance of any kind ; but we are not relieving officers, and except in very exceptional circumstances in visiting, we do not deal with financial appeals. We are commissioned for the stupendous task of presenting every man perfect in Christ and standing for righteousness and social justice in the area where we work. The magnitude of our task should certainly keep us humble. We are to be known by all who are willing to receive us, rich and poor alike. We have no business to miss out certain houses as not being suitable for visiting. Why, for instance, pass by the public-house ? Publicans are often capital fellows from whom we may learn a great deal. Their children are usually particularly well-cared for, and supposing this were not the case, there is all the more reason for a visit. Sometimes it is thought better not to visit those who are reputed to be hostile to religion. This is, of course, absurd. It is unfair and wrong merely to call on people who are not well off. An author of world-wide repute, with distinctly anti-clerical tastes, dates the beginning of his antagonism from the time when his vicar called on his servants without asking to see him.

When it is possible, our visiting should be done at a time when the men are at home, and we should ask to see the man. By most people it is supposed that when the parson calls, he has come to see the lady of the house. Old Bill opens the door, and when he sees who it is, he instinctively calls out before he disappears, " Missus, here's the parson." And other men who are told that the parson is in the hall think it best to retreat to the smoking-room while the ladies deal with him.

All this tends to identify us with the other sex and makes our profession appear to be unmanly. A brother parson who was present some time ago at a mothers' meeting heard himself thus spoken about by the lady super-intendent, " Now, mothers, mind you do what Mr. —— and the other ladies tell you." I do not think we ought to resent it if we are not wanted. It may depress us, but it ought not to make us think that those who do not wish us to enter the house are bad people. The old trick so often recommended by a certain Bishop of wedging your foot in the door when it is an inch or so open so that it cannot be slammed in your face, seemed to me extremely ungentlemanly, unless it is felt that those who do not receive us will be eternally damned, in which case it is a praiseworthy and plucky effort, and should be done in Berkeley Square and Park Lane as well.

In our method of visiting there can be no distinction between the rich and poor; and the type of parson who thinks the poor ought to receive him, but that it is very kind of the Hon. Mrs. Bullion if she does, is most distressing. I often think how marvellously good, patient and kind-hearted the poor are towards us. We always seem to be missionising and visiting them, whereas, as a matter of fact, they do not need nearly as much pastoral care as their better-off neighbours. The nearer men and women are to a carpenter's bench, the more true this is.

The official mind has the souls of the poor more on its conscience than it need. Some of that conscious care might with advantage be transferred to the physical conditions under which he and his family have to work and live. I always notice with distress that whenever authority issues a special service of a missionary character it is suggested that it should be used at Evensong. Whether it be that the official mind really believes that the poor are further removed from the Kingdom of God than other people, or whether officialdom is afraid of upsetting the " quality " (if the new service displace their accustomed Mattins) I know not.

But it is a very evident fact to anyone who has worked east and west of Temple Bar that, if any missionising is going to be done, the morning congregation is the one that needs it.

If you go visiting in the spirit of our Lord and pray quite simply to yourself as you go, you need not think in advance what you are going to say, and you need not feel that it is all a waste unless a Confirmation candidate is the outcome. Remember you are not visiting for the mere sake of obtaining a Confirmation candidate.

What will be said if you visit in the right spirit will be the spontaneous utterance of a man who comes as a humble representative of Divine and human love. I do not believe the man who visits with this intent need ever worry, though his words may be poor and halting, his sympathy ill-expressed, his manner awkward and shy. The great and abounding joy of our profession is our belief that our Lord can make a good deal more of us than we can make of ourselves, and that He can—if we maintain intimacy with Him—use the poverty of our words and even our silent handshakes for His glory. I do not think I should have the courage to go on if, with all my heart and soul, I did not believe that. Forgive a personal anecdote which is only told to give encouragement to any who may feel they have little to give. I am quite clear the worst sermon that was ever preached was my own first attempt. I never heard anything so fatuous or dreadful. I lost both my nerve and my place on the

manuscript, and uttered disconnected plati-
tudes to a bewildered East End audience for
what seemed to me, and certainly to them, an
eternity of time. The only one who tried to
comfort me was an East End lady, who, seeing
my misery, said, " Never mind, I daresay you'll
get a little better when you've had a bit more
practice." There was nothing to be said for
that sermon whatsoever but this, that it had
been prepared in an agony of prayer and with
a passionate desire—such as is in the heart of
any deacon—to be of service to God and man
if He permit. For years the memory of that
sermon haunted me like a ghost. It has ceased
to now, for I have met a man who was in the
church that evening who has told me, strange
as it may sound, that it altered his life. He
acknowledged it would be reckoned a very bad
effort, " but," he went on, " it altered me." It
is the most glorious thing in the world to realise
in hours when the size of our task seems too
big for people like ourselves, that God can take
our tiny, mean offering, our little loaves and our
two small fishes, and having blessed them they
can provide for the hunger of the multitude.

We shall try, in our visiting, to understand
so far as we can the point of view of those we
are with : for instance, how next to impossible
it is to attend Morning Service on Sunday when
the children have to be looked after and the
dinner cooked, and how some souls cannot be
expected to thrive on Mattins. We shall long
to tell them of our Lord and the Fellowship
meal—and we shall, if we can.

We shall be there to help if we can—not to talk of our own busy life, nor to solicit a subscription for the vicar's general fund. We shall speak as naturally as we should in our own home, and we shall not think it a waste of time to sit with our host while he smokes his pipe, or undignified to smoke with him ; and we shall gladly pray in any house, at any hour, if those we visit would like to pray with us, and it will be just simple strong prayer out of our hearts embracing the needs and interests of those we are with. We shall try and say to God on their behalf what they deep in their hearts would like to say. We may add the Lord's Prayer and a Collect or so, but most of the prayer will come not through our lips but from their hearts.

I cannot understand the mentality of men who print books of prayer suitable for special occasions. I came across one the other day, and written, too, by a priest of great experience. There was one prayer suitable—so it was said—for recital to mourners around the body of their dear departed. It was a petitioning that the late departed might have his abode with Abraham. I conclude, if the departed had been of the other sex, Sarah might have been substituted. That sort of thing simply won't do. The tragedy of it is that it reveals the mind of an experienced parish priest as being utterly aloof from the situation.

In all our work we must endeavour to avoid professionalism. It always seems to me that the devil, in the course of a very experienced and not unsuccessful career, has discovered

E

that if he can make a parson proud of his own status and position he can undo a great deal of what might be good work.

There is nothing that so destroys our influence as an attitude that has become pompous, stereotyped and formal. If we cannot secure respect without overstraining our status at the expense of our humanity, it is a very bad look out. I have seen excellent curates become pompous vicars under the weight of their new authority, and even admirably natural and compelling vicars lose all their humour and spontaneity under the dignity of episcopal office. The bishop, vicar or curate who has to be perpetually reminding the people of his status will be in appalling contrast to his Lord —Who seemed almost unwilling that men should know His status until they had companied with Him as a Man among men.

We must keep young and simple-minded and encourage a few people to laugh at us whenever they see any signs of a false dignity, or a professional manner. A certain dignity must be ours, but that will be ours by the integrity of a disinterested life in God's service.

We must be ourselves and not imitate either the Bishop of London or Mr. Studdert Kennedy. We can present our own gifts with the cumulative force of a life's cultivation. We look merely foolish if we attempt anything that is not natural. If our nature is cheerful and what is called hearty, we can use it—without shouting and in season—to the glory of God. If we are not built on those lines, for pity's sake don't let us pretend we are. It is, I think, the quiet folk who get farthest. People who are slapped on the back are not necessarily done good to—they are more often hardened against the clergy in proportion as they are hurt. Noisy breeziness is not necessarily akin to Godliness. I think gentleness is.

We must avoid, too, pretending by our manners that we are still laymen. The kind of layman whom we want to appeal to hates to hear us swearing, and does not think it is fair that we should do some of the things which he is a little ashamed of doing. It injures him quite definitely, I think. He expects us to be in some ways rather different from himself, and in some way, without losing our *joie de vivre*, we ought to be.

CHAPTER V

THERE is, I think, something amiss in a girl being prepared for Confirmation by a man who can know nothing, or almost nothing, of her life and circumstances. She very naturally does not desire to talk about the intimate things of her life with him. I do not think, either, that a curate or vicar is a suitable person to give spiritual counsel or direction to women. I know that in present circumstances this has to be done, and it is often done well, but the system is by no means ideal. It will be a long time before this is recognised, but meanwhile we clergy can at least give to all women the respect and the courtesy that is their due, and allow them as much initiative as is possible. The young deacon who thinks that every parish girl is going to fall in love with him, is an abomination. I know there are foolish women as well as men, and some desperately foolish girls, but it is a poor business to judge women by the few foolish ones we may meet ; it is much better to recognise how much the Church owes to them, and to reverence their gift of a moral courage and patience so far in advance of our own, of an intelligence at least equal to our own, and of a faith and loving loyalty to our Lord that so often leaves us very far behind. Neither the Church nor the State will confront its large moral problem adequately without the assistance, full and unfettered, of women. But let me frankly confess that I think some time must elapse before women will be at their best in public affairs. New power has to become natural before it is used at its best. New authority needs assimilating in order that it may be used naturally. I hope I may be forgiven for saying that nothing frightens me more than the adequate woman who is pleased with her new authority, and nothing surprises and disappoints me more than the harsh judgment she is inclined to mete out to the members of her own sex.

Some of us are called to a life of celibacy, but most of us are, I believe, the better for being married sooner or later. The married parson is likely to have his outlook on life made healthier, and his love more human and deep. If a parson is strong enough to stand to his own deepest convictions, the ideal woman for him is the one who wants sometimes to challenge those convictions. Our wives are like bishops' chaplains—they are not much help if they see no fault in those they live and work with. It is immensely good for the clergy to be told, by someone who really cares for their deepest interests, when they are foolish ; and it is further most stimulating that two partners in a great concern should see their

same Lord from different sides. Always remember that it is about the hardest thing in
the world to be a parson's wife. If she is jolly,
people say " she doesn't look a bit like a
parson's wife " ; if through grinding poverty
(as is now often the case) she cannot be dressed
smartly, then others say " she is just like a
parson's wife ! " Both terms are meant con-
temptuously. There is nothing harder for any
woman than to steer, as a parson's wife has to,
between being considered uninterested in her
husband's work, if she is not present at every
small parochial function, and being identified
with a little clique if she is. And if added to
her difficulties the parson is what is called
" popular," then indeed we may give her our
deepest sympathy. If he is " unpopular,"
then she, of course, must share his odium.

I am inclined to think that the bravest
women in England are the hundreds and
hundreds of vicars' and curates' wives who are
suffering in silence to-day from abject poverty
and yet are cooking, housekeeping, mending,
nursing and sometimes acting as parish drudges.
They get a great deal of abuse. I wish someone
would write their praise in letters of gold ! If
it be your lot to work in surroundings and
circumstances where a little comfort is possible,
do put it upon your conscience that your home
shall remain a place where a modicum of peace
and seclusion and privacy is preserved for the
woman you love, and, so far as you can, protect
it ; never let the vicarage be turned into an
annexe to the vestry, and do not let the happy

girl who gave herself to you be driven against her will into a whirlpool of parochial activities.

If she loves the thing, well and good; if she does not, well why should she? There are many other ways of loving and serving God. And do remember that if it was God's will that you should marry, it is not also His will that you should neglect your wife and your children and your home. The romance that is in the heart of every woman can be crushed out of her if she sees the love and interest that once were hers, and which are her right, waning before the enthusiasm which the new Parochial Church Council excites. It is an ill day in the life of a parson when he is too engrossed to offer his wife those little courtesies which were gladly given in the happy days of courtship. It is a dreadful and devastating day for at least one soul at the parsonage when he forgets that, before the baby arrives and when the baby is ill, it is his duty and his joy to be by his wife's side. Our married life is not a question of either parish or home—it is a question of setting up in the parish a home in which at least two people live in some seclusion as well as in glad contentment, thanking God for His gifts, the greatest of which for each, is the gift of the other's love; yet a home through the windows of which can be heard, and not remain neglected, the cry of a world in pain. If there is no love, no comradeship, no romance in the parsonage, it were better for the parson to refrain from preaching on Love.

In all probability women will be ordained

within thirty years from now. It may take longer than thirty years, but it will come, I think, whether the present generation likes it or not. If I may say exactly what I feel about it, I must confess that I am a little bewildered at the prospect ; but I am not certain that one ought to be bewildered, for I do not see anything but prejudice and practical difficulties in the way. I am perplexed, of course, at the thought of the adjustments and readjustments that will need to be made, but I refuse to be dismayed. I am not an active advocate of the ministry of women, but I am passionately anxious that they should be given the same opportunities for speech within consecrated buildings as are now given to laymen, and that, not because I wish to confer favour upon them, or merely because I think it is insulting that their gift of prophecy should be confined to the parish hall, but because I believe the Church is the poorer without their gift.

The idea of women clergy will be much less strange in ten years' time if the Bishops are able to carry out the resolutions which they framed as to women at the last Lambeth Conference. With those resolutions I am in the warmest agreement. In existing circumstances I should wish to see a woman who had been adequately trained attached definitely to the staff of every large parish, as an expert in the things about which men know next to nothing.

It will be said at once that nearly every parish has its own paid woman worker, but is she really trained, has she any real authority, does she sit with the clergy at their meetings ? Does she shape the policy at all, is she allowed to do anything but act as a general drudge in decorating the church for Harvest Festivals and carrying round the parish magazines ?

At the moment, the Church does not attract the younger woman such as it needs, because it offers no initiative, no prospects, and nothing but a starvation wage. Is there anything more pathetic than the usual parish worker, or anything more deplorable than the way in which she is treated, sometimes by the clergy and often by the congregation ? I know her limitations, I have worked with her for years ; I know she loves those little bits of authority that she wields in the absence of the clergy, but I know also she has had no training, she is generally desperately poor, she is often disgracefully patronised by the morning congregation, she has no future to look forward to.

The kind of enlightened person whom I wish to see attracted to Church work would be concerned not merely with jobs that no one else is willing to do, she would be chosen for the typical excellences of her sex ; she would prepare women and girls of every class for Confirmation ; she would really control the women's work in the parish ; she would give addresses in the church, she would hear confessions and give spiritual direction to those of her own sex who desired it. She would, too, do other things that are now denied her through the sheer prejudice that an out-of-date pagan attitude towards women begets. There will be, of course, some jealousy and some difficulties if this proposal is generally carried out, but there will, I believe, be many advantages. The really competent and trained woman worker will relieve many from doing work which they are not very capable of doing, and will relieve the clergy from tasks which give them no enjoyment, because they realise perfectly well that they do not do them adequately.

There would be many less silly women, and some less silly parsons if, through such a plan as this and as a general rule, women's work was left in the far more capable hands of women, and the clergy were set free for their own work with men and boys.

CHAPTER VI

ON PREACHING

SERMONS are not listened to as gladly as they used to be: now they are tolerated rather than welcomed. It is not because there are no good preachers left. But this is a practical age, and people are very distrustful of moral exhortation: it seems to get so little done. Causes are not now judged by what even their best advocates have to say about them ; men think for themselves.

There was a time when the Church was the only educative force in the country, so that the clergy spoke to an illiterate congregation. To-day the monopoly of wisdom is by no means confined to the pulpit, and the atmosphere of democracy is in the blood of the new generation. It takes the form of an almost unlimited assertion of the right of private judgment, though it is often forgotten that this unquestioned "right" should be conditioned by the pains that are taken to form the judgment. Nevertheless the claim persists, and it affects men's attitude towards the hearing of sermons.

Religion, too, has become more and more a matter of inward and personal experience.

Authority is questioned and distrusted. This was summed up as tersely as possible by the midshipman who wrote from the North Sea: " Our Padre is no damned good, he begins all his sermons with, ' This is the day on which the Church bids us . . ' "

Roughly speaking, the same thing is in the mind of the man in the pew, but if this is remembered, the preacher may still wield an enormous influence for good. There are certain things he does not require, and certain things he cannot do without. He need not, thank God, be an orator ; it will be better for his soul's sake if he is not. Although the scholar who can preach simply has a rare power, no preacher need weight his sermons with profundity, and however much midnight oil he has expended, the sermon should not smack of it. He had much better not work up to periods of heated exuberance, dotting his manuscript beforehand with " ff " like the unreal instructions against the last verse of a combative hymn ; nor need he resort to histrionic devices of lowered voice or long silences. It would be much better to let any tendency to slang, elaborated humour or shouting be rigorously repressed. He had better not talk down to children, or up to the small minority of his congregation whose intellects are coldly critical. His words are for those who are hard pressed in the difficult business of Christian living. He had better postpone as long as possible the day of preaching without manuscript. Many of the best preachers. who are thought to preach *ex tempore*, read their sermons. He must avoid imitating the style of his favourite preacher. It would, for instance, be quite fatal even for Dr. Inge to try and preach like Mr. Studdert Kennedy. It is not advisable to denounce those who do not attend church in the presence of those who do. It is not necessary to say " Brethren," or " Beloved," or even " My Friends," and it had better be remembered that to begin a sermon with the words " The point of view of the Church has always been " is almost fatal in the hearing of the modern congregation.

The preacher must talk of the things he knows something about and in a language that the people can understand. I do not think that the average member of an ordinary congregation has the faintest idea of the meaning of the words his parson uses. I am certain the stranger has not. There is nothing more needed than a new vocabulary for the pulpit and for Confirmation classes. Some of the old words had better be left unsaid. Most of them need translation, they are as Greek or Latin to simple people, that is, to three-quarters of both the morning and evening congregation. The current pulpit phraseology of religion is bank-rupt—by this I mean it is impossible to trade with ; I am not denying its worth in the science of theology, but in daily life its purchasing power is almost nil. Curiously enough, it is at its worst in the Salvation Army. I often think that they could change England if they would suffer Mr. Clutton Brock, in collaboration with

Mr. Edward Woods, to change their vocabulary.
Some preachers seem to be under the impression that those to whom they speak have all
had the benefit of a year at Cuddesdon or at
least at Knutsford. Great-sounding words and
phrases, that have no doubt a noble place in
the science of theology, are hurled at the heads,
or rather over the heads, of uninstructed people,
and often by clergy who have a very imperfect
understanding themselves of what they mean.

Let me make myself a little plainer. Words
like " Incarnation," " Sanctification," " Justifi-
cation," " Mediation," and even phrases like
" The Blood of the Lamb " or, indeed, the
" Holy Ghost," mean no doubt a great deal to
those who use them from the pulpit, but they
are not understood by the majority of those who
are listening. I am not suggesting that these
same words and phrases should not be retained
where theologians meet together, but that they
should be used sparingly in the pulpit, and that
even then they should be accompanied with some
simple statement as to what they really mean.

An excellent discipline for the " would-be "
preacher is to read a work on theology, or the
able writings of someone like the late Dr.
Illingworth, and then to attempt in his own
study to find a language for what he has read
which people who were not deeply read in
theology would understand. Most theologians
who speak and write delight to say they are
addressing themselves to a public of ordinary
people, whereas, as a matter of fact, they are
about as intelligible to those they fondly

imagine they are interesting, as Professor
Einstein is to me. The man who hopes to give
assistance from the pulpit must choose his
words from those that are in current use. Nor
can a man hope to make his utterances intelligible unless he knows something of the mental
condition and attitude of those who will be
listening.

All too often, the preachers of the Gospel
may know the truth of what they affirm, but
they do not know the lives or the thoughts of
those to whom they are trying to bring it. Men
do not ask for a new gospel, they would be
content with the old if only they could listen
to it expressed in terms related to their own
experience and the meaning of life.

Remember that the religious outlook of most
people is largely influenced by the circumstances
and conditions of their lives. The Eton boy will
accept, even if it does not interest him, the
statement that " God is Love," not so the son
of a pauper. We must know how the people
in the pew are thinking. The preacher must
have contact with them before he can speak to
them with power. The suggestion is frequently
made for colleges of itinerant preachers who
would visit parishes and deliver sermons. No
doubt the matter of their sermon would be
excellent, but good matter is not necessarily
effective matter, unless together with its excellence there is also an intimate knowledge of the
conditions under which the hearers are living,
the problems that confront them, and how
those problems can be surmounted. That could

hardly be expected from a preacher who arrived on Saturday and left early on Monday morning.

We must know our people. Every man called to the ministry should have as an inevitable part of his training, at least a grounding in practical psychology. There is such a thing in a congregation as an average mentality towards religion. We have, if we can, to raise the average, but we cannot do that unless we begin where people are : we have to speak to that average in a human dialect. When we forget this, we may give a great impression of intelligence, but we shall not really commend our cause because, though many of the congregation would not own it, most of them will really not understand what on earth we are talking about. There are some people who like being mystified, but I do not think it is good to encourage them. Strange and high-sounding language poured out in a torrent is rather like the comfortable sound of rain to a man who is sitting by his own fireside. The torrent will doubtless do good, but it won't affect him, and it is pleasant to listen to. There were many people who did not understand a word of Welsh, who felt a pleasurable glow of excitement when, some years ago, a certain Bishop in his enthusiastic defence of the Welsh Establishment would break into his native language. There was always tumultuous applause, " Magnificent ! " people would say, but really it did not help them very much, because for most people the arguments stopped when the Welsh began. It is so with any preacher who strains after effect, and uses language not generally understood. A few will enjoy it, but for all the good achieved, for the lives it ought to have converted, for the Christian tasks it gets done, it simply isn't worth the paper it is written on, or the time it takes to prepare and to deliver. Such speech would not have come from Jesus Christ, Who knew the hearts of men. He knew no jargon of technical terms. He would pass by the grand classical speech of religion which was fast becoming a dead language to the living world, and spoke, with the Father and Mother tongue, the dialect of the human heart.

Men and women are not fired to enthusiasm by being asked to resemble Abraham, or other rugged people in the Old Testament. All sarcasm and bitterness and mere denunciation should be avoided in the pulpit. There is often need for moral indignation, but that is quite distinct. No cutting cynical phrases will help the Kingdom of God, and no man is of Christ who talks slightingly of those who are loyal members of other Christian Churches, or indeed of any who are the adherents of other religions which seem to bring them near to God. One further warning—it is not always either necessary or advisable to end the sermon on your paramount Church interest. There are some who hammer Sunday by Sunday on the same ecclesiastical anvil, small missionary interests, confessions, more frequent communion, family prayers, Church reform, and other kindred subjects. These things are all to be spoken about

F

in their time and in their place, but they are not the necessary conclusion of every sermon.

The chief concern of the preacher should be to declare God; the man who desires to give a live message must himself be alive unto God, and this does not happen on Saturday evening because the parson wants to prepare a sermon for the following day. The process of becoming alive unto God is essential for the preacher, but it has nothing directly to do with the preparation of sermons. The things that keep men alive unto God are their constant looking into the face of Jesus Christ, their disciplined prayer, their careful reading, their life of service. These things are independent of whether we have to preach or not, but it so happens that no man can give a live message unless he himself is alive unto God. The preparation of a sermon is the committing to paper the things about God and His purpose which seem to need emphasis—as the result of the preacher's own research into the things of God and his knowledge of those to whom he is speaking. If the life is devoted and the intelligence encouraged, the message that is needful will come.

We have to be careful not to spend our times of devotion and reading in trying to discover points for sermons. I have known a good many hard-pressed parish clergy who have lost all the benefits that they might have had from a retreat, because they have spent most of the time listening to the addresses with a view to their own sermons for the next Sunday. It is a pity, I always think, that students at theological

colleges are encouraged to take notebook and
pencil with them to their quiet days : it is
liable to start what may become a disastrous
habit, as we who still have to fight against it
know. In so far as it is true that it is harder to
missionise the clergy than any other body of
men, it is, I fear, because we have become so
accustomed to listening to sermons either for
the purpose of criticising or of repeating them in
our own. We have been outside the range of
their converting power. Times of devotion and
study are for no other purpose than that we
should be alive unto God. He who is will be
able to declare God through Jesus Christ.

The preacher who will commend our Lord
is he who is really simple and genuine, who does
not ask for tasks to be done that he does not do
himself. He will be alongside of his people,
fellow-pilgrim with them in the search for
truth. He will not think that he has discovered
all truth. He will not attempt to pretend that
there are no mysteries which have not been
revealed to him. He will not be ashamed of
admitting that there are problems he cannot
answer. It is the belief of most people that no
intellectual doubts ever shadow the soul of the
parson. " If only I had a faith like yours " is
the phrase that is used. Why shouldn't they
know by the humility of the clergy's pulpit
speaking that they, too, have been again and
again in doubt and difficulties, and that they,
too, have had periods when, like their Lord,
they murmur, " My God, my God, why hast
Thou forsaken Me ? "

It has come to be believed by many people that it is wrong to doubt, whereas all who have won a living and creative faith in God are bound to go through the Valley of Perplexity. There are many who think there is something wrong with them because they doubt, whereas they are really passing down the way that leads to God. And how much of this conception is due to the cocksure way in which preachers dismiss the largest problems and seem to suggest that God does not approve of intellectual doubt. The attitude of humility that one desires to discover in the preacher is not that of the man who is always apologising for his own view, but that of a man who gives his views respectfully for what they are worth, and knows that some who hear them know more than he does, if only because they have served longer in the school and workshop of Christ. He will respect his congregation, he will remember that it is not necessary or likely that all should think or feel as he does, or find their faith confirmed as he has found his. He will offer what he has as humbly and respectfully as he can, realising that his offering would be much larger if he knew the manifold way in which his people were coming to the knowledge of their Saviour, and had their experience as well as his own. He will not suggest that his is a monopoly of wisdom. He will realise that God has many ways of making Himself known to many people. He will avoid that hard unsympathetic insistence on his own path, as being the only way that leads to God. He may be convinced that for him it is the way, and such things as come to him as he treads it may confirm him in his conviction, but he has no right to say, " This only is the road, take this because it is good for me, accept this because it was proved efficacious by the men of the Oxford or the Evangelical Movement, this is what you must do, this is how you must feel, and this is how you must express your feelings, or something is wrong." I would rather be guilty of being a little too vague than of the charge of being a little too definite in matters that pertain to God. It is the part of a preacher to make people think : it is a primary Christian duty.

The parable of the ferment of leaven in a mass of meal is a vivid forecast of our Lord's effect on the minds of men. He found a world of estab-lished ideas, and the effect of His coming was a struggle between inheritance and experience. " It was said to them of old times—but I say unto you."

Our Lord would have no quarrel with anyone who struck out a new line or was searching for a new truth. There is no one who rejoices more in the adventurer. " Flesh and blood hath not revealed it unto thee, but My Father which is in heaven," He once said to an exploring mind. The very existence of Jesus, says Dr. Glover, has been to humanity one of the greatest stimulants to thought : and one of the greatest factors in developing the human mind.

Historically, one of the marks of the Early Church was that, though it did not come from

the upper ranks of society and had not the
highest culture, it mastered the ancient world
all along the line. A man awakened to one set
of interests is more apt to understand another.
The redeemed man is always ahead of what
he was before ; and the more fully he is remade
by Jesus Christ the more he goes ahead. Con-
quering and to conquer is a true description of
the Christian soldier as well as of his leader.
Remember, Jesus is the Man Who has stirred
mankind to its depths and set the world on fire.

The new preaching, the new evangelisation
for which the world waits, will, I believe, be
concerned with holding up before men God as
known in Jesus Christ—just as truth is held up
without the need of comment or flattery. Men
of certain conditions and men who think will
see and acclaim it. We who know Jesus will
hold Him before men much in the same rugged
simple way as did the Evangelists. It is
amazing that in their narrative they neither
paid Him compliments nor offered sympathy ;
they spoke of Him ; they told things about
Him ; and left it at that—except that later
they died for Him. They seemed almost afraid
of explaining. They saw the Truth and they
may have known that Truth in the end must
prevail.

That is how we must preach Christ.

The longer I live the more certain I become
that if we can induce the men and women who
admire Jesus Christ (and that is practically
everyone) to do more than admire—to attempt
to live in His spirit, they will come to know

God and they will discover that state of Christian orthodoxy into which it will please the Spirit of God to call them.

It may not be the orthodoxy that is ours, but none the less it will be that into which God has called them. We need not worry as to whether they make their confession or how often they come to their Communion. Some will and some will not ; some will need their Communion often, to others it will be more real occasionally. My point is that these things are not especially our business, though naturally we would try to advise in the case of the young and in the case of others who need our advice.

If I have seemed to neglect the duty of the clergy to preach on large social problems or matters such as the bearing of the problem of unemployment and the like, I have not done so intentionally, but I maintain that if a sermon is filled with the Fatherhood of God and the Spirit of Jesus Christ it will of necessity provide the dynamic which will destroy the greatest sin that stalks the world to-day—the sin of separation.

Our sermons will not be comforting : how can they be ? They will be aflame with the burning passionate love of God—they will be spoken in a natural voice—simply and yet with conviction—and in a language understood by the people.

They will come from our own daily prayer and study and Christian adventure, and they will go—we know not whither. About that we need not worry

CHAPTER VII

NEW IDEALS IN PARISH WORK

HAVE we got the organisations that are of service to the people, or are they only those we have told them they ought to like?

It is wrong, I am sure, to impose organisations on reluctant parishioners because we think they ought to be good for them.

We may make suggestions, but we must allow those who are mainly interested to choose what they think will be of service.

For instance, we may think the Church of England Men's Society and the Church Lads' Brigade altogether admirable—our men and boys may not. We may think these societies ought to help—they may know they won't. I know a clergyman so ignorant of the psychology of youth and so devoted to the Church Lads' Brigade that he suspects a propensity to savage vice in any boy who will not enrol in its ranks. His boys want Scouts, but he won't give in, and I maintain he is wrong, and we shall be wrong if we do likewise.

There are, I fear, hundreds of dead branches of various accredited Church societies scattered over the country which are not allowed to be officially reported as defunct because the vicar thinks it would not be seemly if there was no branch of this or that society in the parish.

It is better, I think, to close down and start something fresh than to go on attempting to lash moribund guilds, which no one needs, into a mild activity.

Parochial organisations exist not to make the docile more docile, but to hold and to help those who are most in need of incentives to decent living and Christian service, and for that reason I beg that whatever is started shall not impose at the outset a communicant test —as the condition of membership.

And before I make a constructive suggestion for a new kind of parish guild may I say a word about parish organisations as a whole ? They ought not to claim too much time from their adherents.

I am inclined to think that in these difficult days there is a good deal to be said for Churchmen leaving their coteries of like-minded companions and allowing their Churchmanship to swell the common stock of effort towards reform which is being made by civic authority and citizens at large. I am not certain that we have not attempted, in the past, to shelter our communicants too much from the rude noise of the world, and I do not think they are better in consequence. There is a good deal of machinery which has been created for good purposes in municipal and civic life which is either not working or working badly for lack of men and women with moral courage, high purpose and a sense of civic honour. It is here, I am certain, that Christian virtues are needed, and it is here rather than at those somewhat inconclusive meetings for communicants only (whose main decision is to arrange the date of the next meeting) that the best opportunity for a Churchman's Christian service lies. And this means that instead of begging able Churchmen to assist us in running boys' clubs or taking round the parish magazine, we should frankly say: " Go to your club or trade union or political meeting and let your witness be made there."

Anything that retains Christianity as a static force in the parish hall, when it ought to be a dynamic force in the rough and tumble outside, is to be regretted in days of crisis such as these. For instance, I would wish to see those who are anxious for the restoration and protection of women and girls prefer to struggle for a seat on the local Watch Committee rather than enjoy their safe seat in the chair of the neighbouring Church society for preventive and rescue work. Or again—might it not be well for the members of the parochial branch of the Church of England Men's Society to sacrifice, at any rate occasionally, the pleasure that an attendance at the monthly meeting affords, and as their main interest to carry their zeal for Christian fellowship into regions where there is much enthusiasm for fellowship but little for organised Christianity ?

I think our close Church meetings to discuss, let us say, the tendency to irreligion in the young people of the present generation have had their day—a useful day no doubt it was—but their continued pre-eminence in the life of Churchmen to-day, when Christianity itself is at stake, seems to me to encourage complacent companionship in a clique rather than courageous effort to test and confirm faith and to contribute moral virtues where the din of battle is most fierce and its issues most surely in the throes of decision.

And if the answer is that they are not strong enough to stand alone, I would reply : " Then Christianity, or rather our presentation of it, has no useful place in the world to-day."

And here may I suggest as an ideal for parish work that there should be, under the control of the Parochial Church Council, one main activity in the parish, and one only, and that a Guild of Fellowship open to all who care to call themselves members of the congregation, and with no further test ? Its aim would be fellowship in Christian service, recreation and social intercourse.

The obligations incurred on admission would be a promise of attendance so far as possible at four quarterly meetings of the Guild and a readiness to consider a request for service from the Council of the Guild.

Around that Central Fellowship—controlled by a Council elected by the members themselves—should centre all the smaller activities that the parish needs : the men's and boys' clubs, the girls' guilds, the debating society, the dancing and singing classes, the Scouts, the model Sunday School, and other efforts which cater for those who are not as yet in the Fellow-

ship. But this is the point—every smaller
activity should owe a primary allegiance to the
Guild of Fellowship, on whose Council it shall
be represented. The Council is the G.H.Q. of
the parish. It can look at the parish and its
needs as a whole ; it can regulate the number
of socials and arrange all the smaller fixtures
with a view to co-ordinating activities, prevent-
ing overlapping, and it can scrap all small
organisations that are not needed or are in-
effective. There is one further important rule
that should be laid down as a principle—no
member of the Fellowship may assist in the
control of more than one sub-society. That
prevents " bossy " people bossing everything in
the parish. They can do their worst in one side
show, but only in one. I know this kind of
Fellowship can work and can work extraordinarily well. It works in one parish that I
know intimately—it has revolutionised the
Church life. It has its paid secretary, its office
and its bureau of service, and nearly one thousand members who pay two shillings a year,
the vast majority of whom are doing bits of
service not only just in the parish but all over
London. At the last quarterly meeting of that
Guild of Fellowship there was no hall in the
parish that could hold the members, and an
adjournment had to be made to the church.
The members have a badge, the wearing of
which is entirely voluntary.

This really is a Fellowship with a basis broad
enough to hold any and every one, and with a
spirit warm enough to remind one of a labour

meeting rather than a gathering of respectable
Church-people. It is the best weapon for getting the right kind of spirit into a parish that I
have as yet encountered. In its comprehen-
siveness and its spirit of service and fellowship
it can, I believe, bind together everyone, and
co-ordinate all the activities in a way in which
it is hard for the Electoral Roll of the Parochial
Church Council to achieve the same results.

Finally, I pass to another activity which, I
am certain, is in need of the reformer's hand.
The usual parish magazine. What is the matter
with it ? It does not " bite." It is hard to
understand what public it is aimed at, though,
I suppose, the calendar of Church festivals and
the short stories about choir boys who die young
—largely I suspect from neglect of football and
too close attendance in the sacristy—does
appeal to the milder portion of a congregation.

To begin with, I should alter the word magazine to review—it is easier to get articles
written for it if this is done. People like writing
for monthly reviews, but they don't, alas, for
parish magazines. Parish magazines are under
a cloud—they've had a bad run. Then I should
change the cover. Church bells outside suggest
mildness within ; nor do I like to see the hours
of Mattins and Evensong advertised quite so
aggressively before you have turned over the
first page. It reminds me of a visiting-card for
clergy someone once tried to sell me, which,
beside the vicar's name, contained a list of the
hours of his Sunday services. I thought it
peculiarly ungentlemanly !

And I dislike the vicar's monthly letter which begins " My dear people," and ends " Yours faithfully in Jesus Christ." It gives an air of unreality to a letter which is addressed to everyone in general and to no one in particular.

I should prefer to see that letter disappear and a series of notes—by the vicar if you like—take its place. This would have the further advantage of enabling whoever wrote the notes to avoid those seasonable messages in appropriate language that a letter from the vicar always seems to entail. And I abominate those inside pages of the magazine which, I suppose, are sent round by some well-meaning Church society every month.

I should suggest in our reformed magazine that friends who can write should be asked to write on general topics of public interest from a Christian viewpoint. It is also well to know that nearly all the editors of monthly reviews and Church organs will give their leave for their articles to be reprinted if the source be acknowledged.

There could be reviews of books—our monthly reading, for instance—poetry—a good story—a page of humour and even, if desired, acrostics, though it is to be hoped that the answers need not necessarily be always Biblical names or characters.

Of course the doings of the parish would be chronicled, but I suggest that matters merely parochial should be printed in smaller type. The casual reader cannot be expected, and ought not to be encouraged, to wade through a page and a half in large print on the billiard handicap in the boys' club, or how the G.F.S. nearly won, but ultimately lost, the shield at the Crystal Palace.

A need which I am certain is long overdue, is an attempt to rescue the usual parish magazine from its dullness and trivialities and to bring it into the arena of decent Christian literature—the need for which is so urgent to-day.

It ought to be—that magazine—a monthly challenge to high living and high thinking—it should bring all matters of public importance to the touchstone of Christ. It ought to be concerned with the making of citizens ; it can also be parochial without being narrow. It can be a magnificent tract in capable hands, but usually we have allowed that poor old magazine to become an inartistic chronicle of small activities of no interest to anyone except to those who find their names in print because they sent flowers for the Harvest Festival decorations or made the arrangements for the mothers' annual outing to Blackpool.

And this new kind of magazine can be made to pay, too, for many tradesmen of goodwill will advertise in it, and many people will be glad to buy it if it's worth buying and if, for instance, it is interesting enough to be readable in the local free library. If it does not pay as a piece of propaganda it is worth the extra money it costs, and if finance is still a difficulty, several parishes might combine together—best of all a rural deanery centre—to have a really decent piece of Christian literature.

I have not attempted to deal with the reforms necessary within the Church and at its worship. My plea in this direction is that parish churches to-day should attempt to cater for the whole life of those who live in their shadow—should offer them not only the Blessed Food for the soul but refreshment for the minds and recreation for the bodies of the teeming masses in crowded cities and towns. Reforms are years overdue, I am certain, not that the Church may be popular, but that it may follow in the footsteps of its Divine Master, Who came that we might have life and have it more abundantly.

In conclusion. Everything, I think, goes back to what I ventured to lay down at the beginning. When the morale of the Church is higher ; when she is more ready for a splendid gamble ; when we ourselves, priests and laity, are kneeling more completely at the feet of our Lord in earnest request for a larger measure of His Spirit, then the world will be at our feet and we shall save its soul—through Jesus Christ our Lord.

cil. H. Clough.
17th March. 1951.
Bedford.
7/6d.

RABELAIS

RABELAIS

by
ANATOLE FRANCE

Translated by ERNEST BOYD

Illustrations by EDY LEGRAND
cut on wood by A. and P. Baudier

LONDON
VICTOR GOLLANCZ LTD
14 Henrietta Street Covent Garden
1929

Printed in Great Britain by
The Camelot Press Ltd., London and Southampton

CONTENTS

TRANSLATOR'S INTRODUCTION

W H E N Anatole France went on his lecture tour to South America in 1909 the subject which he prepared was François Rabelais, and the substance of those lectures, with slight modifications, is contained in this volume. We know from the not altogether friendly confidences of M. Jean Jacques Brousson that France's success as a lecturer was mediocre. The Bishop of Buenos Ayres denounced both Rabelais and Anatole France and made it impossible for the pious to attend the meetings. "At the last lecture," M. Brousson writes, "there was not a soul in the boxes and not one woman in the house. In all, three hundred baldpates. It was funereal. The Master, smiling and short-sighted, and fingering sheaves of notes, explained Francis I's subtle policy to empty stalls and boxes peopled with shades, with a little pause for applause at the end of each paragraph. It might have been the Collège de France on a rainy winter day."

According to his secretary, France finally abandoned this heretical and unpopular subject, delivering a lecture on the Argentine which was received with that appreciation which only young nations achieve in the presence of complimentary strangers. One likes to believe that M. Brousson is not relying upon his imagination for his facts when he says that a passage from *Sur la Pierre Blanche*, " where Gallio foretells the future grandeur of the Christian sect, and the new nations which shall tear her hegemony from Rome," was adapted to the needs of the occasion and

7

admirably fulfilled its purpose. The lectures now published have, at least, a more authentic character than the improvisations with which the Master attempted to obliterate the shame of his choice of subject.

That choice may have been determined in some measure by the fact that it was made at the time when France was writing his *Jeanne d'Arc*. M. Brousson declares that there were two bookcases on one of the landings of the Villa Saïd, one containing everything that had been written on " the heroic shepherdess," the other, " topped by a plaster bust of Rabelais, containing everything that he had been able to pick up in the shape of studies, engravings of the Father of Pantagruel. Pointing to the two contrasting bookcases, he used to say : ' Here is the poison ! Here is the counter-poison ! ' " The poison was, of course, the fifteenth century, with its credulous piety, its miracle-mongering, its heresy-hunting. The counter-poison was the discovering of printing, the revival of humanism, the setting up of many books instead of One.

The antithesis represented by those two bookcases will be found throughout the entire course of these lectures. Anatole France sees in his illustrious predecessor the rebel and scholar who made possible a tradition of humanism and scepticism of which France was himself the last distinguished opponent. He has not written a popular life of the author, but a learned commentary on his times and his work. Even had the circumstances been different, if he had not had in mind a mixed audience, it is doubtful if France would have dwelt very much on the " Rabelaisian " side of Rabelais. He is, indeed, at pains to free him from the charge of drunkenness. Although himself an often charming sensualist, there is little in him of the hearty, full-blooded vitality of Rabelais. His kinship with him is of a subtler and purely intellectual order.

As a Hellenist Rabelais attracted France, for was not Greek a heresy to the Church? He is tempted to see in the creator of Pantagruel a forerunner of Voltaire, the first embodiment of the Voltairean spirit in French literature. Nowadays, when a generation of French writers has arisen to set up all the idols which Rabelais, Montaigne, Voltaire, Renan, and Anatole France threw down, when individualism is deprecated, and acquiescence in authority, both ecclesiastical and political, is preached by the new prophets of neo-Thomism, this posthumous work has a special interest. It is the last utterance of a voice which was heard all through the author's life expounding the sane and urbane philosophy whose revival is traced in this study of Rabelais.

Those who were in the habit of viewing Anatole France as a vulgar anti-clerical, those who could not reconcile his socialistic leanings with his personal fastidiousness and pessimistic detachment, will find in the antithesis upon which this study rests an answer to their queries. As between the Middle Ages and the Renaissance, France could not but choose the latter. The reason for that choice becomes clear as he contrasts the free spirit of Rabelais with the spirit of his time. The fashionable medievalists of to-day in Paris did not wait, as so many did, for the death of Anatole France in order to decry him, even if they did leave it for the Surréalistes to discover that he could not write French. They will resent this confession of faith. To those, however, who have admired the superb stylist and appreciated the understanding scepticism of Anatole France, these lectures will have a retrospective interest.

It is fitting that these two great names, François Rabelais and Anatole France, should appear in such a juxtaposition. Each is an incarnation of a particular quality in the French mind which the world at large has valued. France is, perhaps, too much inclined to make that quality a single virtue. He does not see all of Rabelais, but the part that he sees most clearly is assuredly the most valuable. In their present form these lectures can hardly fail to enjoy all the success which was denied to them by the faithful of Buenos Ayres. They are better designed for the reader than for the auditor, and are addressed to the general reader and not to the specialist. After one has closed the book, both Rabelais and Anatole France stand out more clearly in the mind. The two extremes of a tradition have met.

The quotations from Rabelais, Plutarch and Montaigne have been taken from the translations of Urquhart and Motteux, North and Florio respectively, but they are in places slightly modified, as Anatole France's quotations are not always faithful to the text.

PUBLISHER'S BIBLIOGRAPHICAL NOTE

T H E present volume constitutes the first English edition of the lectures delivered by Anatole France at Buenos Ayres in 1909. These lectures were published for the first time in French in December 1928, and formed the seventeenth volume of the complete illustrated edition of the works of Anatole France issued by Calmann-Lévy.

The manuscript belongs to Madame Wulfing Luer ; it is in the handwriting of Anatole France and consists of 218 sheets of quarto paper, written only on one side and preceded by a prefatory letter. The binding is in red morocco.

The points in which the English edition differs from the French are trifling, but are given here for the sake of bibliographical accuracy. The introductory words " Mesdames et Messieurs " are throughout omitted, and so are occasional references to " this beautiful city of Buenos Ayres." Finally, the words Chapter I., Chapter II., etc., are added at the head of Anatole France's own divisions of the material.

Chère madame,

Puisque vous attachez du prix à ces barbouillages, je suis heureux de vous les offrir. Ce manuscrit est inédit et contient un cours élémentaire sur Rabelais. La biographie est exacte, les citations abondantes : ce sont deux mérites.

Croyez, chère madame, à ma respectueuse et fidèle amitié.

ANATOLE FRANCE

Paris, le 10 décembre 1909.

13

AUTHOR'S INTRODUCTION

It is not without prolonged reflection, it is not without a careful weighing of every consideration, that I have chosen the theme on which I have come to address you ; and, if I have decided to speak to you about Rabelais, it is not without reason. I have decided to study with you, if such be your pleasure, the author of Pantagruel because I know him a little ; because he is a very great writer, and moreover, among the great writers, one of the least known and the most difficult to know ; because the history of his life and works has been of late years entirely reconstituted by critical research and I can reveal to you some curious new lights on this old subject ; but finally and above all, because the work of this great man is good, because it disposes the mind to wisdom, to toleration, to gay charity, because the reason derives pleasure and strength from them, because we learn from them the precious art of laughing at our enemies without hatred or anger. Those, I believe, are good reasons. But perhaps also, unconsciously, because the very difficulties of the task have tempted me. To place before you Rabelais, the great Rabelais, the real Rabelais, without wounding, without shocking, without alarming anyone, without offending for a moment the chastest ear, that seems a dangerous enterprise. But I have a complete confidence that I shall be able to carry it through with success. I am sure that I shall not utter a single word that might disturb the most delicate modesty. But that is not all. The life of Rabelais is bound up with those great movements of the Renaissance and the Reformation in which the modern spirit was shaped. And that also helped to decide my choice. The majesty of the theme will transmit a certain strength to my discourse. I shall touch on those questions

15

with a freedom worthy of you. I have too high a regard for you not to tell you all that I consider to be the truth. For you are yourselves men of truth; among you I have—I know it, I feel it—set my foot on a soil of freedom where nothing hinders the soaring of human thought. It would be an insult to you not to open to you my whole soul and my whole heart. It was you who summoned me; and here I am before you without reserve or pretence. But need I assure you that it would be, in my belief, treason to the most hallowed principles of hospitality if I were to deviate in the least degree from the respect due to conscience, to conviction, to faith, to the inner life of the soul?

I also have my convictions, I also have my faith. If it were to happen, by an impossible chance, that they were to be violently attacked on this hospitable soil, I should reply by a calm silence, in the assurance that calm is the proper attitude of reason, disdain the true mark of intellectual independence. But why seek for clouds in a clear sky? We are here in the serene domains of literature, to which you have invited me, where all is concord, peace, friendship, smiles.

It seems to me that the best method of presenting to you the life and work of a great writer is to set forth the facts in chronological order. I shall therefore tell you all that is known about Rabelais from birth to death, and we shall study his books at the dates of their appearance. I know that I am hardly equal to an audience such as yours; but one must avoid all pretence, even that of modesty.

THE LIFE OF RABELAIS

CHAPTER I

THE LIFE OF RABELAIS

IN the garden of France, near a forest, at the foot of a rocky hill surmounted by the ancient castle of the Plantagenets and the Valois, on the right bank of the river Vienne, stands the finest city in the world, according to its most illustrious son ; a famous city, at all events, as its coat of arms declares :

> Chinon,
> Little town, great renown,
> On old stone long has stood.
> There is the Vienne if you look down,
> If you look up, there's the town.

It is a very ancient city, which Gregory of Tours calls Caïno, for which reason a citizen of Chinon, whose acquaintance we are about to make, attributes its foundation to Cain, the first builder of cities. At the end of the fifteenth century, and at the beginning of the sixteenth, Chinon gaily displayed its crooked streets, its spires and towers in the moist sunlight of Touraine. At this time Antoine Rabelais, gentleman of La Devinière, Bachelor of Laws, carried on his profession as a lawyer and, being the oldest lawyer of the circuit, he was entrusted in 1527 with the highest jurisdiction in the district of Chinon, in the absence of the lieutenants general and particular. His father had died young ; his mother, Andrée Pavin, was married for the second time to a certain Sieur Frapin, and presented him with six children, one of whom became Canon of Angers, lord of Saint Georges, and the author of some beautiful and joyful carols in the language of Poitou.

On the death of his mother, which occurred in the year 1505, Antoine Rabelais inherited the property, castle and mansion of Chavigny, together with all seignorial and manorial rights, and all taxes, rents, income and services, all rights of hunting, fishing and grazing reserved to the deceased.

In the town he owned a large house, known as the house of Innocent, the Pastry Cook, which became an inn, " At the Sign of the Lamprey," towards the end of the sixteenth century. There was a cellar connected with the house. In order to go from one to the other, contrary to the usual procedure when going to the cellar, it was necessary to climb up to that cellar by as many steps as there are days in the year, because it stood much higher than the house, on a level with the castle which overlooked the town. After having climbed up, one entered the cellar by going through an archway covered with paintings. For this reason the cellar was called the Painted Cellar.

Antoine Rabelais also owned, in the parish of Sully, a full league from Chinon, opposite to Roche-Clermaut, the farm of La Devinière, after which he was called. The vineyard was planted with *pineau*. That is the name of a dark grape of small size, whose bunches are in the shape of a pine needle. To say that the grapes of La Devinière were exquisite is not enough. Let us rather listen to the remarks made at La Saulaie by a certain drinker, a son of that soil, as he sat on the green grass when Gargantua was born : " O ! Lachryma Christi, it is from La Devinière ! O ! the fine white wine, upon my conscience it is a kinde of taffetas wine, hin, hin, it is of one eare, well wrought, and of good wooll." " Of good wooll," our drinker, who knew the farce of *Pathelin*, talks like a merchant who is praising his cloth, and when he declared that the wine is of one ear, it is because the people of Chinon put the good wine in one-eared flagons, or in other words, flagons with a single handle. Certain connoisseurs declare that this little wine, although quite decent, was nevertheless too rustic and vulgar to be thus clothed in taffetas and velvet. Let us not listen to them. It is better to rely on the drinker at La Saulaie. It ill becomes a Rabelaisian to depreciate the vineyard of La Divinière.

The wife of Antoine Rabelais, who was a Dusoul, had already borne three children to her husband, Antoine, the elder son, Jamet, the younger, and Françoise, when, about 1495, she brought

into the world her last-born, François, who was to rival in knowledge the most learned men of the century and to relate the most
diverting and most profitable stories which have ever been told in
this world. It is believed that François was not actually born at
Chinon but at La Devinière, whose memory was always so dear
to him that I have just been afraid to criticise its vines, lest I
should irritate his cheerful shade.

From his third to his fifth year he spent his time like the little
children of the countryside : " That is, in drinking, eating and
sleeping ; and in sleeping, drinking and eating ; and in eating,
sleeping and drinking : still he wallowed in the mire : he blurred
and sullied his nose : he blotted and smutch't his face, he trode
down his shoes in the heele : at the flies he did oftentimes yawn,
and ran very heartily after the butterflies, . . . dabbled everywhere. . . . His father's little dogs eat out of the dish with him."
What I have quoted is the childhood of Gargantua. That of
François Rabelais was very similar, I assure you.

Towards the age of nine or ten years, the child was sent, not
far from La Devinière, to the village of Seuilly, where there
was an Abbey in which, forty years before, had lived a certain
Guillaume Rabelais, who had kept up his relationship with the
family of young François. Whether his parents sent him there
to make a monk of him and wished to consecrate their last-born
to the Lord, we do not know. We do not even know whether
his mother did not die in giving birth to him, as Badebec ex-
pired on bringing Pantagruel into the world. But one cannot
help recalling in this connection this remark of the little monk

of Seuilly, in his old age, on the subject of mothers whose children are destined from infancy to the cloister : " I am amazed that they carry them for nine months beneath their hearts, seeing that in their homes they cannot bear nor suffer them nine years, nor even seven, more often, and by simply adding an ell to their dress and cutting I know not how many hairs from the top of their head, by means of certain words they turn them into birds." By " birds " he means monks, and he gives the reason which, in most cases, prompts parents to give their children to the Church. The reason is that monks, having renounced the world, are disqualified from inheriting. " Therefore," he says, " when there are too many children, whether male or female, in some good family ; insomuch that the house would come to nothing, if the paternal estate were shar'd among them all (as reason requires, nature directs, and God commands) ; parents rid themselves of their children by making them clerghawks." " Clerghawk," the word is peculiar to our author, but its meaning is obvious.

They say that François Rabelais met at Seuilly a young monk named Buinart, who astonished him by his simple good sense, his faithful heart and his powerful fist, and that later on he made him Friar John of the Trencherites, by improving much upon nature, it is true. But, if it is true that Friar Buinart was angry at the portrait, either he was too simple-minded to understand, or he judged it by hearsay and according to the reports of malicious people.

On leaving Seuilly, the scholar entered as a novice the monastery of La Baumette, founded by King René. There he met the young offspring of an old Touraine family, Geoffroy d'Estissac, who became Bishop of Maillezais at the age of twenty-three, and two of the brothers du Bellay, one of whom was a Bishop and the other a Captain. He made a very good impression upon all three of them and prejudiced them greatly in his favour.

Rabelais finished his novitiate with the Franciscans of Fontaney-le-Comte, went through all the stages of the priesthood, and took orders about 1520. Amidst all these monks, who, they say, made vows of ignorance rather than of piety, he devoted himself ardently to study and, if it is true, as it seems, that later on, when portraying the man of study, he portrayed himself, we cannot doubt that his youth was chaste and thoughtful, thoroughly exemplary. Indeed, it is a pleasure to recognise the young Friar François in this rich and fresh picture which adorns one of the chapters of the Third Book of Pantagruel :

" Contemplate a little, the form, fashion and carriage of a man. Exceeding earnestly set, upon some learned meditation, and deeply plunged therein, and you shall see how all the arteries of his brain are stretched forth, and bent like the string of a cross-bow . . . nay, in such a studiously musing person, you may espy such extravagant raptures, of one, as it were, out of himself, that all his natural faculties, for that time, will seem to be suspended, from each their proper charge and office, and his exterior senses to be at a stand. In a word, you cannot otherways choose than think, that he is by an extraordinary ecstasie quite transported out of what he was, or should be. . . . Therefore, is it, that Pallas, the Goddess of Wisdom, Tutress, and Guardianess of such as

24

are diligently studious and painfully industrious, is, and hath been still accounted a virgin. The Muses upon the same consideration are esteemed perpetual maids : and the Graces for the like reason, have been held to continue in a sempiternal pudicity.

" I remember to have read, that Cupid on a time being asked of his mother, Venus, why he did not assault, and set upon the Muses, his answer was, that he found them so fair, so sweet, so fine, so neat, so wise, so learned, so modest, so discreet, so courteous, so vertuous, and so continually busied and employed : one in the speculation of the stars ; another in the supputation of numbers ; the third in the dimension of geometrical quantities ; the fourth in the composition of heroick poems ; the fifth in the joyful interludes of a comick strain ; the sixth in the stately gravity of a tragick vein ; that approaching near unto them, he unbended his bow, shut his quiver, and extinguished the torch, through meer shame and fear, that by mischance he might do them some hurt or prejudice. Which done, he thereafter put off the fillet wherewith his eyes were bound, to look them in the face, and to hear their melody and poetick odes. There took he the greatest pleasure in the world ; that many times he was transported with their beauty and pretty behaviour and charmed asleep by their harmony ; so far was he from assaulting them or interrupting their studies."

At Fontenay-le-Comte Rabelais burned with an inextinguishable thirst for knowledge, the thirst which then consumed the greatest minds and the noblest souls. The great breath which passed over the whole world at that time, the warm breathing of the springtime of the mind, had touched his forehead.

Humanity was reborn in the genius of antiquity. Italy had been the first to awaken to science and beauty. In the country of Dante and Petrarch, the ancient wisdom had never completely died. A strange fact, related by a capable annalist of the fifteenth century, Stefano Infessura, is a symbol, as it were, of this awakening.

It was the 18th of April, 1485 ; there is a rumour in Rome that some workmen from Lombardy, while digging along the Appian Way, have found a Roman sarcophagus, with these words engraved upon the white marble : JULIA DAUGHTER OF CLAUDIUS. On raising the cover, they saw a virgin of fifteen or sixteen years, whose beauty, by reason of unknown ointments or some magic charm, shone with a dazzling freshness. With her long, fair hair spread upon her white shoulders, she was smiling in her sleep. A troup of Romans, seized with enthusiasm, lifted the marble bed of Julia and carried it to the Capitol, where the people came in a long procession to admire the unspeakable beauty of the Roman virgin. They stood in silence looking long at her, for her figure, the chroniclers say, was a thousand times more admirable than that of the women who lived in their day. In the end the city was so deeply moved by this spectacle that Pope Innocent, fearing lest a pagan and impious cult might be born of the smiling body of Julia, caused it to be removed by night and secretly buried. But the Roman people never lost the memory of ancient beauty which had passed before their eyes.

Such was the Renaissance in Italy and all over Europe. Antiquity was found again, the ancient letters and sciences were restored. What fecund virtue, what powerful life, is contained in the masterpieces of Greece and Rome ! They emerge from the dust, and suddenly human thought tears off its shroud. From these scattered remains, buried for more than a thousand years, welled an eternal fountain of youth. Thinkers, nourished on Scholasticism, formed by the narrow discipline of the Schools, found a liberating inspiration in their commerce with the ancients. In these Greek and Latin fragments, drawn out of the shadows of the cloisters, two great civilisations lived again, governed by wise laws, upheld by heroic virtues, distinguished by eloquence, embellished by poetry and the arts. Let us try to understand more clearly, to understand completely the resurrection of that barbarous world, which had died of ignorance and fear. The Greek genius was in itself a liberator and a saviour ; but what freed the soul was the effort made to understand it. The ideas of Plato and Cicero were fruitful, but the industry and discipline of the minds which endeavoured to understand them, were even more fruitful. At last men dared to think ! Believing that they were thinking through the ancients, they thought for themselves. That is the Renaissance.

Printing, which, " by divine suggestion," as our author would say, was invented about the middle of the fifteenth century, greatly helped this rebirth of learning which, because of its excellence, was called by the single word Renaissance. Hidden and disguised at the beginning, a humble imitator of calligraphy and entirely occupied in copying Bibles, printing grew, spread and became the universal dispenser of sacred and profane letters. Texts were multiplied by the press ; to speak in terms of Pantagruelism, it was an enormous wine-press from which flowed the wine of knowledge for all.

Paris, which had its first printing press under Louis XI, in a cellar of the Sorbonne, very soon had twenty or thirty. The learned city of Lyons had fifty by the beginning of the sixteenth century. At that time Germany had more than a thousand. The book fair was a source of inexhaustible wealth to Frankfort. The treasures of antiquity, which had once been locked up in the coffers of a few humanists, were released and circulated everywhere. Virgil was printed in 1470, Homer in 1488, Aristotle in 1498, Plato in 1512. Men of letters in every country exchanged their ideas and their discoveries amongst themselves. In the city of Bâle, at the back of a printer's shop, a little old man, thin and feeble, Erasmus of Rotterdam, with tireless spirit led humanity in the direction of greater knowledge and consciousness.

While the past was being revealed in its classic glory and beauty, the navigators, Vasco da Gama, Columbus and Magellan, showed the real shape of the earth, and the system of Copernicus, by bursting the narrow limits of the astrological heavens, at once revealed the immensity of the universe.

In France learning was restored ; colleges sprang up everywhere, protected by the bishops against the laziness and barbarism of the monks. Scholasticism, dry and sterile, was dying ; its death, in the domain of the spirit, was the death of death.

Scholasticism died : everything was reborn, everything was revived, everything smiled.

Friar Rabelais, in his monastery at Fontenay, experienced that zeal for knowledge and understanding which fired the minds of the *élite* at the time. There, amongst all those monks who were afraid to study lest their heads should burst, were three or four who, like himself, were devoted to classical studies. One of them is known to us by the Greek surname Phinetos. Another was Pierre Lamy who, being far advanced in his Greek studies when Friar François, his junior, was beginning, had acquired the esteem of the most famous humanists by reason of his knowledge.

In those times, in every country, the disciples of learning knew each other, sought each other out, and formed what were almost secret societies. They visited each other and indulged in learned discourses between themselves, of whose freedom our academic discussions can give no idea. If they could not see each other, they corresponded. Then the correspondence oₗ scholars was the equivalent of contributing to special reviews at the present time and of communications to the Institute. The number of learned letters exchanged by the humanists was prodigious. " I am overwhelmed with letters from Italy, France, England and Germany," said Henri Estienne. Erasmus tells us that he received twenty letters a day and wrote forty.

The Hellenist monks of Fontenay consorted with the best minds of the country : Jean Brisson, King's Advocate, and his relatives, who urged Friar François to throw his habit to the dogs, hoping that afterwards they would enjoy his conversation more freely ; Artus Caillé, first lieutenant particular of Fontenay ; André Tiraqueau, Caillé's son-in-law, a judge at Fontenay ; Aymery Bouchard, president of the court of Saintes, all humanists and great admirers of antiquity, all people who found infinite beauties in the *Pandectes* and who, like Pantagruel, knowing by heart the fine texts of Roman law, could discuss them like philosophers. Did they not hope (and not without reason) to find once more in those ancient texts upright rules and just laws ? With them Rabelais himself became a rather good lawyer and a great admirer of Papinian.

Pierre Lamy was in correspondence with the illustrious annotator of the *Pandectes*, Guillaume Budé, who knew Latin and Greek better than anybody in France, and who joined to his learned studies the important office of secretary to the King. This great man wrote to the monks of Fontenay learned letters in Latin and Greek, and in each letter he had a word for young Rabelais : " My salutation to your brother in religion and science. . . . Farewell and a fourfold salutation in my name to the gentle and learned Rabelais by word of mouth, if he is with you, or in writing if he is away."

The gentle and learned Rabelais aspired to the honour of also receiving a letter from the great man. Pierre Lamy promised to get him one ; but for a long time his efforts were in vain. Friar François, not receiving any, denounced his companion in pleasant terms to Guillaume Budé, as having given himself more credit than he really possessed. Budé entered into the joke which, heavily laden with Roman law, was not exactly light humour. These giants of learning played with the Digest as Gargantua played with the large bell of Nôtre Dame.

Judge Tiraqueau, who had married in 1512, at the age of 24, Marie Caillé, spinster, aged 11, was looking for the best means of instructing, educating and forming the mind of his young wife. To this end he consulted the ancients and, having compared a multitude of texts, he hastily composed a treatise *De legibus connubialibus*, upon which, it is supposed, he made the young Franciscan scholars of Fontenay work, and which was printed in 1513. The doctrine of Tiraqueau as to the rights and duties of married couples is in substance as follows :

Woman is inferior to man ; it is her duty to obey, his to command. That is the will of nature.

Strength and reason are the man's part.

One must choose a wife who is neither too beautiful nor too ugly, whose position in life is analogous to one's own, without, however, avoiding too carefully marriage with a daughter of the nobility. Marriage with widows and women of mature age should be avoided. Men should marry at the age of thirty-six ; women at eighteen. (We have just seen that Tiraqueau had married a girl of eleven when he was twenty-four.) It is well to make inquiry concerning the family, country and character of one's future wife.

Betrothal : Women should not adorn themselves for any man other than their present or future husband. Each one should reveal his or her defects to his or her future partner, but the girl need not undress in the presence of her betrothed.

The husband should not allow his wife to consider herself his equal. However, he must refrain from striking her or maltreating her in any manner whatsoever, for she has two kinds of revenge at her hand. The one is obvious ; the other is poison.

The woman's domain is the garden ; her tool the distaff. A husband may seek his wife's advice, but let him beware of telling her his secrets.

Let those who wish to be loved by their wives love them in return and be strictly faithful to them. Let married couples refrain from having recourse to incantations, philtres and other forms of magic whereby people think hearts may be won. Let it be by dint of mutual affection and other honourable means that they cause conjugal love to be born, endure and grow between them.

Undoubtedly the learned Tiraqueau does not treat women as they were commonly treated at that time all over Gaul, in stories and farces. His tone is not that of the author of *Fifteen Joys of Marriage*. He wishes to be just. And that is what is serious. To be completely just to women is to do them a complete injustice. Despite the praise which Rabelais gave him, in all matters Tiraqueau was lacking in gentleness and charm. He maintained that, as good women were rare, it is not necessary to make laws for them. He made them suffer for the wicked. In a word, although not an enemy of women, he was not their friend, because he was not a friend of the Graces. His book caused some stir. Aymery Bouchard, president of the court of Saintes, a great friend of the Hellenist Franciscans of Fontenay and of Tiraqueau himself,

34

undertook to refute the *De legibus connubialibus* in a Latin work which, by a refinement of elegance, had a Greek title, Τῆς γυναικείας φύτλης, *On the Nature of Women,* an apologia for the sex so harshly treated by the judge of Fontenay.

Rabelais was the friend of Aymery Bouchard ; he was even more, it seems, the friend of André Tiraqueau. The latter consulted the young Franciscan in this lawyer's quarrel, although it was not a matter for the Church.

For Tiraqueau there was one obscure point in the affair. Aymery Bouchard said in his book that the women had engaged him as lawyer, entrusting him with their defence against the author of *De legibus connubialibus.* The judge of Fontenay could not understand how the women had thought of taking a defender in a trial which turned upon a book that they had not read, since it was written in Latin. How did they know that they had been attacked ? the judge of Fontenay anxiously inquired. On this difficult point, Friar François gave an explanation with which Tiraqueau declared himself satisfied.

Aymery, said the young monk to him, who has a taste for women (*mulierarius,* says the text), may well have gone so far, at table or by the fireside, as to translate for them into French, after his own fashion, the passages in the book where the sex is not always spared. He wanted to blacken your character in order to recommend himself to their good graces.

It is evident that already young Friar François was observing and learning to know human nature. But, being too much of a scholar not to consult the ancients, he immediately invoked the authority of Lucian, who recommends the orator, in his ῥητό ρων διδάσκαλος, to make himself agreeable to women if he wishes to succeed.

It is thus that François Rabelais, in the flower of his age, being involved in this learned quarrel, was called upon to consider the advantages and disadvantages of marriage, between the horns of which dilemma, we shall later see Panurge, his other self, suspended.

In 1520, Pierre Lamy went to Saintes, to President Aymery Bouchard's, the defender of women. During his sojourn in this town he wrote to Judge Tiraqueau, the adversary of women, a Latin letter which has been preserved, and which shows us that the mutual friendship of the two champions had not been lost in the quarrel. In it Rabelais is mentioned as a very young man, already full of learning, but who has only lately begun to try to write in Greek.

" I am torn," said Pierre Lamy, " by contradictory emotions when I foresee that if, in the interests of Aymery, I have been obliged to remain for a long time far from those for whom I am consumed with regret, that is to say, you and our dear Rabelais, most learned of our Franciscan brothers, on the other hand, I shall have to tear myself away from the delights of Aymery in order to return to you, which, to my great joy, will be scarce delayed. But I find deep consolation in the thought that, while enjoying one of you, I enjoy the other, so alike unto one another are you in character and learning, and that this same Rabelais, so diligent in fulfilling the duties of friendship, will keep us frequent company by his letters, both Latin, the composition of which is most familiar to him, and Greek, at which he has for some time been striving. . . . I shall wait to tell you more about this until we can at leisure resume our meetings beneath our laurel grove and our walks along the paths of our little garden."

It is not surprising that Rabelais, who was trying in 1520 to write familiar letters in Greek, was able, four years later, to compose verses in this language in imitation of Meleager. He celebrated the *De legibus connubialibus* in an epigram which, according to the custom of the time, Tiraqueau printed at the beginning of the book in the edition of 1524. The following is a literal translation :

" Seeing this book in the Elysian Fields, both men and women will say : ' If Plato had taught us the laws whereby the famous André taught his Gauls the conjugal union and the glory of marriage, would there be amongst men any more illustrious than Plato ? ' "

The work thus celebrated is an indigestible compilation, a collection of texts brought together without any artistic or critical sense. Tiraqueau greater than Plato ! . . . This vain and unmeasured praise was lost in its own immensity. The fault is less that of Rabelais than of the spirit of the times, in which there was no sense of proportion either in praise or invective.

After what we have seen, it cannot be said that the regulations at Fontenay were very severe or that the monks lived separated from the world. But the Chapter and most of the monks looked with an unfriendly eye on the three or four Hellenists of the community. They were afraid that knowledge, and especially knowledge of Greek, would destroy the soul. This fear was not peculiar to them ; it existed in every convent. It was believed that Greek made heretics. At Fontenay a certain Arthus Coultant, amongst others, was very much opposed to the Hellenists, if we may judge by the resentment which he aroused in Rabelais, whose *bête noire* he was. A spy and a calumniator, he rendered every kind of disservice to the studious monks. That is what our author gives us to understand when he calls him, in his joyful indignation, an articulating friar, that is, one looking with curiosity, and a diaboliculating friar, that is, a calumniating one.

Finally the Chapter had a search made in the cells of Pierre Lamy and François Rabelais. Greek books were found, some writings from Germany and Italy, and the works of Erasmus. These books were confiscated. In addition a serious accusation was brought against the two scholars. They were reproached with devoting the profits which they drew from preaching the gospel to the upkeep of a large library, instead of consecrating them to the monastic revenues. That is a grievance of which we cannot judge, but whose seriousness we can feel.

Pierre Lamy and François Rabelais, deprived of books and paper, placed in solitary confinement, suffered great woes and feared worse, through the action of these wretched monks, whom ignorance and fear rendered credulous and cruel. Friar François, prudent and sage, feared the hobgoblins. That was what he called Friar Arthus and all the other diaboliculating friars. Pierre Lamy was not any more confident. At this stage the

learned man remembered that the ancient Romans practised divination by reading a book at the place which they had marked with their nail before opening it, and that, as the works of Virgil were preferably used for this purpose, they called this manner of reading the future the Virgilian lotteries. He took a Virgil, slipped his finger into the closed book, opened it and read at the place so marked this verse :

Heu ! fuge crudeles terras, fuge littus avarum !
(Ah ! fly from this cruel land, fly from this miserly shore !)

Pierre Lamy and François Rabelais did not scorn the warnings of the oracle. Deceiving their gaolers, they escaped by prompt flight from the claws of the cruel hobgoblins and found a sure retreat in the country, for they had friends there. The position of a fugitive monk was none the less precarious and dangerous. From some unknown hiding place, sick with torment and uneasiness, they made powerful personages take action in their favour and found protectors even in the King's household.

The great Guillaume Budé, to whom they both wrote, replied to them with the eloquent and sincere indignation of a Hellenist who saw other Hellenists punished for having cultivated those beautiful studies which he himself cultivated so lovingly. His letter, with its pompous indignation, is in the turgid style proper to all scholars' letters of the period, of which Rabelais was soon to give us some beautiful examples. For he could be Ciceronian if necessary. Here, translated into English, is a sufficiently long passage from the letter from Guillaume Budé :

" O immortal God, Thou who presidest over their holy congregation and over our friendship, what news has reached me ?
I learn that you and Rabelais, your Pylades, because of your
zeal in the study of the Greek tongue, are harrassed and vexed
in a thousand ways by your brothers, those sworn enemies of all
literature and all refinement. O fatal madness ! O incredible
error ! Thus the gross and stupid monks have been so carried
away by their blindness as to pursue with their calumnies those
whose learning, acquired in so short a time, should be an honour
to the entire community. . . . We had already learned and seen
with our own eyes some marks of their insensate fury ; we knew
that they attacked ourselves as the chief of those who had been
seized, as they say, by the fury of Hellenism, and that they had
sworn to annihilate the cult of Greek letters, recently restored, to
the eternal honour of our epoch. . . .

" All friends of learning were ready, each in the measure of
his power, to succour you in this extremity, you and the small
number of brothers who share your aspirations towards universal
knowledge . . . but I have learned that these tribulations ceased
since your persecutors discovered that they were placing themselves in hostility to people of credit and to the King himself.
Thus you have honourably emerged from this trial and will, I
hope, resume your work with renewed ardour."

Rabelais received from the great humanist an almost similar
letter. Budé congratulates him particularly on having recovered
his books and on being henceforth protected from all violence.

" I have learned from one of the most enlightened and most

humane of your brothers, and I made him affirm the news on oath, that they had restored to you your books, your delight, arbitrarily confiscated from you, and that you had been restored to your previous liberty and quiet."

Guillaume Budé was not mistaken. The two Franciscans were out of danger. The affairs of Rabelais were going well : Friar François received from Pope Clement VII an indult authorising him to enter the order of St. Benedict and the Abbey of Maillezais, with the title and habit of a regular Canon and the right to hold benefices. These privileges were not yet sufficient for Rabelais who, but for the hobgoblins, might perhaps have been an excellent monk. But he could not stand the sound of bells and did not like to interrupt his studies to go to matins. He set out on his travels, saying Mass on occasion.

This irregularity was not likely to shock excessively the Bishop of Maillezais, who knew what an exquisite man Friar François was, since he had been a fellow-student of his at La Baumette.

Geoffroy d'Estissac was a young prelate, who was appointed in 1518, when less than twenty-five years old, by a special dispensation, to the see of Maillezais, where he led a lordly and fashionable life. Maillezais, which is situated on a plain in the middle of the Vendean marshes, overlooks one of the two branches formed by the Aulise, a tributary of the Sèvre. There stood an ancient Abbey, raised to a bishopric by Pope John XXII. Geoffroy d'Estissac, who lived in a splendid manner, after the fashion of the Renaissance lords, presented the newly built abbey church with a gateway all glittering with the wonders of the new architecture, and transformed the monastery buildings into a palace in the Italian style, with charming cloisters, a splashing fountain, and broad, noble stairways. Around this beautiful dwelling Geoffroy d'Estissac planted gardens full of flowers and rare plants. On being received at Ligugé, and lodged perhaps in the circular dungeon where they still show his room, Rabelais once more found himself in the congenial company of scholars. He formed a particular bond of friendship with Jean Bouchet, a native of Poitou, like himself, an attorney at Poitiers, author of *Annales d'Aquitaine* and many other writings in prose and verse. There was good fruit and wine, they say, at Ligugé, but above all there were good books and learned conversations. Rabelais boasted of the wine of Ligugé. Perhaps he was not over-critical. I may say in this connection that I suspect our François of having never known much about wine. He is always talking about bottles, but his bottles were books, and he became intoxicated only with wisdom and sound doctrine.

Geoffroy d'Estissac loved the humanists and did not hate the Reformers. At that time in France there were many bishops and cardinals who protected scholars and facilitated the spread of sacred and profane texts. Up to this date, 1524, the Court was favourable to innovations. The Reformation, which was born in France before Luther, had no greater friend than the gentle and pious sister of the King, Marguerite d'Angoulême, duchesse d'Alençon, subsequently Queen of Navarre. The King himself inclined in that direction. The kings of France have always resisted the Popes as much as possible and François I would probably have remained favourable to the French Reformers to the end, if he had not needed the help of the Holy See against Charles V and the Imperialists.

On the other hand, the Sorbonne, the monks and the lower orders clung to the old customs and old beliefs. The common people of the town supported and defended them with a zeal and a fury of which we shall soon have evidence. Consequently, it is not surprising that Friar François, who was suspect to the monks of Fontenay, was favourably treated by the Bishop of Maillezais. Friar François was wonderfully studious. We know from himself that at Ligugé he worked in his bed in his little room. This was not laziness ; the room was not heated. At that time people had no other protection from the cold, save the curtains of their bed and the mantelpiece. François Rabelais acquired such learnings as to astonish the most learned of his contemporaries. He became a philosopher, a theologian, a mathe-matician, a jurist, a musician, an arithmetician, a geometrist, an astronomer, a painter and a poet. In this he was the equal of Erasmus and Budé. But in one respect he is unique, or at least exceedingly rare in his century ; his learning was not only from books, but from nature ; not literary, but intellectual ; not only verbal, but factual and living.

It is not, therefore, surprising that he should have thought of studying medicine as the science which penetrated farthest into the secret of life. At least the hope was permissible at that time of great hope. The School of Medicine at Montpellier was very old. The Arabs and the Jews had brought their teaching there. It was celebrated for its professors, its privileges, and its doctrines. François Rabelais went to Montpellier ; but he did not take either the most direct or the shortest route. That was not his method. He liked fine journeys and, as was said of Ulysses, lengthy wanderings. Like Jean de La Fontaine, who was to imitate him in this as in the art of story-telling, he was always ready to take the longest way. In all probability, as he journeyed he visited the towns and universities of France, Paris, Poitiers, Toulouse, Bourges, Orléans, Angers. Finally, on the 17th of September, in the year 1530, he inscribed his name in these terms on the registry of the School of Medicine at Montpellier : " I, François Rabelais, of Chinon, in the diocese of Tours, have come hither for the purpose of studying medicine and have taken as my sponsor the illustrious Master Jean Schyron, Doctor and Regent of this University. I promise to observe all the statutes of the said School of Medicine which are usually kept by those who have in good faith signed their name and taken the oath, according to custom, and to this I have set my signature with my own hand, this 17th day of September, in the year of our Lord, 1530."

There can be no doubt that François Rabelais was an excellent student of medicine. We know that he acquired a particularly profound knowledge of anatomy and botany. His curiosity, his zeal for learning, were inextinguishable. But he was also eager for pleasure. Having found gay companions at Montpellier, he took a large share in the amusements of the youth of the school. We have it on his own authority that he greatly enjoyed acting in a comedy, or rather a farce, with his fellow-students Antoine de

Saporta, Guy Bouguier, Balthazar Noyer, Tolet, Jean Quentin, François Robinet and Jean Perdrier. It was one of those farces of the type of *Pathelin*, so dear to the people of France in the time of King Louis XII, full of vivid strokes and good comedy. Rabelais entitled it himself : *The Moral Comedy of the Man Who Married a Dumb Wife*, and he gives us a summary of it which is sufficient to describe the action. The wife was dumb. Her good man wanted her to speak. She spoke through the arts of the doctor and the surgeon, who cut the string of her tongue. No sooner had she recovered her speech than she spoke so much that her exasperated husband returned to the doctor to ask him to cure this evil, and to make her silent.

" Truly," replied the doctor, " I have among my arts such remedies as can make women speak. I know none that can make them be silent. The only remedy against a wife's chatter is the deafness of her husband."

The poor husband accepted this remedy, since there was no other. By means of some charm, the doctors made him deaf. The wife, seeing that he did not hear a word, and that she was talking in vain, became mad out of spite at not being able to make herself heard. The doctor claimed his fee. The husband replied that he could not hear his request. The doctor threw a powder on his back by virtue of which he became insane. The insane husband and the mad wife made an agreement to beat the doctor and the surgeon, who lay half dead on the floor. That is the end of the comedy. Rabelais says that he never laughed more than at this farce. That is not surprising. He loved farces and this

47

is an excellent one. What could not but be pleasing to a humanist, there was something of Terence in it. The end is taken from the admirable farce of *Pathelin*. Molière drew largely from the analysis given by Rabelais for his *Doctor in Spite of Himself*. There are many celebrated centuries of drama in this students' entertainment.

Amongst the pleasures which Rabelais enjoyed while study-ing medicine must be mentioned his walks on the Iles d'Or, which are also called Stoechades, and which we call the Iles d'Hyères, which are washed by the blue sea, five leagues from Toulon, all flowering with orange trees, vines, olive trees, ivy, oaks, pines, palms, and rose laurel. He liked those islands so much that later on he decided to call himself their Patriarch, a religious title in use amongst the Christians of the East.

When raised to the rank of Bachelor, according to the custom, he delivered a public lecture and commented upon the *Aphorisms* of Hippocrates and the *Ars Parva* of Galen, and he left the school without having obtained his doctorate. Rabelais could never stay long in the same place.

He was drawn to Lyons. Even more than Paris this was a city of printers. Scholars flocked there, certain of finding work and friends. He went there at the beginning of the year 1532. From November of the same year he discharged the duties of doctor at the Hôtel-Dieu, at a salary of forty livres a year.

In medicine we find him torn between two doctrines, the authority of the ancients, which was then supreme (they swore by Hippocrates), and the study of nature, to which his genius con-stantly turned him. He made dissections, a practice condemned by the Church and disapproved of by custom, and one in which the learned seldom indulged. André Vesale, who was still too young, had not yet begun to hunt for corpses beneath the gallows and in the graveyards. At the Hôtel-Dieu of Lyons, Rabelais publicly dissected a man who had been hanged. Etienne Dolet, who had already made a name for himself amongst the humanists, celebrated this fact as extraordinary and praiseworthy in a discourse in Latin verse which, by a daring fiction, he placed in the mouth of the executed man. He made him say :

" Strangled by the fatal knot, I was hanging miserably on the gallows. Unexpected good fortune which I had scarcely dared ask of great Jupiter ! The eyes of a vast assembly are centred upon me ; I am dissected by the most learned of doctors, who will hold up to admiration in the machinery of my body, the incomparable order, the sublime beauty of the structure of the human anatomy, masterpiece of the Creator. The crowd is looking, all attention. . . . What a signal honour and what excess of glory ! And to think that I might have been the plaything of the winds, the prey of wheeling and rapacious crows ! Ah ! Fate may now do its worst against me. I am transported with glory."

Rabelais was bound in friendship with Etienne Dolet, who was four years younger than he. In the course of his work he observed a little fish in which he thought he recognised the small *garum*, a sort of anchovy which the ancients used in the preparation of a very choice condiment. After various trials, he flattered himself that he had reconstructed the formula of the ancient pickle, and, putting it in Latin verse, he sent it to Dolet with a

D

jar of *garum*. It is wonderful to see the encyclopædic curiosity of the humanists extending to Latin gastronomy and culinary antiquities. Good scholars, with pen in hand they revived the feasts of Lucullus, and in reality regaled themselves poorly on an eel or half an ell of sausage at an eating house. Even then, as often as not, they had to be content with a herring.

At Lyons, François Rabelais divided his attention between the hospital and the shop of Sebastian Gryphius. He was torn between erudition and medicine. Erudition won, at least for a while. He absented himself from the Hôtel-Dieu without leave, and for this offence he was immediately replaced. Then, in order to live, he made books which were sold in the shop in the Rue Mercière, " at the Sign of the Griffin." This Griffin was the emblem of Sebastian Gryphius, printer and bookseller, who had come from Swabia to establish himself in Lyons about 1524, and who, four years later, was celebrated for the beauty of the Greek and Latin texts issued from his presses. Rabelais published with Sebastian Gryphius, in 1532, the *Epistolæ medicinales Manardi*, which he dedicated to Judge Tiraqueau, and the *Aphorisms* of Hippocrates, with an epistle to Bishop Geoffroy d'Estissac. He had not forgotten the days of Fontenay-le-Comte and Ligugé. Our author thought that he should publish this edition of the *Aphorisms*, although there were others in existence, because he had in his possession a beautiful old manuscript of this work, containing abundant glosses. His use of it was more enthusiastic than critical, and he had no scruples in explaining what was already in itself sufficiently clear. If we are to believe M. Jean Plattard, a good judge of such

matters, François had still much to learn in matters of erudition before taking his place amongst the great humanists of the period.

At the same time he published two fragments of Roman law, the Testament of Lucius Cuspidius and a Contract of Sale, with a preliminary Græco-Latin epistle to the defender of women, Aymery Bouchard, now King's Counsel and Master of Requests. In this François had not made a very fortunate choice. Both documents were spurious, very spurious, absolutely spurious. The Testament of Cuspidius had been fabricated a century earlier by Pompeius Lactus and the Contract of Sale was the work of Jovianus Pontanus, who had made it the prologue to a comic dialogue entitled *Actius*. How could so clever a man make such a mistake? He loved antiquity; love blinds and enthusiasm is injurious to criticism. We owe our knowledge of the ancients to these great men of the Renaissance. Let us not employ against them what they have taught us. Since the contemporaries of Rabelais do not seem to have very generally contested the authenticity of these two documents, let us not reproach the editor too seriously with an error which his own period had difficulty in recognising. In short, if the great son of Touraine was not sufficiently suspicious of the compatriots of Poggio, let us not go to the opposite extreme, let us beware of being too cautious, and let us not attribute to Poggio himself the works of Tacitus.

In the sixteenth century the humanists formed a sort of State in the world, the Republic of Letters. The expression dates from that period. Old Erasmus of Rotterdam was the prince of that spiritual republic. Rabelais, who had once so ardently desired a letter from the illustrious Guillaume Budé, seized the opportunity which was offered to him in 1532, at Lyons, to correspond with the great Erasmus. A prelate and friend of letters, like so many others at that time, Georges d'Armagnac, Bishop of Rodez, whose acquaintance he had just made, commissioned him in the month of November to deliver to Erasmus a copy of the works of Flavius Josephus. Rabelais accompanied the package with a letter in Latin to the great man, who was ending a life of labour and glory in Bâle. For some reason which has never yet been explained, so far as I know, this letter is addressed to the unknown name of Bernard de Salignac. But there is no doubt that Erasmus was the person for whom it was intended.

The following are the passages most worthy of interest, literally translated :

" I have eagerly seized this opportunity, O humanest of Fathers, to prove to you by grateful homage my profound respect for you and my filial piety. My Father, did I say ? I should call you Mother, did your indulgence allow it. All that we know of mothers, who nourish the fruit of their womb before seeing it, before knowing even what it will be, who protect it, who shelter it against the inclemency of the air, that you have done for me, for me whose face was not known to you, and whose obscure name could not impress you. You have brought me up ; you have fed me at the chaste breasts of your divine knowledge ; all that I am, all that I am worth, I owe to you alone. If I did not publish it aloud, I should be the most ungrateful of men. Salutations once more, beloved Father, honour of your country, support of letters, un-conquerable champion of truth."

This letter expresses in the grandiloquent manner of the period sentiments that were very true and very sincere. Rabelais was very familiar with the writings of Erasmus ; especially he had read and re-read the *Apophthegms* and the *Adages* ; and often when he was writing he would reproduce some passage from these two works. He felt all the more free to do so because at that time to imitate was praiseworthy and it was an honour to prove that one was well read.

While he was accomplishing works of erudition, which gave him a place of honour amongst men of letters, he gave a few hours from time to time to other works which the learned despised but which we nowadays find well worthy of interest. He made predic-tions and almanacs in the vulgar tongue for the common reader, and into these he put much more of himself than into his learned publications. Into them he gathered a great harvest of pleasan-tries and vulgar jokes, and also maxims of the highest wisdom. His prophecies were simply jibes and sneers at the astrologers and soothsayers. He made fun of those who drew horoscopes and gave excellent reasons for his incredulity concerning them. " The greatest folly in the world," he said, " is to think that there are stars for kings, popes and great lords, rather than for the poor and suffering : as if new stars had been created since the time of the Flood, or since Romulus or Pharamond, at the new creation of kings."

In these popular little books he constantly expresses the idea of a God by whom the universe is governed. Announcing in the almanac for 1533 the future changes of kingdoms and religions, he hastens to add :

" These be secrets of the close Council of the Eternal King, who disposes everything that is and that is done, according to his own free will and good pleasure, about which 'twere better to say nothing and to adore them in silence."

By 1532 Rabelais had accomplished a task which was even more humble, but which was to lead him to make the most peculiar, the most astonishing, the most marvellous book in the world. On a popular theme he had written a story for the entertainment of ignorant and simple people, the story of a giant, *The Great and Inestimable Chronicles of Gargantua*. This Gargantua was not a character invented by Rabelais. His fame extended back into the mists of time ; his popularity was enormous, especially in the country districts. In every province of France the peasants could relate his incredible feats of strength, his miraculous appetite. In a thousand places people pointed out enormous stones, sections of rock, which he had brought there, a hillock or a hill which had fallen from his basket. The story of Rabelais entitled *The Great and Inestimable Chronicles* is just a hodge-podge of traditional funny stories which had long since become popular. He did not take it to the learned printer, Gryphius, but to a bookseller at Lyons called François Juste, where more of them were sold in one month than Bibles in nine years.

How was Rabelais soon led to make of this same Gargantua and his son Pantagruel the weirdest, the merriest, the strangest of novels, a work which resembles no other and can be compared only to the *Satyricon* of Petronius, to the *Gran Tacaño* of Francisco de Quevedo, to the *Don Quixote* of Cervantes, to Swift's *Gulliver*, and to the novels of Voltaire? It is not possible to answer this question as precisely and as accurately as one might wish. Like the sources of the Nile for a long time, the origins of Gargantua and Pantagruel are unknown to us. On this subject I cannot do better than quote the prudent words of the most learned editor of Rabelais, the late lamented Marty-Laveaux:

" It is guessed rather than known that Rabelais re-wrote for the publisher François Juste in Lyons a traditional and long popular joke, which he entitled *The Great and Inestimable Chronicles of the Great and Enormous Giant Gargantua*, that afterwards, amused by his subject, by the success of the little book, he added, as a sequel, his *Pantagruel*, and that finally he substituted for the first formless attempt a new and definitive *Gargantua*, which became the first book of the novel, as *Pantagruel* was the second."

Such are the probabilities. Without entering into an arid and confused discussion on this subject, which would lead to nothing certain, we shall study the first two books and, while refraining from deciding on our own authority whether the second book was composed before the first, we shall examine the latter first of all. The order of the material, although of slight importance in this author, makes this necessary. For it is certain that Pantagruel is the son of Gargantua. This relationship cannot be doubted. We are about to make the acquaintance of these two horrible giants, who are, at bottom, very decent people, and live in their company, which is respectable and even exemplary. With them at every moment we shall pass from the amusing to the serious, from the absurd to the sublime. We shall taste alternately attic salt and kitchen salt. I believe that the taste of both will be enjoyed. But one thing I guarantee is that, in the company of the giants and their friends, nothing will be heard (I shall see to it) which might offend the most chaste, the most timid, and the most delicate ears. I shall be prudent, I shall . . . I must stop. It might seem, in the end, as if I promised too much.

THE FIRST BOOK

CHAPTER II

THE FIRST BOOK

FOR the genealogy of Gargantua the author refers us to the great chronicle of Pantagruel. In connection with this birth he makes a remark upon the greatness and decline of royal families : " I think many are at this day emperours, kings, dukes, princes and popes on the earth whose extraction is from some porters and —pardon—peddlers, as, on the contrary, many are now poor wandring beggars, wretched and miserable, who are descended of the blood and lineage of great kings and emperours. . . . And to give you some hint concerning myself, I cannot think but I am come of the race of some rich king or prince in former times, for never yet saw you any man that had a greater desire to be a king, and to be rich, than I have, and that onely that I may make good chear, do nothing, nor care for any single thing, and plentifully enrich my friends and all honest and learned men." At this point, it may be thought that the mind of Rabelais is revealed, that this great mocker respects neither prince, nor king, nor pope, that he sees far beyond the Renaissance and the Reformation, right down into modern times. Oh ! How wrong that would be, and how mistaken ! Rabelais was very far indeed from thinking anything of the sort. What he says here is quite vulgar and quite popular, and quite common, without being any the worse for that. Here our author merely says very amusingly what had been said before him by all the good preachers, monks like himself. These are gospel words. Nothing is further from the mind of Rabelais than to try to diminish royal authority. King François had no more obedient and respectful subject than Friar François. I say this so that we may be careful not to take a commonplace for a novelty, and also that we may notice how commonplaces are sometimes very daring.

Let us return to our book. The father of Gargantua is called Grandgousier ; his mother Gargamelle ; she was the daughter of the King of the Parpaillots. Grandgousier, we are told, was a good fellow in his time, he loved to drink neat and to eat salt meat, being always well furnished with gammons of bacon, both of Bayonne and Mayence, with store of dried neats' tongues.

One holiday, when they had eaten three hundred and sixty-seven thousand and fourteen beeves and danced upon the grass,

Gargantua issued from his mother's ears. Seventeen thousand, nine hundred and thirteen cows were appointed to furnish him with milk, but he preferred wine to milk.

When he grew up, his father had him dressed in white and blue : nine hundred ells of linen for his shirt, eight hundred and thirteen ells of white satin for his doublet, and for his points fifteen hundred and nine dogskins and a half. " Then was it that men began to tie their breeches to their doublets and not their doublets to their breeches : for it is against nature, as hath most amply been showed by Occam upon the Exponibles of Master Hautechaussade." Occam was a rather Reformist theologian of his time and little inclined towards the Pope ; but he practised Scholasticism ; that was sufficient for Rabelais to make fun of him. Scholasticism was his *bête noire*.

When the time came to give Gargantua a tutor, his father chose a great doctor of theology, Master Tubal Holophernes, who taught him his A B C so well that he could say it by heart backwards, and who instructed him in the old Scholasticism. This great doctor having died, an old coughing fellow named Master Jobelin Bride, succeeded him and, using the same method, reduced instruction to exercises of memory. The child studied with zeal ; he learnt easily, but the more he studied the more he became foolish, doted and blockish. His father complained of this to his friend the Viceroy of Papeligosse, who frankly replied to him :

" It were better for him to learne nothing at all, than to be taught such like books under such schoolmasters, because their knowledge was nothing but brutishness, and their wisdom but blunt foppish toyes, serving only to bastardise good and noble spirits and to corrupt all the flower of youth."

That night at supper the Viceroy sent for one of his pages called Eudemon, his hair in good order, handsome in his apparel, very spruce, comely in his behaviour and more like a little angel than a man ; then he said to Grandgousier :

" Do you see this young boy ? He is not as yet sixteen years old ; let us try (if it please you), what difference there is betwixt the knowledge of the doting Mateologians of old time, and the young lads that are now " (the Middle Ages and the Renaissance are thus confronted, or, to be more accurate, Scholasticism and the Humanities). The trial pleased Grandgousier. Eudemon, with his cap in his hand, a clear and open countenance, ruddy lips, his eyes steady, and his looks fixed upon Gargantua, with youthful modesty began his compliment, and when he had well and duly commended him, he placed himself entirely at his service. All this was delivered with proper gestures, distinct enunciation, eloquent delivery and in very ornate Latin. After which Gargantua's only reply was to cry like a cow and to hide his face in his cap. It was not possible to draw one word from him. To this scene in the old novel, a historic scene corresponds, which took place in France under Louis XIV. The two scenes improve by being compared. I shall remind you that the young Duc de Berry, who had been educated in princely fashion by some Tubal Holophernes and some Jobelin Bride of the seventeenth century one day behaved before the Parliament in a manner

E

which recalled that of the young Gargantua when saluted by Eudemon. This is how St. Simon relates the session, when the prince renounced the crown of Spain :

" The first president presented his compliments to the Duc de Berry. When he had finished it was the Prince's turn to reply. He half took off his hat, promptly put it on again, looked at the first president and said : ' Sir !' . . . After a moment's pause he repeated : ' Sir ' . . . He looked around at those present and again said : ' Sir ' . . . He turned to the Duc d'Orléans, both of them being as red as poppies, then to the first president, and finally he stopped short, without being able to utter a single word except : ' Sir ' . . . In the end, the first president, seeing that there was nothing else to be done, terminated the cruel scene by taking off his hat to the Duc de Berry and bowing low, as if the reply were finished, and immediately made a signal to the courtiers that they could talk.

" On his return to Versailles the Princesse de Montauban came forward to greet him, without knowing anything of what had happened, and she began to cry out, as soon as she saw the Duke, how charmed she had been by the grace and eloquence with which he had spoken to the Parliament. He blushed with vexation and did not reply ; finally, unable to restrain himself further, he took M. de St. Simon to his quarters, began to weep, to shout, and to complain of the King, and of his tutor :

" ' Their only aim has been to make me stupid,' he cried, weeping with rage, ' and to stifle everything I might have been ; they have taught me nothing but gambling and hunting and they have succeeded in making a fool and an idiot of me, an utterly incapable person who will never be good for anything.' "

The two scenes are alike. But it must be admitted to the credit of Rabelais that the scene of Gargantua and Eudemon is just as true and living as the other.

Grandgousier, furious at seeing his son so badly educated, was ready to kill Master Jobelin. Then, his anger having subsided, for he was a decent man, he ordered his wages to be paid to the old coughing fellow, that they should whittle him up soundly, and give him leave to go to all the devils in hell.

When Master Jobelin had left, on the advice of the Viceroy, Grandgousier confided the education of Gargantua to a young scholar named Ponocrates, who was the tutor of Eudemon. No better choice could have been made. And it was agreed that the two young princes should go with Ponocrates to Paris in order to profit by the advantages which that city offers to those who wish to study.

During the voyage Gargantua once more became the horrible giant of legend. He rode on a Numidian mare whose tail was so long that by whisking it a few times she knocked down a forest. Beauce at that time was covered with trees. When the mare of Gargantua drove the flies away, Beauce immediately became the bare plain which we know.

According to our author, Gargantua visited the city and was seen and greatly admired by everybody ; " for the people of Paris are so sottish, so badot, so foolish and fond by nature, that a juggler, a carrier of indulgences, a sumpter-horse, or a mule with cymbals, a blinde fidler in the middle of a crosse lane, shall draw a greater confluence of people together than an evangelical preacher."

Gargantua sat down upon the towers of Nôtre Dame. There he saw the great bells and made them sound very harmoniously. While he was doing this it came to his mind that they would serve very well to hang about his mare's neck, and he carried them to his lodgings. The Parisians, excited by the loss of their bells, assembled at the foot of the Tower of Nesle and, after noisy deliberation, they decided to send the oldest and most respected master of the faculty, Janotus de Bragmardo, to claim them.

Master Janotus, preceded by three beadles, betook himself to the lodgings of Gargantua. On seeing them, Ponocrates at first believed that they were maskers, but, on learning who they were and what they wanted, he informed Gargantua, who had them brought to the goblet-office, where they drank like theologians. Meanwhile the son of Grandgousier returned the bells unknown to Master Janotus who pronounced a gallant oration in asking for them :

" It were but reason that you should restore to us our bells ; for we have great need of them . . . if you restore them unto us at my request, I shall gaine by it six basketfuls of sauciges, and a fine pair of breeches, which will do my legs a great deal of good, or else they will not keep their promise to me . . . ha, ha, a paire of breeches is not so easily got, I have experience of it my self."

To this first argument he adds others of a more general nature :

" A town without bells is like a blinde man without a staffe, an asse without a crocker and a cow without cymbals . . . etc. . . ."

This harangue made everybody laugh heartily, and Master Janotus, seeing them laugh, began to laugh more loudly than they. Thus simple people are happy : everything pleases them. Gargantua caused this fine orator to be given kindling wood, wine, a feather bed, a dish, and seven ells of black cloth to make breeches. Whereupon Master Janotus went to the faculty to claim the payment which had been promised him. But they gave him nothing for the reason that he had already been paid.

Ponocrates, who was an excellent educator, began by making his pupil forget everything that the old Sorbonnists, Tubal Holophernes and Jobelin Bride had taught him. For that purpose he purged him with hellebore. Then he set him to such a course of study that not an hour of the day was lost. Gargantua awoke at four o'clock in the morning. While they were rubbing him, a young page read to him a passage from the Holy Scriptures. While he was dressing, his tutor explained the obscure and difficult points in his previous reading. Then they went and examined the face of the sky, the position of the sun and moon. Gargantua allowed himself to be dressed, combed, trimmed and perfumed while repeating the lessons of the day before, not without drawing therefrom practical conclusions. In this way he was fully dressed and was read to for three hours. After which they went and played ball and tennis, leaving off when they pleased, or when they began to perspire abundantly.

After being well rubbed, they recited some passages from the lesson of the day while waiting for dinner.

At the beginning of the meal they listened to the reading of some romance of chivalry. Sometimes the reading continued after the wine had been served ; sometimes the guests discoursed merrily together ; even this pleasure was profitable, because they discussed the properties and virtues of everything that was served at table, of the bread, the wine, the water, the salt, the meats, fish, fruit, herbs, roots, and in this connection they invoked the testimony of the ancients, Pliny, Ælian, Aristotle, Athenæus and Dioscorides, whom Don Quixote was to read later on with the commentaries of Dr. Laguna. Afterwards the conversation turned to the lesson of the morning and they all gave thanks unto God.

When they rose from the table, cards were brought, not to play, but to discover mathematical tricks ; they designed geometrical and astronomical figures ; they sang in four or five parts, played the lute, the spinet, the harp, the flute, the viola and the trombone. This recreation lasted one hour. It was followed by three hours of study : reading and writing. They had to practice making antique letters, that is to say, the Italic characters brought into favour by the great Hellenist printer of Venice, Aldo Manuzi ; Gothic was left to the pedants of the Sorbonne and to the Scholastics.

Having done this, the young princes left their house. A young gentleman of Touraine, named Gymnast, gave writing lessons to Eudemon and to Gargantua. Gargantua rides a barbed steed, a jennet, a cob, and not that terrible mare who knocked down the forest of Beauce in driving away the flies with her tail. Is Gargantua no longer a giant ? A little earlier he was sitting on the towers of Nôtre Dame ; now he is sitting on the scholar's bench and at the table of Christians. This need not surprise us. The wise man should be surprised at nothing. Gargantua changes his stature at every moment. Rabelais has no difficulty in giving him the stature suitable to every situation : he is a giant when he is the popular hero of the old stories, a prince of respectable proportions and pleasant mien when he mingles with life and is introduced into the human comedy by the profoundest of comic geniuses.

After riding, the son of Grandgousier indulged in all the exercises useful for the training of a warrior. He hunted, swam, shouted like all the devils in hell, to exercise his breast and lungs, swung dumb-bells and collected plants.

While recapitulating the studies of the day they awaited supper, which was plentiful and accompanied by learned and useful conversation. After having given thanks, they had music ; they played cup and ball and, on occasion, paid a visit to some scholar or traveller.

At night they observed the position of the stars in the sky. They briefly recapitulated everything that they had read, seen, known, done and heard during the course of the day, and after praying to God and recommending themselves to His clemency, they went to bed.

When the weather was raining they exercised indoors. They amused themselves by trussing hay, splitting and sawing wood, threshing corn in the barn and, instead of herbarising, they visited the various tradesmen, druggists, apothecaries, and even the mountebanks and quacksalvers, for Rabelais believed that something could be learned even from charlatans and jugglers.

Those were days well filled and varied, with plenty of work and not too much fatigue. A wiser and better system of education cannot be conceived. A French statesman, François Guizot, who was undoubtedly rather too austere and Protestant to enjoy much, and particularly to admit, without reservations, a mind excessively joyful, but who, in his youth, had applied his great intelligence to questions of pedagogy, François Guizot could recognise the merits of our author as an educationalist and teacher. In 1812, he wrote in an educational review these lines, which have since been reprinted in his works :

" Rabelais recognised and pointed out the vices of the systems and methods of education in his day ; at the beginning of the sixteenth century, he perceived almost everything of any sense and value in the works of the modern philosophers, amongst others of Locke and Rousseau."

M. Jean Fleury, in his book on Rabelais, very ingeniously compares Master Jobelin and Ponocrates with two great prelates of the seventeenth century, Court tutors. Disrespectful to the one and flattering to the other, this parallel is rather unexpected so far as both of them are concerned. I shall quote it, because it is curious and fundamentally more just than appears at first sight, making allowances for the restrictions and modifications made by the author.

Here is this striking piece of pedagogical criticism :

" Within certain limits the family of Louis XIV offers us an example of a prince educated after the manner of Gargantua, according to the traditional method, and of a prince educated like Eudemon, according to a more rational method. The Dauphin, educated by Bossuet, remained a deplorable mediocrity ; the Duc de Bourgogne, educated by Fénelon, became a remarkable man. No doubt that depended upon the nature of the pupils, but it depended still more upon the method of education. Bossuet applied the system of Jobelin : learning many things by heart. Fénelon approximated to the system of Ponocrates ; he placed his pupil in direct contact with things, and, in order to raise him to his own level, he began by himself becoming young and ignorant like him. The two systems are written down in the works composed by the two Bishops for their pupils. Bossuet presents knowledge in all its dryness and austerity. One has merely to look at his *Histoire Universelle*, his *Politique tirée de l'Ecriture Sainte*, his *Connaissance de Dieu et de soi-même*. Do they contain a single word which supposes a young and ignorant listener ? Does the illustrious author descend a little from the heights, in order to come within the reach of his pupil ? Never. If he says so, the pupil must believe him ; he must learn without understanding for a second, unless it be later on. His pupil took him at his word ; he did not take the trouble to understand what his teacher did not deign to explain to him. His mind remained in swaddling clothes and never grew up.

" Fénelon, on the contrary, begins by placing himself on his pupil's level ; he composes fables to amuse while instructing him, fables drawn, for the most part, from the circumstances of the young prince's life. In order to teach him history, he does not start by placing in his hands a dry and systematic book ; he talks to him about great men and sometimes, in his *Dialogues des morts*, for example, he allows him to be present at the conversations between them. The child's mind blossoms under this benevolent influence ; in this atmosphere of patience and love the young prince's intelligence grows. He is morally transformed and, if it had been given to him to reign, he would have become a remarkable king, not so brilliant, perhaps, but more sensible than Louis XIV. The Dauphin, on the throne, would have been inferior to Louis XV.

" Bossuet succeeded better than Master Jobelin. Fénelon did not succeed so well as Ponocrates, but at all events the two systems confronted each other. They were put into practice by two equally eminent men and, on a small scale, they produced the results announced by the author of Gargantua."

Even to-day the educators of our youth would have much to learn from the old jester.

While Gargantua was studying in Paris under such good auspices, the affair of the cakes broke out at Chinon. This is what happened : During the vintage season, at the beginning of autumn, while the shepherds of the countryside were looking after the vines, some inhabitants of the village of Lerné happened to pass along the highway, driving into the city ten or twelve horses, loaded with those cakes so dear to the people of Touraine and

Poitou, which they call *fouaces*. The shepherds politely asked these people to sell them the cakes at the market price. The only reply of the cake-bakers to this request was insults ; they called the shepherds by various slanderous epithets : louts, varlets, and knaves.

One of the shepherds, named Forgier, reproached them with their conduct.

" Come hither," replied the cake-baker Marquet, " I will give thee some cakes."

Forgier then offered him a piece of money, thinking to receive some cakes. But Marquet, instead of cakes, gave him a lash of his whip across the legs. The shepherd shouted " Murder ! " and threw his stick at Marquet's head, who fell off his mare. The farmers of Grandgousier, who were shaking down nuts close by, came running when they heard the cries, and thrashed the cake-bakers as if they were green rye. The latter, taking flight, the farmers, shepherds and shepherdesses pursued them, stopped them and took from them four or five dozen cakes, for which they paid the ordinary price.

Then they ate their cakes without remorse and, having thoroughly enjoyed them, they danced to the sound of a bagpipe.

The cake-bakers returned at once to Lerné and lodged a complaint with their king, Picrochole, against the shepherds and farmers of Grandgousier. In revenge for the affront Picrochole immediately assembled his army and invaded the territory of Grandgousier. Thus a dreadful war broke out. The soldiers destroyed and scattered everything on their path ; they spared

neither rich nor poor, neither sacred nor profane places. Thus they pillaged the Abbey of Seuillé or Seuilly, the same place where François Rabelais had been sent about the age of 9 or 10 to become a bird, that is to say, a monk. The good monks, not knowing where to turn, decided to make a fine procession in order to deflect the fury of their enemies. The step was praise-worthy, but it was not certain, for who can foresee the designs of the Lord ? Who can hope to change them ? Now, there was an adroit and frisky young monk in the Abbey, called John of the Trencherites. Hearing the noise which the soldiers were making in the vineyard, Friar John went to see what they were doing and, seeing that they were gathering the grapes, he ran to the choir of the church, where the monks were singing to appease the Lord.

" By the virtue of God, why do you not sing : *Paniers, farewell. Vintage is done ?* " he cried.

At these words the Prior raised an indignant voice :

" What should this drunken fellow do here, let him be carried to prison for troubling the divine service."

" Nay, the wine service," replied Friar John, " let us behave ourselves so, that it be not troubled ; for you your self, my Lord Prior, love to drink of the best, and so doth every honest man."

As he said this, he threw off his great habit, seized the staff of the cross which was made of the heart of a sorb tree, and laid so briskly upon his enemies that he routed them all, to the number of thirteen thousand, six hundred and twenty-two, besides the women and little children.

79

On hearing of the invasion and ravaging of his lands, Grand-gousier was filled with astonishment and grief. He was a good king.

" Alas, alas (said he), what is this, good people ? Picrochole, my ancient friend of old time, of my own kindred and alliance, comes he to invade me ? What moves him ? What provokes him ? What sets him on ? My God, my Saviour, help me, inspire me, and advise me what I shall do. I protest, I swear before Thee, I never did him or his subjects any damage or displeasure ; on the contrary, I have succoured and supplied him with men, money, friendship and counsel. That he hath, therefore at this nick of time so outraged and wronged me, it cannot be but by the malevo-lent and wicked spirit . . . ah, my good people, my friends and my faithful servants, must I hinder you from helping me ? I must (I see it well) load with armes my poor, weary and feeble shoul-ders ; and take in my trembling hands the lance and horseman's mace, to succour and protect my honest subjects : reason will have it so ; for by their labour am I entertained, and with their sweat am I nourished, I, my children and my family. This notwith-standing, I will not undertake warre until I have first tried all the wayes and means of peace."

Words of wisdom ! Happy would be the nations if princes always thought thus !

The good king sent to Picrochole his Master of Requests, Ulrich Gallet, to inquire into the reasons for the war, and he wrote to his son Gargantua, calling him back to his threatened country.

Ulrich Gallet delivered a beautiful Ciceronian speech to Picrochole. The King of Lerné answered him outrageously in these
few words : " They will knead cakes for you ! "

To these threats from an angry prince the holy king, Grandgousier, replied only with further offers of peace. Like Idomeneus
in the ninth Book of *Télémaque* : " Idomeneus is ready to perish or
to conquer ; but he loves peace more than the most signal victory.
He would be ashamed to be afraid of being conquered, but he is
afraid of being unjust."

Picrochole refused to receive the envoys of Grandgousier.

" These clowns are afraid to some purpose," said Captain
Touquedillon, who commanded his armies. " Grandgousier is
trembling in his boots." Picrochole's councillors promised him
the conquest of the universe. The imprudent monarch had no
difficulty in believing them. The scene deserves to be quoted in
its entirety :

" ' Sire, this day we make you the happiest, the most warlike
and chivalrous prince that ever was since the death of Alexander
of Macedonia.'

" ' Be covered ' (said Picrochole).

" ' Grammercie (said they) we do but our duty : the manner is
thus, you shall leave some captain here to have the charge of this
garrison, with a party competent for keeping of the place, which
besides its natural strength is made stronger by the rampiers and
fortresses of your devising. Your army you are to divide into two
parts, as you know very well how to do. One part thereof shall fall
upon Grandgousier and his forces, by it shall he be easily at the

very first shock routed, and then shall you get money by heaps, for the clown hath store of ready coine : clown we call him, because a noble and generous prince hath never a penny, and that to hoard up treasure is but a clownish trick. The other part of the army in the mean time shall draw towards Onys, Xaintonge, Angoulesme and Gascony : then march to Perigourt, Medos and Elanes, taking wherever you come without resistance, townes, castles and forts : afterwards to Bayonne, St. John de Luz, to Fuentarabia, where you shall seize upon all the ships, and coasting along Galicia and Portugal, shall pillage all the maritime places, even unto Lisbone, where you shall be supplied with all the necessaries befitting a conqueror. By copsodie Spain will yield, for they are but a race of loobies : then are you to passe by the streights of Gibraltar, where you shall erect two pillars more stately than those of Hercules, to the perpetual memory of your name, and the narrow entrance there shall be called the Picrocholinal sea. Having passed the Picrocholinal sea, behold, Barbarossa yields himself your slave.'

" ' I will (said Picrochole), give him fair quarter and spare his life.'

" ' Yea (said they), so that he be content to be christened.'

And they continued :

" 'You shall conquer all Barbary ; you shall take in to your hands Majorca, Minorca, Sardinia, Corsica ; going alongst on the left hand, you shall rule all Gallia, Narbonensis, Provence, Genua, Florence, Luca, and then God bi wy Rome. The poor Pope is already dying with fear.'

" 'By my faith (said Picrochole), I will not then kiss his pantuffle.'

" 'Italy being thus taken, behond Naples, Calabria, Apulia and Sicilie, all ransacked, and Malta too. I wish the pleasant knights of the Rhodes heretofore would come to resist you.'

" ' I would (said Picrochole), very willingly go to Loretta.'

" 'No, no (said they), that shall be at our return; from thence we will take Candia, Cyprus, Rhodes, and the Cyclade Islands, and set upon Morea. It is ours by St. Trenian, the Lord preserve Jerusalem; for the great Soldan is not comparable to you in power.'

" ' I will then (said he), cause Solomon's temple to be built.'

" ' No (said they), not yet, have a little patience, stay a while, be never too sudden in your enterprises. It is requisite that you first have the Lesser Asia, Craia, Lycia, Panphilia, Cilicia, Lydia, Phrygia, Nysia, even unto Euphrates.'

" ' Shall we see (said Picrochole), Babylon and Mt. Sinai ? ' "

" 'There is no need (said they), at this time; have we not hurried up and down, travelled and toyled enough, in having transfreted and passed over the Hircanian sea, marched alongst the two Armenias, and the three Arabias ? '

" 'By my faith (said he), we have played the fooles, and are undone : ha' poor soules.'

" ' What's the matter ? ' (said they).

" ' What shall we have (said he), to drink, in these deserts ? '

" ' We have already (said they), given order for that. In the Siriack sea you have 9,014 great ships laden with the best wines in the world : they arrived at Port Joppa, there they found two and twenty thousand camels, and sixteen hundred elephants, which you shall have taken at one hunting when you entered into Lybia : and, besides this, you had all the Mecca caravan. Did not they furnish you sufficiently with wine ? '

" ' Yes, but (said he), we did not drink it fresh.'

" ' By the vertue (said they), not of a fish, a valiant man, a con-querour, who pretends and aspires to the monarchy of the world, cannot alwayes have his ease. God be thanked, that you and your men are come safe and sound unto the banks of the river Tigris.'

" ' But (said he), what doth that part of our army in the mean time, which overthrows that unworthy swill-pot, Grandgousier ? '

" ' They are not idle (said they), we shall meet with them by and by, they shall have won you Britany, Normandy, Flanders, Haynault, Brabant, Artois, Holland, Zealand ; they have passed the Rhine over the bellies of the Switsers and Lanskenets, and a party of these hath subdued Luxumberg, Lorrain, Champaigne and Savoy even to Lions, in which place they have met with your forces, returning from the naval conquests of the Mediterranean sea : and have rallied again in Bohemia, after they had plundered and sacked Suevia, Wittenberg, Bavaria, Austria, Moravia, and Styria. Then they set fiercely together upon Lubeck, Norway, Swedenland, and Greenland, even unto the frozen sea : this done, they conquered the isles of Orkney, and subdued Scotland, Eng-land, and Ireland. From thence, sailing to the sandie sea, and by the Sarmates, they have vanquished and overcome Prussia,

Poland, Lituania, Russia, Walachia, Transilvania, Hungary, Bulgaria, Turquieland, and are now at Constantinople.'

" ' Come (said Picrochole), let us go joyn with them quickly, for I will be emperour of Trebezonde also.'

" ' Shall we not kill all these dogs, Turks and Mahumetans ? And you shall give their goods and lands to such as shall have served you honestly.'

" ' Reason (said he), will have it so, that is but just, I give unto you the Caramania, Surie, and all the Palestine.'

" ' Ha, sir (said they), it is out of your goodnesse : Grammercie, God grant you may always prosper.'

" There was there present at that time an old gentleman well experienced in the warres, a sterne souldier, and who had been in many great hazards, named Ecephron, who hearing this discourse, said :

" ' I do greatly doubt that all this enterprise will be like the tale or interlude of the pitcher full of milk wherewith, a shoemaker made himself rich in conceit ; but, when the pitcher was broken, he had not whereupon to dine : what do you pretend by these large conquests ? What shall be the end of so many labours and crosses ? '

" ' Thus it shall be (said Picrochole), that when we are returned, we shall sit down, rest, and be merry.'

" ' But (said Ecephron), if by chance you should never come back, for the voyage is long and dangerous, were it not better for us to take our rest now ? ' "

This marvellous dialogue, full of broad and subtle humour, this scene which flows abundantly and rapidly, is one of the finest flights of the rich genius of Rabelais. Nevertheless, the idea, the structure of the scene is not his. He took it from the conversation between Pyrrhus and Cineas, as reported by Plutarch in the Life of the Tyrant of Epirus.

This original must be read, in order to admire all the more the richness of the copy, to appreciate better, if I may so express it, the originality of the imitation. I will quote this passage from Plutarch, for it is excellent in itself. I shall take it from the translation of Jacques Amyot, because it is very agreeable, and in order to have an opportunity of comparing the style of Rabelais with that of a writer who is a few years later than he, and who contributed, as he did, to the perfection of the French language. Here is the passage from Plutarch ; it is short, and I will first mention its brevity as an element of the comparison.

" Cineas perceiving that Pyrrus was marvellously bent to these wars of Italy, finding him one day at leisure, discoursed with him in this sort : It is reported, and it please your majestie, that the Romaines are very good men of war, and that they command many valiant and warlike nations : if it please the gods we do overcome them, what benefit shall we have of that victory ?

" Pyrrus answered him again, thou doest ask me a question that is manifest of it selfe : for when we have once overcome the Romaines, there can neither Grecian nor barbarous city in all the countrey withstand us, but we shall straight conquer all the rest of Italy, with ease : whose greatnesse, wealth, and power, no man knoweth better then my selfe.

" Cineas pausing a while, replied : and when we have taken Italy, what shall we do then ?

" Pyrrus not finding his meaning yet, sayd unto him : Sicilia as thou knowest, is hard adioyning to it, and doth as it were offer it self unto us, and is a marvellous populous and rich land, and easie to be taken : for all the cities within the land are one against another, having no head that governes them since Agathocles died, more than orators only that are their counsellors, who will soone be won.

" Indeed it is likely which your grace speaketh, quoth Cineas : but when we have won Sicilia, shall then our wars take end ?

" If the gods were pleased, sayd Pyrrus, that victorie were achieved, the way were then broad open for us to attaine great conquests. For who would not afterwards go into Africke and so to Carthage, which also will be an easie conquest, since Aga-thocles secretly flying from Syracusa, and having passed the seas with a few ships, had almost taken it ? And that once conquered, it is most certaine there durst not one of all our enemies that now do daily vex and trouble us, lift up their heads or hands against us.

" No surely, says Cineas ; for it is a cleare case, that with so great a power we may easily recover the realm of Macedon againe, and command all Greece besides, without let of any. But when we have all in our hands, what shall we do in the end ?

" Then Pyrrus laughing, told him againe : we will then (good Cineas) be quiet, and take our ease, and make feasts every day, and be as merry one with another, as we can possible. Cineas, having brought him to that point, sayd againe to him : My Lord, what letteth us now to be quiet, and merry together, sith we enjoy that presently without further travell and trouble, which we will now go seeke for abroad, with such shedding of blood, and so manifest danger? And yet we know not whether ever we shall attaine unto it, after we have both suffered, and caused others to suffer infinite sorrowes and troubles."

Such is the graceful and clear stream which Rabelais flooded with the impetuous torrent of his inspiration. Boileau, in his turn, drew from the same passage in Plutarch the best lines in his *Epistle to the King* :

> " Why all these elephants? This train and host?
> These ships prepar'd to quit the crowded coast?"
> To Pyrrhus said a sage, whom oft he heard
> And loved. Yet never did enough regard.
> The King too mad, the councillor too wise,
> This shews the danger, and that shuts his eyes.
> *By Empire and by Fame I'm call'd to Rome,*
> *And fly from an inglorious ease at home ;*
> *Thither I go—* The boastful Prince replies.
> " For what? A siege? A glorious enterprise.
> Worthy alone of Philip's son and you ;
> What shall we, Sir, when Rome is taken, do?"
> *We'll then with ease all Italy subdue.*
> " Yours I allow that Italy may be,
> But what will you do next?" *Have Sicily ;*
> *She'll soon surrender, nor will Syracuse*
> *Free entrance to my dreadful fleet refuse.*

"Here do you stop, my Lord?" *A tempting gale*
Presents, and thence we will to Carthage sail:
Can Carthage deal with our victorious pow'rs?
Or long resist our arms when Rome is ours?
Say what can stop us? When the way's so fair?
All Africa will be mine without a war.
"I understand you, Sir. When we have past
The Lybian Desert and Ægyptian waste.
When we've enslav'd the Arabs in our way,
Ganges and Indus shall your laws obey.
And Scythians yet untam'd confess your sway.
When this vast hemisphere is ours, what then,
Shall we not see Epirus once again?"
Yes, yes, victorious and content, we there
Will live the life of gods, and laugh at care.
No time for anything but joy allow.
"What hinders, Sir, but you may do it now?
Why should you for the joy of laughing roam?
What lets, but you may laugh your fill at home?
Who, or what dares deny you that delight?
Stay where you are, and laugh from morn to night."

These lines are solid and well turned, but how far superior is the prose of Rabelais in abundance, colour, movement and life! In a word, how much more poetic! But let us resume the story of the great Picrocholinal War.

Young Gargantua, who has resumed his gigantic stature and his Numidian mare for the purpose, defeats Picrochole in a great battle in which Captain Tripet gives up four potfuls of soup and his soul amidst the pottage. The words are our author's. A buffoon could be pardoned for talking that way. A philosopher who expressed himself with the same liberty about the immortal soul would have been roasted alive.

It was to the advantage of Rabelais to pretend to be mad and he never forgot it. But let us continue. When combing his hair, after the battle, Gargantua caused the cannon balls to fall out which the enemy had lodged there, and at one of his meals he swallowed six pilgrims with his salad.

The good king Grandgousier distinguished himself in this war even more by his humanity than by his victories.

Picrochole fled in despair to the Island of Bouchart. Alone, and without a mount, he tried to take an ass from a mill. But the millers prevented him from doing so. They beat him black and blue, and having stripped him, they threw over him a wretched old canvas jacket. Thus the poor choleric wretch went off, and passing the waters near Langeais, he related his misfortunes to an old gypsy, who predicted that his kingdom would be returned to him at the coming of the Cocklicranes. " What is become of him," says our author, " we cannot certainly tell, yet was I told that he is now a porter at Lyons, as testie and pettish in humour as he ever was before, and would be alwayes with great lamentation inquiring at all strangers of the coming of the Cocklicranes, expecting assuredly, according to the old woman's prophecie, that at their coming he shall be re-established in his Kingdom."

Such was the end of the Picrocholinal War. Observe that this quarrel between kings, this formidable struggle, in which fabulous giants are engaged, illustrious captains, and a monk of such unheard of valour that he alone is worth a whole army, all takes place in a flowery corner of Chinonais, in the little corner where Rabelais spent his childhood. If the field of battle is the author's cradle, should the heroes of the war not come from the same place ? There can be no doubt that they do. The wicked Picrochole and the good Gargantua are two country-men of Friar François. The Gargantuan and Picrocholinal War represents the rivalry of two famous houses in Chinon. This Pyrrhus of Touraine, this insatiable king, this choleric Picrochole, is a doctor in Chinon whose real name was Gaucher-de-Sainte-Marthe. His son, Charles, was later to belong to the Queen of Navarre, a good and wise man, who would, however, never pardon Rabelais for Picrochole, and this gigantic and debonair king, the good man Grandgousier, who warms himself after supper at a fine, big, clear fire where chestnuts are roasting, who writes by the hearth with a stick burnt at one end, with which the fire is stirred, and who tells his wife and all his family the beautiful stories of old times, is none other, we may be sure, than the father of our author, Antoine Rabelais, licentiate of laws, and lawyer in Chinon. At first François merely thought of relating amusingly the dispute of Gaucher and his own father, and this quarrel amongst neighbours, this affair of the stolen cakes, became a burlesque epic, as long as the *Iliad*. It is the gift of Rabelais to render immense everything that he touches. They say that, in order to make fun of a Hidalgo against whom he had a grievance, Miguel Cervantes began to write his *Don Quixote*, which was destined to contain so many joyful specimens of

93

humanity. Thus this first book is a comic poem like *Le Lutrin*, in which unimportant facts and unimportant people are comically elevated to an epic grandeur. And why not? What is great, what is small in this world? All depends upon the feelings of the observer and the tone of the speaker. Some commentators may have said that Rabelais wrote the comic history of his time in this first book, that Picrochole is Charles V, Gargantua François I, and the mare of Gargantua—no offence meant—the Duchesse d'Etampes. There is not a word of truth in that. It is nonsense. It is the misfortune of great writers to inspire all sorts of absurdities in swarms of commentators. In the Picrocholinal War Rabelais related his memories of childhood. He always drew from nature. It is for that reason that his pictures are so true and of such vivid interest.

Friar John, as we have said, is a young monk whom Rabelais knew at Seuillé in his childhood. In the chronicle, this Friar John greatly aided Grandgousier in the defence of his territories. As a reward, the good King founded and endowed an Abbey which was not called after any Saint in the calendar, but was called the Abbey of Thélème, because every one there did what he pleased.

This foundation provides Rabelais with an opportunity of showing his taste for art and his knowledge of architecture. Unlike the humanists of his time, most of whom were little concerned about the beauty of form and the charm of colour, he lived as much by his eyes as by his mind, and his attention was particularly captivated by the art of building, which had been restored by the Italian Renaissance, deriving its inspiration from Vitruvius and the ruins of antiquity. He appears greatly to have admired the Roman amphitheatre at Saintes. However, his Abbey of Thélème preserves a rather Gothic appearance, with the six turrets at each angle. It is so minutely described in its structural proportions that an attempt has been made to draw a plan of it. This has been attempted twice ; first, about 1840 by François Lenormant, then, more recently, by M. Arthur Heulhard. These two archaeologists have drawn plans, both vertical and horizontal, which are by no means identical, but which show a considerable resemblance to each other. This proves that Rabelais is an accurate and exact writer, who describes objects perfectly. Reading him, we can form a very good idea of the Abbey of Thélème. It is a beautiful building in the style of the first French Renaissance. On a fountain in the middle of the courtyard the three Graces can be seen. Over the entrance stood the words : *Do What Thou Wilt.* In this Abbey of his dreams Friar François, whose mind revolted against all constraint, adopted the reverse of the usual regulations of monastic life, and ordered everything in a way contrary to what he had observed and experienced at Fontenay. Women are admitted to Thélème in the company of men. They are free, gallant and wealthy. These were the three essential points. The two first are dependent upon the humour of the Thélèmites. The third is guaranteed solely by the munificence of Grandgousier. This prince endowed the Abbey liberally enough to enable the Thélèmites to spend their time in liberal studies, in the practice of the arts, in merry talk and pleasant intercourse. Rabelais does not trouble to tell us to what sum this wealth amounted, nor how it was administered. Nowadays people would expect more details in this connection, if one were to offer a plan for a phalanstery.

It will not be amiss to point out that this monk, who has been described as a drunkard and a glutton, forgot the kitchens, when drawing up the detailed plan of his Abbey.

THE SECOND BOOK

CHAPTER III

THE SECOND BOOK

THE Second Book, which was the first to be written, it is believed, begins with the genealogy and birth of Pantagruel, son of Gargantua and Badebec. Badebec did not survive the birth of her son. That is why the good man Gargantua laughed like a calf and cried like a cow over this birth and this death. The expression, which is our author's, must be excused. It is by no means the worst of the improprieties which he allowed himself.

When the time came to study, Pantagruel went to Poitiers, where he learned a great deal. One day he took from a ledge of rocks a great stone about twelve fathom square and set it upon four pillars in the middle of a field : " To no other end," said Rabelais, " but that the scholars, when they had nothing else to do, might passe their time in getting up on that stone, and feast with a store of gammons, pasties and flaggons, and carve their names upon it with a knife."

Here we are in the midst of popular tradition. The peasants attributed to the caprices of giants the moving of these rough stones, which have since been called Druidic, Celtic, Prehistoric, although no better proven origin has been found for them than that attributed by Rabelais to the raised stone of Poitiers, by hearsay, where the students used to go to eat and drink in his day. For the moment, Pantagruel is a giant, capable, like his father, of swallowing three pilgrims in his salad. But wait ! Soon he will become a man of reasonable stature like ourselves. Would to the gods that we were all as wise as he ! For, on all occasions, Pantagruel will prove himself reason and kindness personified.

One day, after supper, when he was walking near the gates of Orléans with some of his fellow-students, he met a scholar who was coming along the road from Paris, and as soon as they had saluted each other, he asked :

" My friend, from whence comest thou now ? "

The scholar answered :

" From the alme, inclyte and celebrate Academie, which is vocitated Lutetia."

To another question of Pantagruel's, the scholar replied :

" We transfretate the Sequan at the dilucul and crepuscul ; we deambulate by the compites and quadrives by the Urb."

Still talking in this Latinised fashion, he described in these terms the problems of France, where he was born :

" The primeval origin of my aves and ataves was indigenare of the Lemovick regions."

" I understand thee very well," said Pantagruel, " when all comes to all, thou art a Limousin, and thou wilt here by thy affected speech counterfeit the Parisiens."

With this the good giant took him by the throat and almost strangled him.

This episode of the Limousin student is celebrated. Chancellor Pasquier refers to it in his *Recherches sur la France* :

" We should make use of Greek and Latin, but not to butcher them stupidly as in our youth Hélisenne did, of whom our gentle Rabelais rightly made fun in the person of the Limousin scholar."

It is possible, as Pasquier says, that Rabelais made fun of a certain Hélisenne, and it is possible that it was a good joke, but it did not cost him any great effort. This conversation of the Limousin scholar may be found in a book which the printer Geoffroy Tory published at least four years before the second book of *Pantagruel*. It was probably a traditional joke amongst the students of the University of Paris. But we have been warned : Rabelais, like Molière, borrowed on all sides. Great inventors are great borrowers. It would seem as if one could not grow without stealing. I may add that, in taking these " Latial verbocinations " from the printer Geoffroy Tory, Rabelais provided a stick with which to beat himself, for we shall sometimes see him Latinising as the young Limousin did. And the latter had at least an excuse :

he was a Limousin ; he knew only his dialect and the Latin of the Schools. How could he have spoken French ?

While at Orléans, Pantagruel was asked by the inhabitants to place in the steeple an enormous bell which they could not move. It was child's play for the young giant to go through the streets shaking this bell as if it had been an handbell. The delighted inhabitants smiled at the kindness of the young prince. But they were glum the next day when they discovered that this bell ringing had spoiled all their wine. Now, at that time, the wine of the slopes of Saint-Jean-le-Blanc was regarded as a divine elixir. It may be noted in this connection that Rabelais hated bells. He could never pardon them for having governed his life and disturbed his Greek studies at Fontenay. Undoubtedly many churchmen then shared his aversion. The philosophers of the eighteenth century were no better pleased by the great chimes of the cathedrals. André Chénier, a confessed atheist, begged in beautiful verses that the funereal bronze should not moan over his coffin. His wish was granted. The Romantics, I believe, were the first to discover poetry in these aerial verses of towers and spires. Chateaubriand celebrated the poetry of bells. He would have loved them less if they had made him, like Rabelais, get up in the middle of the night.

Scarcely had Pantagruel arrived in Paris than he visited the Library of St. Victor. There he saw the books of which our author gives the imaginary and ridiculous titles. Great efforts have been made to identify them with real works, but not always successfully. It appears that Rabelais was chiefly mocking the

Scholastics. He was a humanist ; humanism had either to kill
Scholasticism or be killed by it. However, we must be careful not
to praise François for all sorts of fine intentions which he never
had. He himself made fun in advance of commentators who
might try to credit him with too much wit. It is true that he also
said it was necessary to break the bone in order to find the marrow.
What a number of doubtful problems ! If we had to probe them
all to the bottom, we should never have finished, and time presses.
As in the poem of Dante, a voice exhorts us : " Look and pass
on."

While in Paris, Pantagruel received from Gargantua, his
father, a very beautiful letter, which has the distinction of showing us the progress of studies in France under François I, and of
drawing a vivid portrait of parents and children at this ardent
hour when the human mind was reborn :

" Although my deceased father of happy memory, Grandgousier, had bent his best endeavours to make me profit in all
perfection and political knowledge, and that my labour and study
was fully correspondent to, yea, went beyond his desire : neverthelesse, as thou mayest well understand, the time then was not so
proper and fit for learning as it is at present, neither had I plenty of
good masters such as thou hast had ; for that time was darksome,
and savouring a little of the infelicity and calamity of the Gothes,
who had destroyed all good literature, which in my age hath by
the divine goodnesse been restored unto its former light and
dignity, and that with such amendment and increase of the knowledge, that now hardly should I be admitted unto the first forme

of the little grammar school-boys : I say, I, who in my youthful days was (and that justly) reputed the most learned of that age.

" Now is it that the mindes of men are qualified with all manner of discipline, that the learned languages are to their pristine purity restored, viz. Greek (without which a man may be ashamed to account himself a scholar), Hebrew, Arabick, Chaldæan, and Latine. Printing likewise is now in use, so elegant, and so correct, although it was found out but in my time by divine inspiration as by a diabolical suggestion on the other side was the invention of ordnance. All the world is full of knowing men, of most learned schoolmasters, and vast libraries ; and it appears to me as a truth, that neither in Plato's time, nor Cicero's, nor Papinian's, there was ever such conveniency for studying, as we see at this day there is : nor must any adventurer henceforward come in publick, or present himself in company, that hath not been pretty well polished in the shop of Minerva. I see robbers, hangmen, free-booters, ostlers, more learned now than the doctors and preachers were in my time.

" What shall I say ? The very women and children have aspired to this praise and celestial manna of good learning. . . .

" Wherefore (my sonne) I admonish thee, to imploy thy youth to profit as well as thou canst both in thy studies and in vertue. Thou art at Paris, where the laudable examples of many brave men may stirre up thy minde to gallant action, and hast likewise for thy tutor and pedagogue the learned Epistemon, who by his lively and vocal documents may instruct thee in the arts and sciences.

" I intend, and will have it so, that thou learn the languages perfectly : first of all, the Greek, as Quintillian will have it : secondly, the Latine : and then the Hebrew, for the holy Scripture-sake : and then the Chaldee and Arabick likewise, and that thou frame thy stile in Greek in imitation of Plato, and, for the Latine, after Cicero. Let there be no history which thou shalt not have ready in thy memory ; unto the prosecuting of which designe, books of cosmographie will help thee much. Of the liberal arts of geometry, arithmetick, and musick, I gave thee some taste when thou were yet little, and not above five or six yeares old ; proceed further in them, and learn the remainder if thou canst. As for astronomy, study all the rules thereof, let passe nevertheless the divining and judicial astrology and the art of Lullius as being nothing else but plain abuses and vanities. As for the civil law, of that I would have thee to know the texts by heart, and then to conferre them with philosophie.

" Now in the matter of the knowledge of the works of nature, I would have thee study that exactly, and that so there be no sea, river nor fountain, of which thou doest not know the fishes, all the fowles of the aire, all the several kindes of shrubs and trees, whether in forrests or orchards : all the sorts of herbes and flowers that grow upon the ground : all the various mettals that are hid within the bowels of the earth ; together with all the diversity of precious stones that are to be seen in the Orient and South parts of the world ; let nothing of all of these be hidden from thee.

" Then faile not most carefully to peruse the books of the

Greek, Arabian and Latine physicians, not despising the Talmudists and Cabalists ; and by frequent anatomies get thee the perfect knowledge of the other world, which is Man ; and at some houres of the day apply thy minde to the study of the holy Scriptures : first in Greek, the New Testament, with the Epistles of the Apostles ; and then the Old Testament in Hebrew. In brief, let me see thee an abyss and bottomless pit of knowledge : for from hence forward, as thou growest great and becomest a man, thou must part from this tranquillity and rest of study. Thou must learn chivalrie, warfare, and the exercises of the field, the better thereby to defend my house and our friends, and to succour and protect them at all their needs against the invasion and assaults of evil doers.

" Furthermore, I will that very shortly thou try how much thou hast profited, which thou canst not better do than by maintaining publickly theses and conclusions in all arts, against all persons whatsoever, and by haunting the company of learned men, both at Paris and otherwhere.

" But because, as the wise man Solomon saith, Wisdome entereth not into a malicious minde ; and that knowledge without conscience is but the ruine of the soule, it behooveth thee to serve, to love, to feare God, and on Him to cast all thy thoughts and all thy hope, and by faith formed in charity to cleave unto Him so that thee mayest never be separated from Him by thy sins.

" Suspect the abuses of the world : set not thy heart upon vanity ; for this life is transitory, but the Word of the Lord endureth for ever. Be serviceable to all thy neighbours and love them as thyself : reverence thy præceptors : shun the conversation of those whom thou desirest not to resemble, and receive not in vaine the graces which God hast bestowed upon thee : and when thou shalt see that thou has attained to all the knowledge that is to be acquired in that part, return unto me, that I may see thee, and give thee my blessing before I die. Gargantua."

Now we encounter an interesting person to know, because he is a summary of humanity. He has great needs, he is ingenious, naturally perverse, sociable, and his soul is restless. His name is Panurge. Pantagruel met him by chance on the Charenton Bridge in tatters and rags and half dead with hunger. Panurge begged alms of him in Arabian, Italian, English, Basque, Low Breton, in Old Dutch, Spanish, Danish, Hebrew, Greek, Latin, and Low German, before asking in French. In this might be seen a reference to the stupidity of clever people who try to complicate everything. More probably our good Rabelais is just amusing himself and it is a conceit of no consequence. It must be confessed that he amuses himself somewhat carelessly, since he shows us the studious and learned Pantagruel unable to understand Panurge's Latin, which is quite good. But every language, known and unknown, had to pass before his French mother tongue, which Panurge speaks excellently, for he was brought up in his youth in the garden of France, that means Touraine !

The manners of Panurge are far from displeasing to Pantagruel, who is seized with a sudden friendship for the stranger and says to him a little prematurely :

" By my faith, I have already stamped in my minde such a deep impression of love towards you, that, if you will condescend unto my will, you shall not depart out of my company and you and I shall make up another couple of friends, such as Æneas and Achates were."

One day Pantagruel, who was fortunately not too tall to enter a doorway (we know that Rabelais increases and diminishes his stature at will), announced that he was ready to sustain an argument with all comers. Challenges of this kind were frequent amongst scholars. Pico della Mirandola, at the age of twenty-three, carried on disputations *de omni re scibili*. Equally young and no less learned, Pantagruel set up nine thousand, seven hundred and sixty-four conclusions which he was ready to defend. For six weeks he argued every day at the Sorbonne, from four in the morning until six in the evening, and acquired great renown. At that moment, the Parliament had to try a case which was so difficult and so involved that nothing could be made of it. In its extreme plight, the court decided to consult the learned Sorbonnist.

" Make the two gentlemen come personally before me," said Pantagruel.

They appeared and the arbiter allowed the plaintiff to speak, who began as follows :

" My Lord, it is true, that a good woman of my house carried eggs to the market to sell " : " Be covered," said Pantagruel. " Thanks to you, my Lord," said the plaintiff. And he continued.

" But to the purpose. There passed betwixt the two tropicks

the summe of threepence towards the zenith and a halfpeny, forasmuch as the Riphæan Mountaines had been that yeare opprest with a great sterility of counterfeit gudgions, etc., etc."

The few words I have quoted show that the case was obscure.

The plaintiff talked for a long time without throwing any more light on it.

The defendant was more vehement but he was not any clearer :

" Should I endure," he shouted indignantly, " that, when I am eating my pottage, and that without either thinking or speaking any manner of ill, they rudely come to vexe, trouble, and perplex my braines with that antick proverb which saith,

" Who in his pottage-eating drinks will not,
When he is dead and buried, see one jot."

It was most decidedly an arduous case. In spite of the diffi- culties which it presented, Pantagruel gave judgment in a sovereign manner and rendered a memorable decision, of which this is the gist :

" Having seen, heard, calculated and well considered of the difference between the two lords here present, the court saith unto them, that in regard of the sudden quaking, shivering and hoarinesse of the flittermouse, bravely declining from the estival soltice, to attempt by private means the surprisal of toyish trifles, etc."

The decision was as obscure as the case. Doubtless it was for that reason that it seemed equitable to both parties, who with- drew, pleased and satisfied. From that time, Pantagruel was rightly reputed to be as just as Solomon. But let us return to Panurge.

When Pantagruel met him on the Charenton Bridge, Panurge was on his way back from Turkey, where the infidels had broached him on a spit all larded like a rabbit. At least, that is what he said. And he further swore that he had been miraculously saved by the powerful intervention of the good Saint Lawrence, not without assisting the miracle, as is only right, by his own efforts. With a firebrand, which he held in his teeth, he set fire to the house of the Pacha who was cooking him and who, in his peril, invoked all the devils, calling them by their names, Gringoth, Astaroth, Roppalus, and Gribouillis. This was very terrifying to Panurge on his spit, for he was larded, and the devils are quick to carry off people who smell of fat, at least on all Fridays during the year, and during the forty days of Lent, unless they have a special dispensation.

Panurge related many other Turkish tales. The sixteenth century was less polite than the seventeenth. The Turkish tales of Rabelais are more ferocious clowning than those of Molière. Now that there is a Parliament in Constantinople, all those Turks of the old comedies have been relegated to the museum of dreams. And how dead those dreams are, labelled in their glass cases !

At the age of thirty-five Panurge was of medium height, neither too tall nor too small, he had a rather aquiline nose, made like the handle of a razor, a very gallant and proper man in his person, but naturally subject to a kind of disease which at that time was called " lack of money." It is an incomparable grief. Notwithstanding, he had threescore and three tricks to come by it at his need, of which the most honourable and most ordinary was a manner of thieving, secret purloining and filching ; for he was a wicked rogue, a drinker, a royster, a rover, and a very dissolute fellow, if there were any in Paris. Otherwise the best man in the world. In short, a man like the rest of us.

He was always contriving some plot against the sergeants and the watch. If he saw a man and a woman sitting side by side in church he sewed them together. One day he sewed a priest's chasuble to his shirt, in such a way that after Mass the priest removed both together, to the great scandal of those present.

At that time there stood in the churches great copper founts with round plaits, or with figures, representing Adam and Eve and the Marriage Feast at Cana, which are now well known to collectors of antiquities. The faithful who bought indulgences under the Pontificate of Leo X (then, as we know, Rome sold a great many) placed their offering in the fount. When he was short of money, Panurge bought indulgences. It was pure profit for him because, while he put a small coin into the plate, he withdrew a larger one.

" You damn yourself like a snake," said Rabelais to him (for it is Rabelais who intervenes in person in this matter of indulgences) ; " you are a thief and a sacrilegious person."

Panurge, quoting the holy Scriptures : " You shall receive an hundredfold what you give," prided himself, on the contrary, upon conforming to the Gospel. In this industry he had not the merit of invention, for we read in one of the colloquies of Erasmus : " There are those so devoted to the Virgin that, while pretending to put in an offering, they skilfully subtract what another has placed there."

Like Pantagruel, Panurge argued at the Sorbonne. He argued with an English doctor ; the argument was peculiar in this respect, that it took place in silence, by signs. It was Panurge who was victorious. This victory gave him a reputation in the city of Paris ; he was publicly praised ; he was made welcome in all company ; he became presumptuous and fell in love with a great lady of the city. He went to see her at her house and engaged with her in a conversation which cannot really be reported. Fortunately, it is not necessary ; suffice it to say that in love the speech of Panurge went straight to the point, and was pressing and urgent. The lady became angry ; she would have preferred a little more delicacy.

" Wicked villain," she replied, " is it for you to speak such words to me ? To whom do you think you are talking ? Go ! never let me see you again."

As he did not stop, she threatened to call her neighbours and have him beaten.

" Ha (said he), you are not so bad as you say, or else I am deceived in your phisiognomie, for sooner shall the earth mount up to the heaven, and the highest heavens descend unto the hells, and all the course of nature be quite perverted, than that in so great beauty and neateness as in you is, there should be one drop of gall or malice. Your beauty is so excellent, so singular, and so heavenly, that I believe nature hath given it to you as a paragon, to make us know what she can do, when she will imploy all her skill. There is nothing in you but honey, but sugar, but a sweet and celestial manna : to you it was, to whom Paris ought to have adjudged the Golden Apple, not to Venus, nor to Juno, nor to Minerva ; for never was there so much magnificence in Juno, so much wisdom in Minerva, nor so much comelinesse in Venus as there is in you. O heavenly gods and goddesses ! how happy shall that man be to whom you will grant that favour. . . ."

As Panurge returned to the point with his customary exactness, the lady went to the window to call the neighbours.

" I will call them myself," said Panurge.

He went away without much caring for the repulse which he had received.

The next day at church, he approached the lady, took her beads, and caused her dress to be ruined by dogs. An unworthy revenge. Such are the love affairs of Panurge ; they are not at all decent.

Meanwhile, Pantagruel was informed that Gargantua, his father, having been transported to the land of the fairies, his kingdom of Utopia was invaded by the Dipsodes who, under the leadership of their King, Anarchus, were besieging the capital. The young prince at once set out for the land of the Dipsodes, which is a long distance from Chinon, for it is in South Africa. Rabelais springs these surprises ; but a wise man should be surprised at nothing.

Rabelais, as is well known, took the name of Utopia from Thomas More, who had imagined an island of that name and made it the seat of a better social order than the one in which he lived. In the Utopia of Thomas More, socialism reigns, collectivism is put into practice. Goods are held in common, goods but not women ; each man jealously keeps his own. There is no love outside marriage, and adultery is punished by death. Such is the dream of Paradise of a councillor of King Henry VIII. It is true that, in order to avoid as much as possible unhappy unions, Sir Thomas More authorises betrothed couples to see each other without concealment, under the supervision of a matron and a patriarch. . . . But we are not here concerned with studying Utopian civilisation, since Rabelais took from More the name of his island without taking its customs, and there is nothing in common between the English and the French Utopia, the latter being merely a sham. O ! how little we shall study social questions there !

Once landed in Utopia, Pantagruel, calling together his companions, Panurge, Epistémon, Eusthenes and Carpalin, said to them with his accustomed wisdom :

" Let us advise well what is to be done, that we be not like the Athenians who never took counsel until after the fact."

Pantagruel, having become a swaggering giant once more in Utopia, encountered there an adversary of his own stature, Captain Loupgarou, whose mace weighed nine thousand, seven hundred quintals and two quarterons, at the end of which were thirteen pointed diamonds, the least of which was as big as the largest bell

of Nôtre Dame in Paris. Before measuring himself against Loupgarou, the son of Gargantua recommended himself to God, and
promised him that if he emerged from the adventure with honour
he would cause to be preached in his Kingdom the holy Gospel,
purely, simply and entirely, and to exterminate the abuses sewn by
the hypocrites. Usually giants are pagans; this one is a Christian.
He calls himself a Catholic, but he is in favour of the Reformation,
and we should like to know whom he calls hypocrites. I am afraid
they are good Catholics submissive to the authority of the Pope.
Loupgarou and his giants were defeated and exterminated. But
Pantagruel suffered a cruel loss : in the battle the faithful Epistémon lost his head. Contrary to appearances, the evil was not without a remedy. Panurge, whom we had not suspected of being a
surgeon, anointed the head and body with a certain ointment,
adjusted the one to the other, vein against vein, sinew against
sinew, vertebræ against vertebræ, gave it fifteen or sixteen stitches
with a needle, and put all round it a little resuscitative ointment.
Suddenly Epistémon began to breathe, then opened his eyes, then
yawned, then sneezed.

Somewhat hoarse, Epistémon began to speak. He had seen the
devils, he said, and had talked familiarly with Lucifer. He declared that the devils were good companions and complained
that Panurge had called him back to life so soon.

" I took a wonderful delight," said he, " in seeing the damned
in hell."

" How so ? " said Pantagruel.

" They do not use them there (said Epistémon), so badly as

you think they do : their estate and condition of living is but only changed after a very strange manner ; for I saw Alexander the Great there, amending and patching on clowts upon old breeches and stockins, whereby he got but a very poor living. Xerxes was a crier of mustard ; Romulus a salter."

In this manner our author gives some mechanical or manual trade to the heroes of antiquity, the knights of Brittany and France and to all the princes of Europe. Pope Julius, Papa Giulio, who, in his lifetime, had ordered Michaelangelo to represent him, sword in hand, is a crier of pudding pies in hell. He no longer wears his great beard. Cleopatra sells onions and Livia cleans vegetables. Piso is a peasant, Cyrus a cowherd, Brutus and Cassius land-surveyors, Demosthenes a vine-dresser, Fabius a threader of beads, Artaxerxes a rope-maker, Æneas a miller, Achilles a scurvy pate, Agamemnon a lick-pot, Ulysses a hay-mower, Nestor a beggar, Ancus Martius a ship-trimmer. . . . The list stretches out longer than a breadless day. Most of the time, unfortunately, not the slightest connection can be seen between the person and his condition ; whenever, by chance, the connection is seen, it is much worse, because then it is apparent that they are simply incongruous puns and absurd clashes of syllables. Our François, who, alone and unaided, thinks more and better than his entire century, freely exercises the divine gift of thinking of nothing, whenever the humour seizes him. It seizes him suddenly like a blessing, then he tells his beads of words. What a blessed author ! And that is and always will be well !

"I saw," continued Epistémon, "Epictetus there most

gallantly apparalled after the French fashion, sitting under a pleasant arbour, with store of handsome gentlewomen, frolicking, drinking, dancing, and making good cheare, with abundance of crowns of the sunne. . . . When he saw me, he invited me to drink with him very courteously, and I being willing to be entreated, we tipled and chopined together most theologically. I heard Master Frances Villon ask Xerxes, how much the messe of mustard ? 'A farthing,' said Xerxes." Whereupon Villon called him a rascal and harshly reproached him with overcharging for food.

The Middle Ages have left several narratives of journeys into the other world, not to mention the *Divine Comedy* of Dante. Rabelais must certainly have known some of them, but he took nothing from any of these Christian stories. He borrowed the principal traits and even the spirit of his little Nékyia from an ancient writer, his favourite author. The *Nekyomanteia* of Lucian was his only model. It was there that he found those changes in human condition which astonished and pleased Epistémon. In this dialogue, the philosopher Menippus, questioned by Philonides, tells him of the excursion which he has just made amongst the dead.

PHILONIDES

Tell me, Menippus, are not those who have on earth lofty and magnificent tombs, columns, statues and inscriptions more highly considered in Hades than the common dead ?

MENIPPUS

You cannot be serious, my friend. If you had seen Mausoleus himself, that Carian celebrated for his tomb, I am certain you would have laughed loud and long, on seeing him lying shamefully in a corner, lost in the crowd. . . . But you would have laughed even more, I am sure, on seeing kings, satraps, reduced to the state of beggars, compelled by poverty to become vendors of salted meat, or schoolmasters, exposed to the insults of the passer-by, and beaten like the vilest slaves. I could not restrain myself when I saw Philip of Macedonia in a corner mending old shoes for money. Others could be seen begging for alms at the cross-roads, Xerxes, Darius, Polycrates.

PHILONIDES

What you tell me about the kings is amazing and almost incredible. But what were Socrates, Diogenes, and the other sages doing ?

MENIPPUS

Socrates was walking about there also, arguing with everyone. Near him were Palamedes, Ulysses, Nestor and all the dead who love talking. The legs of Socrates were still swollen as a result of the poison he took. As for good Diogenes, he is the neighbour of Sardanapalus, the Assyrian, of Midas, the Phrygian, and other wealthy men. When he hears them groaning at the memory of their lost riches, he laughs and is in a good humour. Usually he lies on his back and sings so loudly, in a hoarse and savage tone, that he drowns the complaints of those unhappy men : it is a great sorrow for them, and they have resolved to go and live far from the intolerable company of Diogenes.

What a difference, what a contrast, between the original and the copy ! Rabelais does not limit himself, does not stop. He is amused. He plays with words as children play with stones ; he piles them up. To him is given wealth, abundance, childish and sonorous merriment, that immense strength which is unaware of itself. A refined elegance, measure and order belong to his model ;

it is rapid, sober, economical. It seems dry when translation deprives it of the harmony of its native language. But we can feel that it is as polished as a finger-nail. If it were otherwise, the Greeks would not be the Greeks.

It is one of the most unexpected, the most paradoxical, and yet the strongest and most certain proofs of the genius of Rabelais that, having known, read, and imitated Lucian so much, he always remained so far removed from his favourite model. He borrowed on all sides, as was the custom of his time. But unconsciously he transformed everything he touched.

King Anarchus, in this second book, meets with almost the same fate as King Picrochole in the first book. Having made the unfortunate Anarchus prisoner, Panurge marries him to an old lantern-carrying hag. Pantagruel gave them a little lodge near the lower street and a mortar of stone wherein to bray and pound their sauce. Anarchus became as pretty a crier of green sauce as ever was seen in Utopia. After the capture of Anarchus, the only people of Utopia who still resisted were the Amaurots. At the head of his army, Pantagruel went to conquer them. A storm overtook them on the plains and the rain fell in a downpour. Pantagruel put out his tongue halfway and covered his army. " Meanwhile," says Rabelais, " I, who relate you these so veritable stories, hid myself under a burdock-leafe, but when I saw them thus covered, I went towards them to shelter myself likewise ; which I could not do, for that they were so (as the saying is) ' at the yard's end there is no cloth left.' Then as well as I could, I got upon it, and went along full two leagues, upon his tongue, before I came into his mouth. But, O gods and goddesses, what did I see there ? I saw there great rocks, I believe that those were his teeth. I saw also faire meadows, large forrests, great and strong cities, not a jot lesse then Lyons or Poictiers. The first man I met with there, was a good honest fellow planting coleworts, whereat being very much amazed, I asked him : ' My friend, what dost thou make here ? ' ' I plant coleworts.' "

That is more Lucian. Long before Friar François explored the mouth of the giant, Lucian had discovered a world in the belly of a whale. He relates that travellers, swallowed by the monster, met in his inside an old man and a young one, cultivating a garden. " The old man," says the Greek author, " takes us by the hand and leads us to his dwelling, which he had made very comfortable. There he serves us with vegetables, fruits, fish and wine."

This second book is perhaps inferior to the first, whose main themes it repeats, but it is still excellent in places. It ends with the cleaning out of Pantagruel's stomach. Only doctors can judge the technical merits of this. In my opinion the passage is far from pleasant. Is this a reproach against Rabelais ? Why, certainly not ! This Pantagruel is a whole world, a world with its lands, its oceans, its plants, its animals. It is as right that we should find there dirt and manure as flowers and fruits.

CHAPTER IV

THE LIFE OF RABELAIS (continued)

THE *Gargantua* and the *Pantagruel*, printed in the shape of popular little booklets, with crude wood engravings, were very popular and had many readers, for they had several editions in a short space of time. But the theologians were exceedingly wroth. They were very much excited at this time. The King's own sister, the good Queen of Navarre, was, in this year 1533, denounced, insulted, threatened with the gallows and the stake, and ignominiously represented on the stage of the College of Navarre. A book written by her, an austere, edifying, ascetic work, *Le Miroir de l'âme pécheresse*, caused a scandal. It was not enough to be pious, it was necessary to be pious in the Sorbonne manner. *Pantagruel* was condemned at the Sorbonne, together with a book which I have never, I confess, read, *La Sylve d'Amours*. For a long time, things had not been so bad in France. Numerous heretics were being burned in Paris and Rouen, but the common people did not think that enough were being burned. The winds of anger and cruelty were blowing up from below, rising from the mob which applauded the tortures and eagerly breathed the odour of roasting flesh. The King was not wicked ; he was no fanatic ; he was a frivolous man, completely given up to gallantry and sport, who liked art and letters and was as favourable to scholars and artists as his frivolity and selfishness permitted him. He was undecided, powerless before this flood of popular and monastic fury. But, if only from self-interest and in order to defend his independence against the enterprises of the Pope, he was inclined towards a wise, moderate and royalist reformation of the Church of France. Suddenly, in the month of October, 1534, an audacious gesture on the part of the Reformers, a piece of insolent bravado on the part of those known as Sacramentarians, drove him on to the side of the hangmen.

On the 18th of that month, in Paris and several other cities, and even in the King's own chamber, placards were found which were violently hostile to the Mass. François I was irritated and frightened by this. From that moment he gave the theologians a free hand ; everywhere the stakes were lighted. At one moment he even thought of forbidding the printing of books. It was very dangerous to write about matters of faith and, at that time, everything was a matter of faith, or was connected therewith. However, we need not believe that the author of the censored *Pantagruel* was in very grave danger of being burned. On the contrary, amongst the suspects he was one of those least threatened. Like Brutus in the Rome of Tarquinius, François Rabelais played the fool in his books and was thus enabled to say what no man reputed to be in his senses could have said with impunity. His *Gargantua* and his *Pantagruel* were regarded, it is true, as detestable buffoonery, but of no consequence, which were censored only in the interests of decency and good manners. Further, Master François was physician to the Bishop of Paris. It will be remembered that the young monk of La Baumette had made the acquaintance of two very great and very powerful personages, the brothers Guillaume and Jean du Bellay, of a very illustrious Anjou family. Now, in 1534, Rabelais was in the service of Jean du Bellay, Bishop of Paris, whom the King was sending that year on an embassy to Rome.

At this point it is necessary to say a few words about this prelate whose protection was so valuable to our author. Jean du Bellay, while quite young, had astonished the University of Paris by the extent of his learning, sacred and profane. Trained in the exercise of dialectic and in public debate, he had held his own against the most obstinate theologians. That is how the finest minds of the Church liked to employ themselves. They had posted up at every cross-road in the city the theses which they wished to maintain, like those which we recently saw young Pantagruel post, to the number of nine thousand, seven hundred and sixty-four at one time, in Paris, " touching in them the hardest doubts that are in any science." Subtle, agreeable, persuasive, Jean du Bellay succeeded very well in the negotiations with which the King had entrusted him. Having been sent to England, to the court of King Henry VIII, he had won him over and, on his return to France, he had obtained the Bishopric of Paris. In 1533 he was present at the interview in Marseilles, where Pope Clement VII and King François I concluded an agreement of which the Reformers in France were to pay the costs. Being agreeable, both to the Pope and to Henry VIII, he was obviously designed to negotiate in Rome for the divorce of the King of England. He set out with his household. Passing through Lyons, he found Friar François Rabelais, whom he had previously known as a

I 129

novice at La Baumette, and out of his love for Greek, he took him with him as his physician.

Delighted at travelling over the soil of Italy, which had nourished one of the most beautiful civilisations in the world, and where the ancient learning had awakened from its long sleep, Rabelais looked forward to talking to the scholars, studying the topography of Rome ; and looking for plants unknown in France.

The Bishop and his suite set out in the month of January, 1534, and, being pressed by the inclement weather and the urgency of their business, they scarcely stopped in the towns along the way. Rabelais explored Rome with two studious companions, Claude Chapuis, librarian to the King and French poet, and Nicolas Leroy, a jurist with Lutheran leanings. There is often an odour of heresy about the people with whom Rabelais associated. He undertook a complete description of the Eternal City, whose smallest *vicolo* he was beginning to know, but he abandoned this work when he heard that an antiquarian of Milan, called Marliani, had undertaken the task and had just successfully completed it.

Jean du Bellay, however, employed in vain his keen mind and his abundant eloquence. He could not bring the cardinals over to the side of the King of England. He spoke well, and if Rabelais may be believed, he spoke better than Cicero. None the less, the Consistory decided that the marriage of Henry VIII was valid. Thus was provoked the schism which still lasts. Without being personally involved in the negotiations, Rabelais was present at the meeting, when the Pope and the Sacred College discussed this question, so trifling in itself and so important in its consequences. He was keenly interested, for he was as curious about matters of his own time as about Greek, Latin and Hebrew antiquities.

On the 15th of April the Embassy was back at Lyons. In this city Rabelais published an edition of Marliani's topography with a Latin epistle to Bishop Jean du Bellay, in which he eloquently expressed his gratitude to his master and protector.

"You have conferred on me," he said in this Ciceronian epistle, "that which has been the dearest wish of my heart ever since I have had any feeling for the progress of *belles lettres*, viz., that I might be able to traverse Italy and pay a visit to Rome, the world's capital ; and you have brought it about for me, not only to visit Italy, but also to visit it in your company, you who of all men under Heaven are distinguished for learning and courtesy—the value to be set on which I have not yet fully realised. To me indeed it was more to see you at Rome than to have seen Rome itself. To have been at Rome may fall to any one's lot, and lies before all, except those who are maimed and disabled in all their limbs ; but to have seen you at Rome successful, with incredible congratulations of every one, was a source of pleasure ; to have taken part in affairs at the time when you were conducting that illustrious embassy, on which you had been sent to Rome by our most triumphant King Francis, was a matter for boasting ; to have been by your side when you pronounced your speech on the affairs of the King of England, in the most sacred and dignified conclave in the world, was a point of high felicity."

Jean du Bellay returned to Italy in the month of July, 1535, and once again François Rabelais accompanied him. On the 18th they were at Carmagnola, on the 22nd at Ferrara. There the ambassador had recourse to the arts of his physician ; he was not well and in no state to travel with post-horses, he said. At Florence, where they stopped, Master François, in the excellent company of scholars, contemplated the beautiful situation of the city, the structure of the cathedral, the sumptuousness of the churches and palaces. As he vied with his companions as to who should most worthily praise all this magnificence, a monk from Amiens, named Bernard Lardon, expressed his surprise and dissatisfaction :

" The devil take me," said he, " if I know what you find here so worthy of praise. I have gazed as well as you and am no more blind. What is there ? Beautiful houses, and nothing more. But, God and our good patron, St. Bernard, be with us ! In the whole city I have not yet seen a single cook-shop and I have looked and searched with curiosity. . . . In four times, in only three times the distance which we have covered in our observations, I could show you at Amiens more than fourteen old and sweet-smelling cook-shops. I do not know what pleasure you found in looking at the lions and tigers near the belfrey and the porcupines and ostriches of the Strozzi Palace. By my faith, my children, I should like to see a good and plump young goose on the spit. These porphyries, these marvels, beautiful ? I say nothing against them. But the cream cakes of Amiens are better to my taste. These ancient statues are well made, I have no doubt. But, by

St. Ferréol of Abbéville, the young lasses of our country are a thousand times more engaging."

Need I say that this is Rabelais, word for word. The lions and the tigers mentioned by Friar Bernard Lardon are not, as might be imagined, carved in marble. They are animals in a princely menagerie. The great Italian lords kept wild beasts in their palaces. A picture by Giovanni Bellini, preserved in the Louvre, shows a rich Renaissance palace, with wild beasts chained in the cellars. Towards the middle of August, Jean du Bellay was in Rome, where he received the Hat. Although he was there in grave and difficult circumstances, he found the time to look for antiques. In order to make excavations, he purchased a vineyard near San Lorenzo in Palisperna, between Viminal and Esquiline. He received from a Roman Cardinal a beautiful old mortar. This present to a foreigner caused such a clamour in Rome that du Bellay had to return the mortar to the Governor of the Capital.

At this period, the palaces of the Eternal City were orna-mented, as they still are to-day, with ancient fragments, marbles, bronzes, jaspar, porphyries. The nobles had them placed in the courtyards, in the gardens, on the steps and at the entrances of the rooms. It happened that a young Frenchman, who was later to become renowned as a cosmographer, André Thévet, was in Rome during the embassy of Jean du Bellay and went about the city examining the sculpture with passionate ardour. One day, when his curiosity had drawn him into the courtyard and gardens of a nobleman, and he was lost in the contemplation of the remains of so great a past, the lackeys, misunderstanding what attracted him into a private dwelling, took him for a spy. They would have given him a bad reception if young Thévet had not declared to the master of the house that he was known to Rabelais. Rabelais introduced his compatriot to this nobleman as a great traveller and collector of antiquities. From that moment Thévet was freely admitted into all the Roman houses. This single fact shows that Cardinal du Bellay's position was in good repute with the Italian nobility.

In the Eternal City Rabelais frequented the priests who had come from the East. The Bishop of Caramith, who gave him some lessons in Arabic, abused the credulity of his pupil, who was not, however, very ingenious, by persuading him that the noise of the cataracts of the Nile is audible at three days' distance, that is, from Paris to Tours.

Rabelais had no regular position in religion. From fear of the hobgoblins, as he called them, or rather, in order to be in a position to profit by all the advantages which he might expect from his illustrious protectors, he addressed to the Pope a supplication *pro apostasia*. In it he confesses to have deserted the religious life, to have gone abroad through the world, and he asks the Sovereign Pontiff for full and complete absolution, permission to renew the habit of St. Benedict, to re-enter a monastery of that Order, where they are willing to receive him, and to practise everywhere, with the permission of his superior, the art of medicine, in which, he said, he had taken the degrees of bachelor, licentiate and doctor. To practise it within the limits canonically

imposed upon priests, that is, up to the application of the knife and fire exclusively, for purely humanitarian reasons and without any hope of lucre.

I may point out, without unduly dwelling on the fact, that Rabelais at this time held the degree of licentiate in medicine, and was not yet a fully qualified doctor, although amply equipped with the talent and knowledge requisite.

His request was granted by a letter of Pope Paul III Farnese, dated 17th January, 1536, in the second year of his pontificate. The latter is conceived in the most flattering terms for Rabelais :

" Wishing to succour with gracious favour one who hath received manifold commendations for zeal in religion, knowledge of letters, honesty of life and morals, and other merits of probity and virtue, having these things in view, do hereby absolve you, etc."

We must be careful not to see in this document the opinion of the Holy Father concerning the author of *Pantagruel*. This is the formal style of diplomacy. What must have touched Friar François more than these testimonials to his qualities and virtues was the fact that, contrary to usage, the Pope granted him gratis and without expense the privilege of composing bulls of absolution. The grantee had only to bear the cost of copying, that is to say, as he himself irreverently put it, the honorarium of the " referendary, proctors and other blotters on parchment."

From Rome Rabelais kept up a correspondence, of which a few letters remain, with the pleasant Bishop of Maillezais, Geoffroy d'Estissac. On the 29th November, 1535, he notified the Bishop that he was sending him some seeds from Naples for the garden of Ligugé, the best seeds which the Holy Father had sown in his private garden at the Belvedere. He also sent him some pimpernel ; if he does not send him salads of nasitord and arrousa, it is because he found them too tough and much less grateful to the stomach than the variety cultivated at Ligugé. It is touching to see Master François thus striving to enrich the gardens which he had enjoyed as a poor monk, and to provide vegetables for the table at which he used to sit when he was exposed to the resentment of the hobgoblins. He furnished advice as to the time of planting these seeds which he sent, and the care to be given to the plants. He offered Alexandria pinks, matronal violets, and also an herb with which the Italians keep their chambers fresh in summer called belvedere. " But," he added, " this would be rather for Madame d'Estissac." He meant young Anne de Daillon, married to Louis d'Estissac, nephew of the Bishop. In return, he asked for some crowns. The ambassador of the king of France was always in need of money. His physician, as may be imagined, was even more so. Rabelais never had any money ; it was a disease with him, and he had experienced all the feelings which he attributes to Panurge in this connection. He is always ready to ask of the great, believing that to beg from them is to do them a favour.

One day he wrote to the Bishop of Maillezais :

" If I am short of money I shall appeal to your charity."

This he did a few days later : " I am again obliged to have recourse to your alms. For the thirty crowns, which you were pleased to have paid to me here, are all but come to an end ;

and yet I have spent nothing for any ill use, nor yet upon eating ; for I eat and drink with my Lord Cardinal du Bellay or my Lord de Mascon. But in these little trumperies of dispatches and hiring of chamber-furniture and keeping up one's dress, a great deal of money goes ; although I regulate myself as frugally as I possibly can. If it is your pleasure to send me a bill of exchange, I hope to employ it only in your service and to be grateful besides. I see in this city a thousand little knick-knacks to be bought cheap, which are brought from Cyprus, Candia and Constantinople. If it seems good to you, I will send you anything that I shall see suitable for you, as well as my Lady d'Estissac. The carriage from here to Lyons will cost nothing."

I hasten to say that Master François gave Monsignor d'Estissac plenty for his money. I do not speak of the little knick-knacks, which must have been very like the amber beads, the copper trays, the many-hued fabrics and the embroideries of our Oriental bazaars, nor of the seeds, salads and vegetables from Naples. The Bishop of Maillezais entrusted him with the most important business which he had at the court of Rome and Rabelais acquitted himself with skill. We have this on the authority of Colletet, one of the oldest biographers of our author. Finally, he gave his correspondent news of Rome and the whole of Christendom, which was very valuable at a time when it was hardly possible to learn about public affairs save by private letters.

Very important events were occurring in Christendom at the time, and Rabelais, although not in a position to disentangle the intrigues which were being concocted in Italy, was fairly well informed of the facts as they occurred. So far as the King of France was concerned, he had particular sources of information and, if certain rumours are to be believed, sometimes less discretion than is necessary in matters of this kind. Charles V, who had made an expedition into Tunis that year, on his victorious return to Sicily, was preparing for the conquest of France, and making plans after the manner of Picrochole. Knowing that prophecies sometimes bring about the accomplishment of the facts which they predict, his partisans were uttering all sorts of prognostications which conformed to the plans of the Emperor, and a certain book, full of such oracles, was creating a considerable stir in Rome. Rabelais, who had the work to his hand, sent a copy to M. de Maillezais. " For my own part," he added, when sending it, " I put no faith in it. But none hath ever seen Rome so given over to these vanities and divinations as she is at present."

Meanwhile Charles V, who was expected at Rome, remained in Naples, forming alliances, raising troops, and collecting money. Rabelais informed the Bishop of Maillezais that the Emperor had postponed his arrival until the end of February, and he added :

" If I had as many crowns as the Pope would give days of pardon to whosoever would put it off to five or six years from now, I should be richer than Jacques Cœur ever was."

It is easy to understand the feeling of the Sovereign Pontiff. Rome had just been sacked and despoiled of all its riches. People feared that, if the Emperor and his troops fell upon it, nothing would remain of the unfortunate city.

" They have begun in this city," Rabelais continued, " great preparations to receive him. By command of the Pope they have made a new road by which he is to enter. To make and level this road they have demolished and thrown down more than two hundred houses and three or four churches, level with the earth. This is taken by many as an evil presage."

Meanwhile the Emperor was approaching and Cardinal du Bellay no longer felt safe in Rome. Busybodies advised him to look to his sword and his poison. Believing that his life was threatened, and resolved to escape this mortal danger by flight, he caused his doctors to spread the report of a headache which confined him to bed, jumped on his horse and fled alone through Romagna, Bologna, Montecalieri, into France. For two days the Cardinal's servants were unaware of his departure. Rabelais, who was doubtless no better informed than the others, rejoined his master in Paris.

At this time Charles V, in his attempt to realise long cherished projects, crossed the Var and entered Provence with fifty thousand men, while the Imperialists entered France by the north, took Guise, beseiged Péronne and marched on Paris. Cardinal Jean du Bellay, Bishop of this city, having been named the King's lieutenant-general, by a decree of the 21st July, 1536, was trying to put his episcopal city into a state of defence, as Bishop Synesius formerly did in Pentapolis. His task was difficult, for the walls of Paris were worthless. On this point we have the authority of *Pantagruel*. In the fifteenth chapter of the second book it is said that Panurge, looking at them derisively, spoke of them with contemptuous irony.

" O ! " cried he, " how strong they are, and well fitted to keep geese in a mue or coop to fatten them ! By my beard, they are competently scurvie for such a city as this is ; for a cow with her tail would overthrow above six fathoms of them."

" Oh, my friend (said Pantagruel), dost thou know what Agesilaus said, when he was asked why the great city of Lacedemon was not enclosed with walls ? Lo, here (said he), the walls of the city, in showing them the inhabitants and citizens thereof, so strong, so well armed, and so expert in military discipline ; signifying thereby that there is no wall but of bones, and that towns and cities cannot have a surer wall, nor better fortification than the prowesse and vertue of the citizens and inhabitants ; so is this city so strong, by the great number of war-like people that are in it, that they care not for making any other walls. Besides, whosoever would go about to wall it, as Strasbourg, Orléans, or Ferrara, would finde it almost impossible, the cost and charges would be so excessive."

" Yea, but (said Panurge), it is good neverthelesse to have an out-side of stone, when we are invaded by our enemies, were it but to ask, who is below there ? "

Cardinal du Bellay put into practice the wise maxims of Panurge and tried to give Paris an outside of stone to receive the Imperialists. He fortified the city with ramparts and boulevards and took in provisions.

But the peril which they feared disappeared of itself ; the imperial army melted away, exhausted by famine and dysentery. The siege of Péronne was raised and almost at the same time

Montmorency obliged Charles V to recross the Var. You may be sure that these events were not indifferent to Rabelais, who had a great love for France and his King, and in whom the feeling of military glory blew in great gusts.

The Bishop of Paris was the Abbot of the Benedictine Abbey of Saint-Maur-des-Fossés. We know that Rabelais had obtained by a letter from the Pope permission to be a monk in a monastery of the Order of St. Benedict where they were willing to receive him. He was received as a monk at St. Maur and lived in this house. But the Abbey of St. Maur, having been raised to the rank of a collegiate church by the Pope, at the request of the Cardinal Abbot, the monks there had the rank of Canons. This seemed to exclude Rabelais, unless there were another letter authorising his Canonicate. To leave St. Maur, according to him, was to leave Paradise ; a Paradise, he said, of healthfulness, amenity, serenity, delight, and all honest pleasures of agriculture and rustic life. We do not know what became of this request, and there is little interest in knowing it. Rabelais could not remain in a Paradise, any more than Eve ; like her, he was too full of curiosity for that.

We find him again in Paris when the humanist printer, Etienne Dolet, who had been persecuted as a murderer and pardoned by the King, gave a banquet in that city to celebrate the royal clemency, to which he invited a distinguished crowd of scholars, men of letters, and poets, Guillaume Budé, Danès, Toussain, Macrin, Bourbon, Voulté, Clément Marot, the Gallic Virgil, and François Rabelais, who had been invited in his capacity as an excellent physician. Etienne Dolet himself has transmitted to us in

Latin verses the names of the guests and the subjects of conversation. They talked *sub rosa* about the cleverest writers of which foreign countries could boast : Erasmus, Melanchthon, Bembo, Sadolet, Vida, Jacques Sannazar, and each of these names was greeted with loud acclamation. If the ancient Muse of Etienne Dolet has not exaggerated the austerity of the speeches, this banquet was a banquet of sages, and the orgies in which those present indulged were what a Greek poet called the quiet orgies of thought.

Very shortly after this celebration, Rabelais went to Montpellier, where, on the 22nd May, 1537, he was raised to the rank of a doctor, a title which he had already taken before he had obtained it, but not without being worthy of it, for everything points to the belief that he was a very good doctor. As we have seen, he was a botanist and an anatomist, a cook, a scholar, and according to his learned friend, Sussanneau, he had that joyful, serene, gracious, open countenance which cheers the patient, and is a notable part of the art of Hippocrates and Galen.

In 1537, he made another sojourn in Lyons, his favourite city, which was disturbed by a misadventure about which we have very little information. A letter which he sent to some friend in Italy was handed over to Cardinal de Tournon who, whether rightly or wrongly, finding blameworthy indiscretions, sent it to Chancellor du Bourg, with a few lines which indicate his anger towards the physician of Jean du Bellay.

" Sir," he writes, " I am sending you a letter which Rabelasus wrote to Rome, from which you will see what news he was communicating to one of the worst rakes in Rome. I have given him orders not to leave this city (Lyons) until I learn what are your wishes. If he had not spoken of me in the said letter and avowed his fealty to the King and Queen of Navarre, I should have had him thrown into prison, in order to set an example to all these scribblers of news. You will write to me what is your pleasure, and I rely upon you to let the King know of this what shall seem best to you."

Whatever Cardinal de Tournon may say, Rabelais belonged to Cardinal du Bellay, Ambassador of the King, and consequently, to the King himself. He was not in the service of the Queen of Navarre ; but it is possible that he may have used the name of so helpful a princess, the certain refuge of poor or persecuted humanists. One of her servitors said that she was the port and refuge of all who were unhappy. We do not know whether the complaints of Cardinal de Tournon were well founded. What is certain is that the matter had no unpleasant consequences for Rabelais, whom we find, in 1538, accompanying François I to Aigues-Mortes and being present at those interviews which, by bringing together the Emperor and the King, won the latter over to the Spanish Catholic party, to the great detriment of the humanists, who are all more or less Reformers and inclined towards Lutheranism in the light French manner. An exclusive devotion to the cause of Roman orthodoxy animated the conduct of François I and Charles V, when they were reconciliated.

Rabelais returned to Lyons with his master, the King, at the end of July, 1538.

It is time to reveal a fact which was long unknown but is certain, of his private life. François Rabelais had a child in this city of Lyons by a mother who is unknown to us, a son who received at the baptismal fount the name of Théodule, and one is tempted to believe that it was his father who gave him this name, which means Adorer of God. Rabelais never lost an opportunity of showing his love for Almighty God. He loved Him as a philosopher, for love of Plato and against his priests. Far from hiding this child as a disgrace, François showed him to everybody and little Théodule was rocked in the purple on the knees of cardinals. The princes of the Church could not be severe upon a monk who, after all, did not surrender more than they to the desires of the flesh. Cardinal Jean du Bellay, to mention only one, lived in a sort of conjugal union with the twice widowed sister of that Cardinal de Tournon whom we have recently seen so irritated against Master François. Théodule, upon whom the princes of the Church smiled, died at the age of two. A friend of Rabelais, Boyssonné, a jurist and poet, consecrated to this child, torn so young from life, a whole flora of Latin elegies, distichs, hendecasyllabics, and iambic verses. The following is a translation of these little poems, which imitate in form the Greek Anthology, but are deeply stamped by Christian thought. I have used the translation of M. Arthur Heulhard, slightly modified in places :

OF THÉODULE RABELAIS DEAD AT THE AGE OF TWO YEARS

You ask who lies in this tomb so small ? It is little Théodule himself ; in truth everything about him is small, age, shape, eyes, mouth, for he is a child in body. But he is great through his father, the learned and erudite, versed in all the arts which a good, pious and honest man should know. Little Théodule would have learned them all from his father if destiny had allowed him to live, and from the small child that he was he would have one day become a great man.

TO THÉODULE RABELAIS DYING AT THE AGE OF TWO YEARS

Why leave us so soon, I ask thee, Rabelais ? Why this wish to renounce the joys of living ? Why fall before the day, betraying thy tender youth ? Why prepare to die a premature death ?

REPLY

It is not, Boysson, from hatred of living, that I abandon life. If I die it is in order not to die for ever. I thought that life with Christ is the only life which should be precious to good souls.

DISTICH (TO THE SAME)

By going to Heaven so young, Théodule, thou showest that only those who share your fate are loved by God.

ANOTHER

I who was called Théodule, that is, slave of God, I pray that you may be like me in word and deed.

ANOTHER

He whom you see reposing in this narrow tomb was the friend, when living, of Roman Pontiffs.

ANOTHER

Lyons is his country, Rabelais his father. He who is ignorant of both is ignorant of the two greatest things in the world.

RABELAIS

Fearing lest I become the slave of men and wishing only to obey God, the All-Highest and All-Good, lest I be compelled to descend from horses to asses, I, who had two years here below, leave the mortals and fly to Heaven.

These verses have a flavour of Christian Platonism which may appear affected to us, but which was very much the fashion of the time. Philosophy, like clothing and headdress, is subject to fashion, and there is nothing which better marks a place and an epoch than the idea entertained of the absolute and the infinite. We even represent eternity itself in our own image and to our own taste. The abstract has its picturesque quality, like the concrete. I like to find a literary comparison which illustrates the style of the period and the manner of the author. That is why I shall quote, after the Latin verses of Boyssonné, a little poem, more than 200 years later, on a similar subject, an elegy of André Chénier on the death of a child. As the Latin Muse of the old jurist of Toulouse is stiff and solemn, so the French Muse of the son of Santi L'Hommaca is subtle, graceful and pathetic.

SUR LA MORT D'UN ENFANT

L'innocente victime, au terrestre séjour,
N'a vu que le printemps qui lui donna le jour.
Rien n'est resté de lui qu'un nom, un vain nuage,
Un souvenir, un songe, une invisible image.
Adieu, fragile enfant, échappé de nos bras ;
Adieu, dans la maison d'où l'on ne revient pas.
Nous ne te verrons plus, quand, de moissons couverte,

La campagne d'été rend la ville déserte :
Dans l'enclos paternel, nous ne te verrons plus,
De tes pieds, de tes mains, de tes flancs demi-nus,
Presser l'herbe et les fleurs dont les nymphes de Seine
Couronnent tous les ans les coteaux de Lucienne.
L'axe de l'humble char à tes jeux destiné,
Par de fidèles mains avec toi promené,
Ne sillonnera plus les prés et le rivage.
Tes regards, ton murmure, obscur et doux langage,
N'inquiéteront plus nois soins officieux :
Nous ne recevrons plus, avec des cris joyeux,
Les efforts impuissants de ta bouche vermeille
A bégayer les sons offerts à ton oreille.
Adieu, dans la demeure où nous nous suivrons tous,
Où ta mère déjà tourne ses yeux jaloux.

In 1537, the brother of Cardinal du Bellay, Guillaume du Bellay, lord of Langey, in the absence of Marshal d'Annebault, was charged *ad interim* with the function of the King's lieutenant-general in Piedmont. The King of France had conquered this country without difficulty ; the difficulty was to keep it. Langey had to put Turin, which was threatened by the Imperialists, in a state of defence, set up a Parliament in this city, with instructions to apply French law, fill the offices of the judiciary, prepare the fortifications of the castles and towns all over the country, and bring from France oil, groceries, salt fish for Lent, and medicaments, of which Piedmont had been denuded.

Master François was called to Turin in 1540, and discharged there the function of physician to the Viceroy, who was in great need of his services, for Langey, being a little over 50, was greatly worn and the superhuman labour which he undertook completed the ruin of his shattered health.

A universal man, the Pantagruelist rendered his master other services than those of a doctor. He was his intermediary with several scholars. He corresponded particularly with the juris-consult Jean Boyssonné, whose Latin verses we have just quoted, with Guillaume Bigot, with Guillaume Pélicier, Bishop of Nar-bonne, then of Montpellier, and, at this time Ambassador of the King of France at Venice. We have two letters from this prelate to Rabelais. One of the 23rd July, the other of the 17th October, 1540, written in a friendly and familiar tone. In the second of these letters, it is a question of Hebrew and Syriac manuscripts and Greek books whose purchase the French Ambassador was negotiating. Pélicier asked the Hellenist monk to use all his credit to help the success of the negotiations. We do not know whether Rabelais made himself useful in this matter, but it succeeded according to the wishes of Pélicier, and the Oriental manuscripts acquired by the Ambassador still enrich our public institutions to-day.

It would appear that Master François, whom a prelate like the Bishop of Montpellier treated with such consideration, got into another scrape at Turin, owing to his indiscretion. He was so terrified by what he had done that he re-crossed the Alps madly and was found at Chambéry, out of his wits and not knowing where to go. We do not know what his error was, but it was doubtless less serious than he supposed, for, in the month of March, 1541, he was back in Turin, in the good graces of the Viceroy and receiving further letters from the Ambassador of the King of France at Venice.

After three years of dogged labour, Langey assured the defences of Piedmont ; but tortured by gout, exhausted by fatigue, powerless and unable, as he said, to serve his King any longer, save with his brain and his tongue, he asked for his *congé* and was carried back to his country on a litter. This valiant and clever man died at Saint-Symphorien, at the foot of Mount Tarare, between Lyons and Roanne, on the 9th January, 1543. François Rabelais, who was present at his death, relates that the last thoughts of this great captain were concerned with the future of the kingdom. " He employed the three or four hours before his death in vigorous words, serene and tranquil in sense, predicting what we have since seen in part, and expect in part to happen, although then the prophecies seemed strange, in no wise credible, and no prognostication had appeared of what he was predicting."

Langey's papers were not found after his death. A German servant was suspected of having stolen them, although this man seemed little capable of knowing their value. Questioned as to their disappearance, Rabelais replied that he had never thought of looking for these papers, as he thought they were locked up in the mule boxes, which had not been opened at all.

The will of Langey reads :

" *Item* to Sieur Rabelais and Messer Gabriel Taphenon, Doctors, the aforesaid testator wills and commands that there be paid to them, in addition to their salaries and fees, videlicet, to the said Rabelais, fifty Tours livres per annum until his heirs have furnished him or caused to be furnished to the Church a total of three Tours livres per annum ; to the aforesaid Taphenon, fifty crowns in one payment."

It is supposed that it was in execution of this clause that René du Bellay, Bishop of Mans, brother of Guillaume and Jean du Bellay, conferred upon Rabelais the living of Saint Christophe-du-Jambet, in the diocese of Mans, from which the former physician of Langey drew the revenue without being compelled to reside there.

Rabelais preserved a tender memory of his protector. In his Fourth Book, to which we shall soon come, he associated the end of the good knight Guillaume du Bellay with everything great, noble, mysterious, and terrible related by Plutarch about the death of geniuses, of heroes and of the great god Pan himself.

To one of the wisest heroes of his book he attributed the hyperbolic statement that, so long as Langey was living, France lived in such happiness that the entire universe envied her, and that, immediately after his decease, she fell into the contempt of the whole world during many long years. Finally, he wrote in Latin a book about the high deeds of Langey, which another friend of that nobleman, Claude Massuau, translated into French, under the title : " *The Stratagems, that is, the Prowesses and Tricks of War of the Valiant and Very Celebrated Knight Langey at the Beginning of the Third Cæsarian War. Lyons. Seb. Gryphius, 1542.*" The Latin text and the French translation have both been lost.

About this time the friendship of Etienne Dolet and François

Rabelais was violently sundered, and the worst faults were not, perhaps, on the side of Etienne. This bookseller, greatly suspected of heresy, having reissued *Pantagruel* with all the passages likely to irritate the Sorbonne pedants, who had become more and more violent and cruel, Rabelais became frightened, and not without reason. The danger was real, and the austere Dolet could rightly be reproached with having been as imprudent with others as he was with himself. He might be accused of trying to compromise, betray and expose a friend. It is not surprising that Rabelais hastened to disown so dangerous a publisher. Rabelais was prudent, he feared the stake : " I am by nature," said he, " sufficiently thirsty without becoming any more heated." Who can reproach him with this ? As he was publishing at the same time an expurgated edition, he included a letter in which he makes the printer speak, but the style betrays him. There he says expressly that Dolet " out of avarice subtracted a copy of this book while it was still in press." The accusation is inconceivable. Dolet had merely to take one of the numerous copies of the old editions ; and, if he had fraudulently procured copies of the new emended and expurgated edition, in order to copy them, his edition would have been equally expurgated and emended. Under the name of his printer, Rabelais added that Dolet was a monster " born to injure and upset decent people." He was not very perspicacious, for he had taken ten years to discover this. It is a sad adventure and an eternal one. Whether it be humanism, intellectual and moral liberty, justice, or any other generous impulse, minds are stirred up in a powerful movement. Between defenders of the same cause, between workers at the same task, men unite, support each other, encourage each other, and excite each other ; in this way the great task is lightened and easily achieved. Then men grow tired and stop. That is the bad moment for quarrels, recriminations, disputes, and the breaking up of friendships. Let us not be too severe upon Rabelais. After all, he was only a man, and the exquisite qualities of his mind only rendered him more sensitive, more restless, and more irritable. The brutal Dolet had brought him within an inch of imprisonment, of the stake ; he had frightened him. Alas ! we are cruel only when we are afraid.

THE THIRD BOOK

CHAPTER V

THE THIRD BOOK

MY friend Seignobos, Professor of History at the Sorbonne, speaking of a historical work of mine, reproached me, in gracious terms, with having concealed gaps in the texts, and also the sometimes narrow limits of our knowledge, by means of a closely knit narrative and a harmonious style. It was a flattering reproach, which my book did not deserve, and which this work will deserve even less. The biography of Rabelais, owing to the ravages of time and the negligence of man, is full of gaps which I shall not try to fill with any patches. All through his life there are gaps. These gaps occur during the entire period which must now be covered. After the death of the good knight, we lose sight of Master François, only to find him for a moment in Orléans at the table and in the house of Etienne Lorens, of Saint-Ay, whom he had known as a soldier in Langey's company and a Captain at Turin. Saint-Ay zealously served the King of France in secret negotiations. In 1545 Saint-Ay received Rabelais in his castle, which stood on a slope covered with vines on the banks of the Loire between Meung and Orléans. At the foot of the slope a well bubbled, by the side of which our author, they say, used to work. Later they used to point out a round stone table upon which he used to write. Etienne Lorens, who was one of the King's men, apparently liked to associate with scholarly people, with leanings toward the Reformation. Such was Antoine Hulot, to whom Rabelais wrote a letter from Saint-Ay, which has been preserved, by some chance, in which the inventor of Pantagruelism invited him philosophically to come and join the guests of Langey's old friend. He tries to lure him with the attraction of fish moistened with the wine of the country, which was excellent. Undoubtedly Rabelais was fond of food, but note that, when he speaks of banquets, he is usually thinking of a banquet of the Muses, and the wine which he extolled is the wine of wisdom. When inviting Antoine Hulot to the table of Saint-Ay, whose fish he praises, he says : " You will come, not when you please, but when you are impelled by the will of the good God, who was full of pity and never created Lent, but did create salads, herrings, haddocks, carps, pike, perch, umbrina, ablets, etc., *item*, good wines, especially one which is being held here for your arrival, as if it were the Holy Grail and a second essence, nay, the quintessence. *Ergo veni, domine, et noli tardare.*"

In 1545, Rabelais obtained from King François I the privilege of printing the Third Book of *Pantagruel*, which appeared the following year, under the title : *The Third Book of the Heroic Deeds and Sayings of the good Pantagruel, composed by Master François Rabelais, Doctor in Medicine and Patriarch of the Isles of Hyères. The Author aforesaid beseeches the courteous readers to reserve their laughter till the Seventy-eighth Book.*

The First Book appeared in 1532, the Second Book about 1524, eight years earlier. During this long interval the author had lost the slender thread of his story. There is no link, so to speak, between the Third Book and its predecessors, yet Rabelais, when he resumed his story in his maturity, seems to recall the old days at Fontenay-le-Comte and to like working out the ideas which he exchanged with Judge André Tiraqueau, in the laurel grove, about women and marriage. The Third Book, in fact, is three-quarters full of the very detailed and very amusing consultation of Panurge on the question as to whether he can marry without disadvantage.

We shall now go through this marvellous Third Book, the richest and perhaps the most beautiful, the most wealthy in comic scenes of the entire *Pantagruel*. But let us remember first that this year 1546, which is marked by the appearance of this luminous and joyous work, was painful and sombre. François I, uneasy and in bad health, could no longer resist the cruel exigencies of the Sorbonne and of Parliament. The persecutors of

thought were raging cruelly against the humanists, the philosophers, the scholars, the poets, against every one who favoured the
Reformation of the Church and inclined, however little, towards
Lutheranism. Clément Marot was dragging out his days in poverty
and exile ; Bonaventure Despériers had committed suicide.
Etienne Dolet had been hanged and burned in the Place Maubert in Paris ; at Meaux, the cradle of the gentlest Reformers,
fourteen stakes were lighted. In this melancholy atmosphere, in
this smell of burning flesh, the voice was heard of this buffoon,
full of wisdom.

When the Third Book opens and, after a long interval, the
author continues the narrative of the high deeds of the good
Pantagruel, we discover the son of Gargantua organising the
country which he has just conquered. He transports a colony of
Utopians to Dypsodie and assigns to Panurge the lairdship of
Salnygondin. But Panurge conducts his affairs so badly that in a
short time he is loaded with debts, but is not worried thereby. As
Fantasial says : " When you have debts and do not pay them
you might as well not have them." Panurge, who is much wittier
than Fantasial, is not content merely to enjoy his position as a
debtor, he exalts it, he glorifies it and, on the basis of his debt, he
not only establishes a theory of public credit but a whole philosophy of man and nature.

" Debt," he says, " is as an union or conjunction of the Heavens
with the Earth, and the whole cement whereby the race of mankind is kept together. Represent unto your self a world wherein
it is to be supposed that there is no debtor or creditor. There,

amongst the planets will be no regular course and all will be in disorder. . . . The moon will remain bloody and obscure : for to what end should the sun impart unto her any of his light ? He owed her nothing. . . . In such a world, without order and array, owing nothing, lending nothing, and borrowing nothing, you would see a more dangerous conspiration than that which Æsop exposed in his epilogue, and the chafing soul, full of indignation, will take its flight to all the devils. . . . On the contrary, be pleased to represent unto your fancy another world, wherein every one lendeth and every one oweth. . . . O how great will that harmony be, which shall thereby result from the regular motions of the Heavens ! What sympathy will there be amongst the elements ! O how delectable then unto nature will be our own works and productions ? Whilst Ceres appeareth loaden with corn, Bacchus with wines, Flora with flowers, Pomona with fruits ; then will among the race of mankind peace, love, benevolence, fidelity, tranquility, rest, banquets, feastings, joy, gladness, be found. . . ."

Pantagruel is not convinced by these fine speeches. " Preach it up and patrocinate it, even from hence to the next Whitson-tide," he replies to Panurge, " yet will you be astonish'd to find how you shall have gained no ground at all upon me, nor per-suaded me. . . . From henceforwards do not hang upon creditors nor tie yourself to them ; I make account, for the time past, to rid you freely of them."

Pantagruel is a liberal and magnificent King, but an enemy of foolish prodigality.

Panurge, freed from his debts, and seeing his youth slip away from him, thought of marriage and consulted his master Pantagruel on this subject, as he did not wish to take any action without his advice.

"It is my judgment (quoth Pantagruel), and I advise you to it."

"But if it were much better for me to remain as I am, I would rather choose not to marry."

"Then do not marry."

"Yea, but would you have me so solitarily drive out the whole course of my life without the comfort of a matrimonial consort ? You know it is written *vae soli*, and a single person is never seen to reap the joy and solace that is found with married folks."

"Then marry in the name of God ! "

"But if my wife should make me a . . . as it is not unknown to you how this hath been a very plentiful year in the production of that kind of cattel."

"Then do not marry, for this sentence of Seneca is infallibly true without all exception : what thou to others shalt have done, others will do the like to thee."

"Yet seeing I can no more want a wife, then a blind man his staff, were it not a great deal better for me to apply and associate my self to some one honest, lovely, and vertuous woman ? "

"Marry then ! "

"But if it were the will of God, and that my destiny did un-luckily lead me to marry an honest woman who should beat me, I would be stor'd with more than two-third parts of the patience of Job, if I were not stark mad by it."

"Do not marry then."

" But being alone and not married, nobody will be so regardful of me, or carry towards me a love like that which is said to be in conjugal affection. And if by some mishap I should fall sick, I would be lookt to very waywardly. The wise man saith, where there is no woman (I mean the mother of a family and wife in the union of a lawful wedlock) the diseased are in danger. . . ."

" Marry then, in the name of God ! "

" But if being ill at ease and made unable to discharge the matrimonial duty, my wife should not only then not help and assist me in my extremity and need, but withal flout out and make sport of my calamity, or (which is worse) embezzle my goods and steal from me as I have seen it oftentimes befal ? "

" Do not marry then."

" Yea, but, I shall never by any other means come to have lawful sons and daughters, in whom I may harbour some hope of perpetuating my name and arms, and to whom also I may leave and bequeath my inheritances and with whom I may make merry, as I do perceive daily by the gentle and loving carriage of your kind and gracious father towards you."

" Marry then, in the name of God ! "

An amusing consultation, of which we find the idea in the literature of the Middle Ages, and which Molière imitated in his *Mariage forcé*. Can one say anything better than the wise Pantagruel ? There are good marriages and there are bad. So what advice can one give ?

Let us consult, said Pantagruel, the Virgilian and Homeric lotteries.

This consists, as we have already seen, in sticking a pin three times into a volume of Homer or Virgil and of taking as an oracle the lines picked. Panurge had recourse to this form of divination. Unfortunately he could draw no conclusion from the verses so marked. Pantagruel advised him to adopt divination by dreams.

" In sleep," said the good King, " our soul delighteth to disport it self, and to take a review of its native country, which is the Heavens, where it receiveth a most notable participation of its first beginning, and in contemplation of that infinite and intellectual sphere, whereof the centre is every-where and the circumference is in no place, to which no new thing hap'neth, which nothing that is passed escapeth and unto which all things are alike present, remarketh not only what is preterite, and gone in the inferior course and agitation of sublunary matters, but withal taketh notice what is to come ; then bringeth a relation of those future events unto the body by the outward senses and exterior organs, it is divulged abroad unto the hearing of others. Whereupon the owner of that soul deserveth to be turned vaticinator, or prophet."

This famous definition of God, which is remarkable in that it perfectly defines the non-existence and absolute absence of God, occurs again, I need hardly say, in Pascal. To find its author we should have to go back to the Alexandrine philosophers and perhaps even to the Greek Empiricists. That would be a little long. Let us not leave Panurge.

He had recourse to divination by dreams and dreamt that he was married, that his wife caressed him in a thousand ways and attached to his forehead a pretty little pair of horns. He also dreamt that he was transformed into a tabor and she into a chough. This dream did not appear to be open to plausible and convincing explanation.

Pantagruel proposed that they should consult the Sibyl of Panzoust, and the good King immediately set out with Epistémon and Panurge. In three days they were transported from Utopia to Chinon. How was that? Let us be truthful, when it is agreeable. The truth is, Rabelais had forgotten that his Pantagruel was in Utopia in the North of China, or in some country thereabouts, it had completely slipped his memory. A delicious lapse, a sweeter sleep than that of old Homer. Cervantes makes Sancho ride on an ass which he has lost and for which he is searching with tears. Rabelais no longer knows on what Continent he has left his characters. How adorable is the negligence, the carelessness of genius!

Here, then, are our friends at Panzoust, near Chinon. So much the better! I prefer sweet Touraine to the prodigies of Utopia.

On the top of a hill, under a large and spacious chestnut tree, they were shown the house of the Sibyl. They entered and found in the chimney corner the old woman, ragged, toothless, blear-eyed, crook-shouldered, snivelling, making a soup of green cabbage with a rind of yellow bacon and an old unsavoury broth, *savorados*. An old *savorados*, I may explain, is a hollow bone, a marrow bone which is put into soup to give it a taste. In order to save expense, it is used several times, but when old it has less taste than in its fresh and savoury beginnings. It is a proof that, like the sorceresses of Thessaly, who stopped the course of the moon, like the witches who predicted the crown of Scotland to Macbeth on the Heath, like the fortune-tellers who live in garrets, like the trans-mediums who follow fairs in caravans, like all such people from ancient times to our own day, the old woman of Panzoust earns with difficulty her miserable livelihood, and we may well be astonished that people who attribute to themselves such extraordinary faculties derive such meagre profits from them. The Sibyl of Chinon remained silent for some time, pensive and showing her teeth, then she sat down on the bottom of a bushel, took her spindles and yarn-windles and placed her apron over her head. . . .

When in Rome Rabelais had seen in the Sistine Chapel the recently discovered Sibyls of Michelangelo. The Cumæan Sibyl is prouder, the Delphian nobler, but the Sibyl of Panzoust is more picturesque. Her words and gestures frightened Panurge, who took her for one possessed by the devil and invoking demons, and his only thought was to run away. He was afraid of devils, particularly because devils attracted theologians, who inspired him with a not unreasonable terror. Finally, the Sibyl wrote her article on eight sycamore leaves, which she scattered to the winds. Panurge and his companions breathlessly pursued them. Unfortunately, these verses were obscure and open to different interpretations. Pantagruel's reading was that Panurge would be deceived and beaten by his wife. As Panurge did not wish either to be deceived or beaten, he naturally understood them quite differently. That is human. We like to interpret things in a sense which flatters us.

In a word, as Pantagruel said, what was very clear was that the oracle was not clear. The good giant was inclined to consult a dumb man, oracles by gestures and signs being more truthful, they say. A dumb man whom they sent for made signs, but it was impossible to understand them. Pantagruel then proposed to question a decrepit old man who was near his end. The wise prince credited dying people with sibylline powers. " Angels, heroes and good demons," he said (according to the doctrine of Platonicks), " when they see mortals drawing near unto the harbour of the grave, free from the troubles and solicitudes of this tumultuous and tempestuous world, hail and salute them, cherish and comfort them, and speaking to them lovingly, begin even then to bless them with illuminations, and to communicate unto them the abstrusest mysteries of divination."

Here Pantagruel seriously expresses his belief, and apparently Rabelais himself was not far from sharing it, for he cites, in a tone whose gravity and emotion cannot be denied, the example of Guillaume du Bellay, lord of Langrey, whose death he witnessed at Saint-Symphorien, as has already been related. Guillaume du Bellay, Rabelais says, employed the three or four hours before his death in vigorous words, serene and tranquil in sense, predicting what has since happened, in part.

Pantagruel, Epistémon, Panurge and Friar John, whom we had almost forgotten, went to the house of the old French poet, Raminagrobis, and found the good old man dying, with cheerful mein, open countenance and luminous eyes.

Panurge requested him to express his judgment on the problem of marriage. Raminagrobis sent for ink and paper and wrote a little poem, which begins as follows :

" Take, or not take her,
 Off or on :
Handy-dandy is your lot,
When her name you write, you blot."

As these lines are also found in the works of Guillaume Crétin, there is reason to recognise this old poet in Raminagrobis.

The dying man gave Panurge and his companions the verses which he had written and said : " Go, my lads, in peace, the great God of the Highest Heaven be your guardian and preserver ; and do not disquiet me with this or any other business whatsoever. I have this same very day (which is the last both of May and of me) with a great deal of labour, toil and difficulty, chased out of my house a rabble of filthy, unclean, and plaguily pestilentious rake-hells, black beasts, dust, dun, white, ash-coloured, speckled, whose obstrusive importunity would not permit me to die at mine own ease : for by fraudulent and deceitful pricklings, ravenous, harpie-like graspings, waspish stingings, forged in the shop of I know not what kind of insatiabilities ; they went about—withdraw and call me out of those sweet thoughts, wherein I was already beginning to repose my self, and acquiesce in the contemplation and vision ; yea, almost in the very touch and taste of the happiness and felicity which the good God hath prepared for His faithful saints and elect in the other life, and state of immortality."

Who were the filthy rabble that were besieging the dying man's bed ? The scandalised Panurge recognised them without hesitation as monks of all orders, Franciscans, Dominicans and other mendicant orders. There were four orders, grey and brown, of which we have made the four mendicants which are served at dessert in France during the winter : Dried raisins, fried figs, almonds and walnuts.

" But what harm, in the devil's name," said the seeker of oracles, when he came out, " have these poor devils, capucins and minims done unto him ? Are not these beggarly devils sufficiently wretched already ? Are they not thoroughly besmoaked and besmeared with misery, distress and calamity, these poor snakes, the very extracts of ichthyophagy ? . . . He goeth, before God, as surely damn'd to thirty thousand basketsfull of devils, as a pruning-bill to the lopping of a vine-branch. To revile with opprobious speeches the good and couragious props and pillars of the Church, is that to be called a poetical fury ? " [I am rather afraid that in the mind of our author the words should be pronounced pillagers of the Church.] He hath transgressed most enormously ; his soul goes infallibly to thirty thousand panniersfull of devils." He wrote *âne* (ass) instead of *âme* (soul), a misprint, no doubt, but it looks deliberate.

These are evil-sounding words on the immortality of the soul. In this year, 1546, they are enough to have the author and the book burned. That year Etienne Dolet was burned and hanged in the Place Maubert in Paris for less, for three words translated from Plato. But he was a serious man. The jokes of Rabelais were not of any consequence. He could say everything. Nevertheless,

I think that he believed in the immortality of the soul, I think that he believed in it, at least five days out of seven, which is a lot.

Panurge has run down the stairs. Nothing in the world will make him return to the bedside of the old, dying poet. He is too much afraid of the hobgoblins. Rabelais is just as much afraid of the hobgoblins as Panurge. He fears them and defies them ; he defies them while fearing them ; he fears them while defying them. Before he expresses his opinion, he plays the fool. His audacity is wrapped up in buffoonery. He crams his text with all sorts of obscurities, as the nymph, surprised in her bath, troubles the waters of the fountain.

Then Panurge consults on the subject so near to his heart an astrologer named Her Trippa, who prophesies that his wife will deceive him. There is a learned consultation ; all the methods of divination are enumerated ; names succeed names interminably. They are drowned by them, and Panurge cannot forgive himself for having lost his time in the lair of this befrocked devil. On the advice of Friar John he listens to what the bells say. But he does not succeed in discovering what they say : marry, marry, marry, or marry not, marry not, marry not.

All forms of divination having proved vain and deceptive, the noble Pantagruel called a theologian, a doctor, a jurisconsult and a philosopher, to put an end to the complexities of Panurge.

The theologian, Hippothadee, the first to be consulted, spoke very well. To Panurge's question : " Shall I be deceived ? " he replied, " By no means, if it please God." From which Panurge concluded : " I shall be, if it please God." Thereupon, for his enlightenment, the good Father described the kind of wife he should take, descended of honest parents, instructed in piety and virtue, loving and fearing God.

" You would have me then (quoth Panurge) to espouse and take to wife the prudent and frugal woman described by Solomon. Without all doubt she is dead. . . . Nevertheless, I thank you, Father ! "

As for the doctor, Rondibillis, a great explorer of the secrets of nature, he frankly declared that the misfortune so greatly feared in advance by Panurge, naturally attended marriage. He compared women to the moon and reproached them with their hypocrisy : " When I say womankind, I speak of a sex so frail, so variable, so changeable, so fickle, inconstant, and imperfect, that, in my opinion, nature (under favour nevertheless of the prime honour and reverence which is due unto her) did in a manner mistake the road which she had traced formerly and stray exceedingly from that excellence of providential judgment, by the which she had created and formed all other things, when she built, framed and made up the woman. And having thought upon it a hundred and five times, I know not what else to determine therein, save only that in the devising, hammering, forging and composing of the woman, she hath had a much tenderer regard, and by a great deal more respectful heed to the delightful consortship, and sociable delectation of the man than to the perfection and accomplishment of the individual womanishness, or muliebrity. The divine philosopher Plato was doubtful in what rank of living creatures to place and collocate them, whither amongst the rational animals, or with the irrational."

In this connection Ponocrates tells a story, which was told before Rabelais, which has been told since, and which the reader doubtless knows. It is as follows :

" Pope John XXII, passing one day through the convent of Fontevrault, was asked by the Abbess and the Mothers to authorise them to make their confessions to each other, alleging that there are certain sins which the nuns could not reveal to a man without unbearable shame.

" ' We shall be able much more easily to tell them to each other.'

" ' I would willingly grant you what you ask,' replied the Pope, ' but I see one disadvantage. Confession must be kept secret, and you women would have great difficulty in keeping a secret.'

" ' We shall keep it very well,' they replied, ' and better than men do.'

" Before leaving them the Holy Father gave them a little box to keep in which he had placed a linnet, and he asked them to lock it up in some secure and secret place, promising them, on his Papal faith, that he would grant what they asked if they kept the box well hidden, and strictly forbidding them to open it under pain of ecclesiastical censure and eternal excommunication. This warning was no sooner uttered than they were dying to see what was in the box, and they longed for the Pope to go in order to satisfy their desire. Having given them his blessing, he retired. He was not gone more than three steps from the convent

when the good Mothers rushed to open the forbidden box to see
what was in it. The next day the Pope paid them a visit and they
expected him to give them the written permission to hear each
other's confessions. Before taking this matter up, he asked for
the box to be brought to him. It was given to him, but the little
bird was no longer in it. The Pope then pointed out to them that
it would be too difficult for them to keep the secrets of the con-
fessional since they had kept the secret of the box for so short a
time."

Grécourt, having put this story into charming verse, added a
rather clever stroke. In his version, when the Pope, finding the
box empty, refused to give the nuns permission to take the place
of their confessors :

> Tant mieux, reprit tout bas une nonnain,
> Je n'étais pas pour la métamorphose.
> Un confesseur est toujours quelque chose.

The philosopher, Trouillogan, was consulted in his turn.

" Now, go on, in the name of God, should I marry?" Panurge
asked.

" There is some likelihood therein."

" But if I do not marry ? "

" I see in that no inconvenience."

" You do not ? "

" None, truly, if my eyes deceive me not."

" Yea, but I find more than five hundred."

" Reckon."

" This is an impropriety of speech, I confess ; for I do no more thereby, but take a certain for an uncertain number. When I say, therefore, five hundred, my meaning is, many. . . Is it possible for me to live without a wife, in the name of all the subterranean devils ? . . . Shall I marry ? "

" Perhaps."

" Shall I thrive or speed well withal ? "

" According to the encounter."

" But if in my adventure, I encounter aright, as I hope I will, shall I be fortunate ? "

" Enough."

" What if I encounter ill ? "

" Then blame not me."

" But, of courtesie, be pleased to give me some advice : what must I do ? "

" Even what thou wilst."

" Wishee, washee ; trolly, trolly."

Panurge grows impatient, but he does not cease to ask questions :

" Shall I marry? If I never marry, I shall never be a cuckold."

" I thought so."

" Well, then, if I marry, I shall be a cuckold."

" One would say so."

" Yet, if my wife prove a vertuous, wise, discreet and chaste woman, I shall never be cuckolded."

" I think you speak congruously."

" Will she be discreet and chaste ? This is the only point I would be resolved in."

" I question it."

" You never saw her ? "

" Not that I know of."

" Why do you then doubt that of which you know not ? "

" For a cause."

" And if you should know her ? "

" Yet more."

At this point Panurge became very angry, and called his page :

" Page, my pretty little darling, take here my cap, go down to the lower court, swear there half an hour for me, and I shall in compensation of that favour, swear hereafter for thee as much as thou wilt."

Molière, a great Rabelaisian, has introduced this scene into his *Mariage forcé* :

Sganarelle. I wish to marry.—
Marphurius. I know nothing of that.—
Sganarelle. I tell you so.
Marphurius. That may be.
Sganarelle. The girl I wish to take is young and very beautiful.
Marphurius. That is not impossible.
Sganarelle. Am I right or wrong in marrying her ?
Marphurius. Both.
Sganarelle. I am greatly drawn to the girl.
Marphurius. That may be.
Sganarelle. Her father has given his permission.
Marphurius. Quite possible.

Sganarelle. But if I marry her, I am afraid I shall be deceived.

Marphurius. The thing has happened.

Sganarelle. But what would you do in my place?

Marphurius. I do not know.

Sganarelle. What do you advise me to do?

Marphurius. Whatever you please.

Judge Bridlegoose (the reader might be pardoned for having forgotten him), Judge Bridlegoose had been called to the consultation, but had not been able to come because he had to depart in haste for Myrelingues, where he had been called before the Parliament to answer for a judgment which he had pronounced. Pantagruel, who was anxious to follow this case, travelled to Myrelingues with his friends, Panurge, Epistémon, Friar John and the others.

When they entered the Parliament Hall, President Trinquamelle was asking Bridlegoose how he had pronounced a certain judgment which did not seem at all equitable.

His only reason and excuse were that he had become old, that his sight was not as good as it used to be, that he could not recognise the points of the dice as distinctly as in the past and that, in pronouncing sentence in the case concerned, he must have taken a four for a five. There was nothing reprehensible in this, as the infirmities of nature should never be imputed unto any one for a crime.

" What kind of dice (quoth Trinquamelle) do you mean, my friend Bridlegoose ? "

" The dice of sentences at law, which your worships do, as

well as I, use, in this glorious sovereign court of yours ; so do all other righteous judges, in their decision of processes."

" But how is it that you do these things ? "

" My practice is therein the same with that of your other worships, and as the custom of the judicatory requires. Having well and exactly seen, surveyed, read, and read over again, turned and tossed over, seriously perused and examined the bills of complaint, requests, inquiries, rejoinders, duplies, triplies, etc., etc., as a good judge ought to do, I posit on the end of the table in my closet all the poaks and bags of the defendant [they used to put in bags the documents which are now put on file], and then allow unto him the first hazard of the dice. That being done, I thereafter lay down upon the other end of the same table the bags of the plaintiff, then do I likeways, and semblably throw the dice for him and forthwith livre him his chance."

Then Bridlegoose explains how he throws the dice. He has small dice for difficult cases and large, fair and goodly ones for clearer cases. He pronounces judgment according as the dice fall, and has no doubt that in proceeding in this manner he is conforming to the usual practice of magistrates.

" Yea, but (quoth Trinquamelle), my friend, seeing it is by the lot, chance and throw of the dice that you award your judgment, why do you not livre up the fair-throws and chances the very same day and hour without any further procrastination or delay, that the controverting party-leaders appear before you ? To what use can those writings serve you, and other procedures contained in the bags ? "

" In three things," replied Bridlegoose. " First, for formality sake, the omission whereof that it maketh all whatever is done, to be of no force nor value is excellently well proved. Secondly, in lieu of some other honest and healthful exercise. Thirdly, I consider, as your own worships used to do, that time ripeneth and bringeth all things to maturity, that by time everything cometh to be made manifest patent, and that time is the father of truth."

Bridlegoose, in this connection, tells the story of Peter Dandin, who was a very different person from his namesake in the *Plaideurs*. The Peter Dandin of Bridlegoose was not a judge ; he was an old farmer of Poitou, known for thirty leagues around as a reconciler of law-suits. There was not a hog-kill within three parishes of him, whereof he had not some part of the haslet and puddings. He was invited almost every day to some banquet and he never made the litigants agree without having them drink together. In short, he alone ended more suits than were settled by the entire law-courts of Poitiers.

Now, his son, Tenot Dandin, also wanted to take up this business of reconciling litigants, but he could not succeed at all and could not even manage to compose the slightest difference ; on the contrary, he irritated and exasperated more than ever the parties whom he wished to soothe and calm.

" Thou hast not the skill and dexterity of composing differences," said the old man to him. " Why ? " " Because thou takest them at the beginning, in the very infancy and bud as it were, when they are green, raw and indigestible ; yet I know handsomely and featly how to compose and settle them all." "Why?" "Because I take them at their decadence, in their weaning, and when they are pretty well digested, when the purses of the parties are empty. At that moment the fat of bacon is not more relishing to boiled pease than I."

" For this cause," Bridlegoose concluded, " I temporise, waiting patiently for the maturity of the process."

Bridlegoose having finished the speech in his defence, the court ordered him to withdraw, and looked to Pantagruel to pronounce judgment. The wise prince, in consideration of the fact that, of the innumerable judgments pronounced by Bridlegoose, only one seemed to be ill-founded, was of the opinion that there was no ground for proceeding against him.

That is one of the best stories of Rabelais, one of the best that has ever been related at any time and in any country, even in the country of La Fontaine and in the country of Quevedo.

The author of *The Barber of Seville* borrowed Bridlegoose from our author and made him into Bridoison. Bridoison was stupid. Bridlegoose was naïve and we learn a great truth from him. We should meditate upon it and never forget it. Whether the decisions of the courts are founded on law, or decided by the chance of dice, they are neither better nor worse. That is the valuable conclusion to be drawn from this story. It was written by the son of a man of the law. Rabelais, as we know to-day, was cradled in lawyer's bags, and nourished on chicanery.

Still concerned about marriage, Panurge questioned the fool

named Triboulet. Sometimes, indeed, the truth is heard in the mouths of simpletons. Mad though he was, Triboulet did not speak any more clearly than the doctors and lawyers, and his last hope was disappointed like the others. The great consultation ends with Triboulet. Panurge decided to go and question the Oracle of the Holy Bottle.

" I am acquainted," he said to Pantagruel, " with a prudent, understanding, and discreet gentleman, and besides a very good friend of mine, who knoweth the land, country and place where its temple and Oracle is built and posited ; he will guide and conduct us thither sure and safely. Let us go thither, I beseech you. I have a long time known you to be a great lover of peregrination, desirous still to learn new things and still to see what you have never seen before."

Pantagruel agreed to guide Panurge to the Oracle of the Holy Bottle, but not without first having obtained the permission of King Gargantua, his father, who had got back mysteriously from the land of the fairies. At the same time, this dutiful son declared that he would never marry without his father's consent. This gave Gargantua an opportunity to pronounce an eloquent, generous, indignant discourse against those who induce children to marry without the knowledge and consent of their father and mother.

" Could the Goths, the Scyths, or Massagets, do a worse or more cruel act to any of the inhabitants of a hostile city, when, after a long siege they shall have stormed and taken it by a violent and impetuous assault ? May not these fathers and mothers be sorrowful and heavy hearted when they see an unknown fellow, a vagabond stranger, a barbarous lowt, by an open rapt, snatch away before their own eyes their so fair, delicate, richly provided for, and healthful daughter, on whose breeding and education they had spared no cost nor charges, by bringing them up in an honest discipline, to all the honourable and vertuous employ-ments, hoping by these commendable and industrious means in an opportune and convenient time to bestow them on the worthy sons of their well-deserving neighbours and ancient friends, who had nourished and schooled their children with the same care and solicitude, that from them might issue an offspring and progeny no less heirs to the laudable endowments and exquisite qualifications of their parents, than to their personal and real estates, movables and inheritances ? "

Against whom is Rabelais (for it is certainly he who is speaking through the words of the giant) so eloquently and powerfully indignant ? Against the Nysts, he says. He does not dare to indicate them more clearly. But, when the book appeared, every one recognised in these Nysts the monks who suborned daughters and married them without the knowledge and against the wishes of their parents. This was one of the most greatly feared plagues which attacked the home at that time. These monks based their detestable practices on canon law. " I well know," says Pasquier in his *Recherches sur la France*, " that for several hundred years certain monks, patching together ancient glosses, have insinuated this brutal and barbarous opinion that, according to canon law, the consent of parents to the marriage of their children was required only as a point of honour and not as a matter of necessity." It was against these suborners and clandestine marriage-makers that Rabelais protested vehemently. The reader will observe on this occasion how he can employ every tone, the most noble and the most familiar, and how he can pass, when he pleases, from the comic to the pathetic.

After having taken leave of the good King Gargantua, his father, Pantagruel set out for the Court of Thalassa, near St. Malo, accompanied by Panurge, Epistémon, Friar John and others of the royal household.

He began to equip his ships, and particularly he had them loaded with great quantities of an herb called Pantagruelion. What is this herb? To judge by the description which Rabelais gives of it, it is hemp. In four chapters the author defines its characteristics, describes its various uses, praises its qualities, and recommends its virtues. In this section, which closes his Third Book, he proves himself to be a botanist as accurate as he is enthusiastic. This great man may be mentioned amongst the creators of botany, for he was the first to have any idea of the sex of plants.

Thus, in a magnificent and unforeseen manner, this marvellous Third Book closes, so rich in excellent comedy scenes, from which Molière freely borrowed. In the whole of French literature I know of no pages so rich in style and so full of sense.

CHAPTER VI

THE LIFE OF RABELAIS (continued)

AFTER having given his Fourth Book to the printer, during the first days of 1546, Rabelais went to the imperial city of Metz with the former Captain of Turin, the same Etienne Lorens who had received him so well, a few years earlier, in his castle at Saint-Ay, on the banks of the Loire. Etienne Lorens, a secret agent of the King, was engaged in negotiations for his master. It has been thought that his friend Rabelais had fled as far as the walls of Metz from the fury of the hobgoblins. It is true that Pantagruelism was not in good odour with the Sorbonne nor the Parliament, and that the King and his sister, the Queen of Navarre, could no longer do anything for their friends suspected of heresy and impiety. It is true that Judge Tiraqueau, having become a member of Parliament and very zealous in the defence of orthodoxy, erased the name of François Rabelais from all his writings. But our author still had powerful protectors, the Bishops of Paris, of Mans, of Tulle, of Montpellier, Cardinal de Châtillon, and *Pantagruel* was regarded, quite wrongly, it is true, as a buffoonery of no consequence. According to the happy researches of M. Henri Clouzat, it would seem that Master François quietly installed himself in the house which the Lord of Saint-Ay owned in the city of Metz.

From there he wrote to Cardinal du Bellay a very humble request for a little money.

" If you do not take pity upon me," he said, " I know not what will become of me, unless, as a last despairing refuge, I place myself in the service of somebody here, to the obvious loss and damage to my studies."

He protests that it is impossible for him to live more frugally than he does. All that he asks is to be able to " keep body and soul together " and live decently, as he has done up to that time, for the honour of the house to which he belonged when he left France. This letter is very humble, no doubt, but it is remarkable for its threats. Master François, Doctor of Medicine, says politely to the Cardinal Bishop : " If you continue to subsidise me, I am yours ; if you do not, I shall give myself to another, as my condition and station in life demand." The du Bellay family were distinguished and honourable, but they were not very well

off. It will be remembered that Langey, on his death, owed his Doctor a great deal. Rabelais was well aware that, in order to be heard by the great, one must knock loudly and often and not be afraid of seeming importunate. Saint-Ay undertook to transmit the letter to the Cardinal Bishop, but he did not add the slightest word of recommendation, doubtless because he knew that in his house Rabelais was not lacking in the necessities of life.

Rabelais was so much the less to be pitied in Metz that, in April 1547, he had been accepted as a stipendiary physician at the Hôtel-Dieu. He remained a full year in the service of the Republic, at an average salary of one hundred and twenty livres, and the inhabitants of Metz were so pleased with him that the authorities granted him three months' salary as a gratification, so he " kept body and soul together " fairly well.

François I died on the 31st March, 1547. Henri II, who succeeded him, unlike his father, had no taste for art, literature, and the graces of the mind. His intelligence was limited, his heart small, and it could be foreseen that the French Lutherans, under the new prince, would be more bitterly persecuted than they had been even during the last years of the late King, which were so filled with torture. The first act of the sovereign confirmed all the fears of the Moderates. Henri II established in Parliament a special chamber to expedite trials for heresy.

Cardinal du Bellay, whose credit was not so great at the new Court, preferring to serve his King from a distance, returned to Rome and lived there in an exile disguised as an Embassy. This time again he called Rabelais to him, and the latter was in the

Eternal City in the month of February, 1549, at the time of the birth of Louis of Orléans, the second son of Henri II and of Catherine de' Medici. We know in what contempt this great mind held astrologers and how he mocked at those who believed that there are stars in the heavens for princes but not for beggars. However, whether to please the Ambassador, or to obtain the King's favour, he drew the horoscope of the new-born child, and predicted a favourable fate for him, provided he escaped a certain sad phase of the Western angle of the Seventh House. This astrologer, in spite of himself, who knew his Virgil, probably remembered those lovely lines in the Sixth Book of The Æneid :

> Heu, miserande puer, si qua fata aspera rumpas !
> Tu Marcellus eris.

But Virgil, when he made the old man, Anchises, predict the premature death of Octavia's son, was merely announcing an event which had happened. Rabelais risked a happier prophecy. The royal child did not even reach the Seventh House, and his death proved the falseness of a horoscope whose imposture was known as well and better to Master François than to any one else, for he had denounced the abuses and the vanity of the art of Ramon Lulli and of divination by reading the Heavens.

On the occasion of this birth, Cardinal du Bellay and the Ambassador of France held a fête in Rome and, particularly a sciomachia, or mimic battle, of which Rabelais sent a description to the Cardinal de Guise, whom we are not surprised to find protecting the old age of Rabelais, for the Civil War had not yet broken out, the Guises were not yet the leaders of the Roman and Spanish Catholics, and Friar François, if he was not a Papist, was even less a Calvinist. The Reformer, Théodore de Bèze, who had formerly praised him, now regarded him as the Beast of the Apocalypse, and a monster full of iniquity. This was no reason why he should be spared ; on the contrary, he received the blows of both parties, to the Catholics he was a Reformer, a Papist to the Reformers. While he was living in Rome with Cardinal du Bellay, in France a monk of Fontevrault named Gabrielle de Puits-Herbault, in Latin Putherbus, attacked him violently in a book called *Theotimus*, which was widely read. It is possible, as has recently been said, that the animosity of this monk against Pantagruelism was for particular reasons, and that it owed its origin to the fact that Rabelais, in his great Pantragruelian comedy, had made fun, under the name of Picrochole, of a Sainte-Marthe, a friend of Puits-Herbault. However, it is impiety, disbelief, Calvinism, with which the *Theotimus* reproaches Master François, and the attack is quite general and comprehensive, since it includes du Bellay and the indulgent prelates of the Church in France. The angry monk sends Rabelais to Calvin and wishes he could send him to the devil :

" Would to God," he cries, " that he were in Geneva, he and his Pantagruelism, if he is still alive ! For at the beginning of this reign, he had followed the rabble of dismissed Cardinals relegated to Rome."

He paints for us a drunken, gluttonous, cynical Rabelais, a false portrait, which for a long time was to be considered true.

If he had numerous enemies, he had also powerful protectors, and perhaps he had more at the Court of Henri II than he had at that of the late King, who nevertheless was a reader, they say, and an admirer of *Pantagruel*. He was well considered by the Guises and by Cardinal Odet de Châtillon. When he returned to France, not only was he never disturbed, but, already Curé of St. Christophe-du-Jambet in the diocese of Mans, on the 18th of January, 1550, he was appointed Curé of Meudon, near Paris. If we may rely on ancient testimony, which is not without its value, he fulfilled the duties of his curacy with great dignity and devotion.

" His house (at Meudon)," according to Antoine Leroy, his oldest biographer, " while closed to women, was open to scholars, with whom he loved to converse. He detested ignorance, especially in ecclesiastics, and when characterising illiterate priests, he would recover the satirical verve of the author of Pantagruel. *Quos vocaret Isidis asellos*. For the rest, these were the only people towards whom he was lacking in charity. The poor were always certain of receiving help from his purse. His integrity was so great that he was never known to fail to keep his word with anybody. His medical knowledge had rendered him doubly useful to his parish."

Guillaume Colletet afterwards bore witness also to the virtues of the Curé of Meudon :

" He filled his curacy with all the sincerity, all the kindness and all the charity to be expected of a man who is anxious to fulfil his duty. At least, neither by tradition, nor otherwise, can we find any complaint lodged against his morals or his care of his flock. On the contrary, there is every evidence that his flock was very pleased with him, as may be inferred from certain letters which he wrote to some of his friends, which have still been preserved by the curious and which I have seen, where he says, amongst other things, that he has good and pious parishioners in the persons of Monsieur and Madame de Guise (the Duke and the Cardinal de Guise had just bought the castle of Meudon), a proof of the great care with which he discharged his duty and won the affection of those whose spiritual direction had been entrusted to him by his Bishop."

We cannot doubt that Rabelais acquitted himself becomingly and devotedly of the ministry which he had assumed. But that he could for long submit to a sedentary existence is denied by his whole wandering, vagabond, curious life, the insatiable desire of his soul to see and know. Despite what Colletet and Leroy say, it is not certain that this good man resided very strictly in his parish, and, as a matter of fact, we learn that, on the occasion of the pastoral visit of his bishop, Eustache du Bellay, nephew of Cardinal Jean, in the month of June, 1551, Pierre Richard, Vicar, and four assistants were present in the parish of Meudon ; the Curé was absent.

For the rest, Rabelais, who never settled down anywhere, remained Curé of Meudon only for the space of two years, less a few days. He resigned both his curacies on the 9th of January, 1552, why we know not. The end of his life, which we are approaching, is wrapped in profound obscurity.

A few days after this double resignation, the Fourth Book of *Pantagruel* appeared for the first time in its entirety. The first chapters had been published at Grenoble in 1547. The Fourth Book, complete, was finished by Michel Fezandat, bookseller in Paris, on the 28th January, 1552, and appeared with the privilege of the King and an epistle to Monsignor Odet, Cardinal de Châtillon.

This book, whose publication was separated from that of the Third Book by only a very short interval of time, is a continuation of the latter, and contains the journey of Pantagruel and his companions in search of the Oracle of the Holy Bottle. We shall now go through it, and not without pleasure assuredly, for it is full of excellent and precious passages. Further excellent scenes of human comedy are unfolded, although allegory, with its frigid fictions, too often takes the place of that movement, that tumult of life, which is so entertaining in the earlier books.

THE FOURTH BOOK

CHAPTER VII

THE FOURTH BOOK

THE Fourth Book is entirely filled by the journey of Pantagruel
and his companions in search of the Holy Bottle. What is this
journey? M. Abel Lefranc, professor at the Collège de France,
believes that the answer is certain : " It is the journey which so
occupied the minds of geographers and navigators from the time
of the Renaissance down to our own day : the journey from the
coast of Europe to the Western Coast of Asia, through the famous
North-West passage in the North of America, which had been so
often sought in vain, and whose practical impossibility has been
definitely established only a few years ago."

The good giant and his court embark at Thalassa, quite close to St. Malo. Now St. Malo is the port from which Jacques Cartier set out and to which he returned when, from 1534 to 1542, he traced the course of the St. Lawrence River and the map of New-foundland. At St. Malo they still said in the seventeenth century that Rabelais had learned his marine and piloting terms from this navigator, and M. Abel Lefranc believes that the pilot Xenomanes, who conducts the Pantagruelian fleet, is none other than Jacques Cartier himself, pilot of the King of France. It is possible. We shall not argue about it.

There is no interest in knowing whether the pilot Xenomanes is Jacques Cartier or anybody else, since Rabelais has not given him any particular character, any appearance peculiarly his own. Neither do we need to follow too attentively on the map the itinerary of Pantagruel, who puts in only at allegorical islands, and whose voyage is mainly satirical.

What is true, however, is that the author, very jealous of the greatness and power of France, as usual, and very careful to praise the King, his master, shows here as elsewhere his great interest in the progress of the naval forces of the Kingdom, and when King Henri II, at the beginning of his reign, in 1547, had new ships constructed, Master François in the Second Edition of his Fourth Book adds triremes, galleons, men of war, and feluccas to the fleet of the good Pantagruel, who did not know what to do with them. But it pleased him to endow with these new and mag-nificent vessels the navigators who had set out in search of the Oracle of the Holy Bottle, in order to exalt the Navy of his King, at a time when French navigators were trying to get a share of the New World. Rabelais was in favour of large armaments. I do not know whether he encouraged naval construction without foreseeing the excess of expenditure; one thing certain is, that he was not working for a syndicate of ship-builders, furnishers, and financiers. Then, as now, there were greedy contractors who robbed the King. When they were too rich, the King despoiled them. Such were the order and economy of finance in the matter of public works at this period.

On the fourth day the navigators put in at the island called Medamothi, " of a fine and delightful prospect, by reason of the vast number of light-houses, and high marble towers in its circuit," but which, as its Greek name means Nowhere, might well not exist. I should not mention it, if Gymnast had not bought there for Pantagruel the story of Achilles in seventy-eight pieces of silk tapestry, embossed with gold and silver, which made a fine suite. It is not out of vain caprice that the author shows us these tapestries. At that very time Henri II, in order to encourage the cloth industry in his Kingdom, had had executed, at his own expense, tapestries of the finest quality, and Rabelais, whom this luxury did not cost much, unfolds the history of Achilles in seventy-eight pieces to the glory of French industry.

In the course of the Journey, Pantagruel drew the *gozal* from the basket in which it was shut. The *gozal* is a pigeon, from the dove-cotes of Gargantua. Attaching a knot of white silk to its foot, as a sign that all was well, Pantagruel released it on the deck and the *gozal* flew in rapid flight towards the distant dove-cote, bearing news of the navigators in his white knot. It is a messenger pigeon, a carrier pigeon, which is not, as we see, a modern invention.

On the fifth day of the crossing, they sighted a ship. The passengers on board came from Lantern-land and they were all natives of Saintonge. They saluted and hailed each other. Panurge, who was taken on board the vessel from Lantern-land, got into a quarrel with a sheep-merchant named Dindenault, who called him a dark lantern of anti-Christ. I forgot to say that Panurge had fastened his spectacles to his cap, which Dindenault found extremely ridiculous. The quarrel became very venomous. However, Pantagruel succeeded in calming him down. Panurge and Dindenault drank each other's health. Panurge, who was seeking revenge and was not frank, emptied a second bumper of wine to the merchant's health and begged him to sell him one of his sheep. Dindenault, who was really rather a difficult person to approach and very ungracious, took these overtures in bad part.

" Nay," said he to Panurge, " you seem a rare chapman ! O what a mighty sheep-merchant you are ! In good faith, you look liker one of the diving trade than a buyer of sheep. . . ."

Panurge would not be put off and became more pressing.

" Be so kind (as to sell me one of your sheep, come, how much ? "

" My friend," replied the merchant, " they are meat for none but kings and princes ; their flesh is so delicate, so savoury, and so dainty that one would swear it melted in the mouth. I bring them out of a country where the very hogs, God be with us, live

on nothing but mirabolans. The sows in their styes when they lie-in (saving the honour of this good company), are fed only with orange flowers."

"But," said Panurge, "drive a bargain with me for one of them, and I will pay you for't like a king."

Dindenault replied only with hyperbolical and prolix praise of his sheep. He praised their shoulders, legs, chests, livers, spleen, tripes, ribs, heads and horns.

The skipper of the ship suddenly interrupted :

"What a fidle fadle have we here ? There is too long a lecture by half, sell him one if thou wilt ; if thou won't, don't let the man lose more time."

"I will for your sake," said the merchant, "but then he shall give me three livres French money for each, and pick and chuse."

"'Tis a woundy price," cry'd Panurge, "in our country I could have five, nay six, for the money."

"A murrain seize thee for a blockheaded booby," cried Din-denault, whose language was rough but who was very learned, "the worst in this flock is four times better than those which the Coraxians us'd to sell for a gold talent each."

"Sweet sir, you fall into a passion, I see," return'd Panurge. "Well, hold, here is your money."

Having paid the merchant, he chose from the flock a large and beautiful sheep and carried it off, crying and bleating. Meanwhile all the others began to bleat and watch where their companion was being taken.

Dindenault was saying :

" Ah ! how well the knave could chuse him out a ram, the whoreson has skill in cattle ! "

Suddenly, without saying a word, Panurge threw his sheep, crying and bleating, into the sea. Crying and bleating, all the other sheep began to throw themselves overboard after him. They competed as to who should jump first. It was not possible to restrain them. It is the nature of sheep, as we know, to follow the leader wherever he may go. Wherefore, Aristotle says that the sheep is the most inept and stupid animal in the world.

The merchant, frightened at seeing his sheep drowning and perishing before his eyes, tried to prevent them and to hold them back with all his strength. But it was in vain. At last, he laid hold of a large sturdy one by the fleece on the deck of the ship, hoping to keep it back and thereby save the others. But the sheep was so strong that he dragged the merchant with him into the sea. . . . The ship being freed of the merchant and of the sheep : " Is there," asked Panurge, " ever another sheepish soul left lurking on board ? Where are those of Toby Land, and Robin Rand, that sleep whilst the rest are a feeding ? Faith, I can't tell my self. This was an old coaster's trick : what think'st thou of it, Friar John ? "

" Rarely perform'd," answer'd Friar John, " only methinks you ought not to have paid your man, and the money had been sav'd."

" A fig for the money," cried Panurge, "have I not had about fifty thousand pounds' worth of sport ? Come, now, let's begone, the wind is fair, hark you me, my friend John, never did man do me a good turn, but I return'd or at least acknowledg'd it. No, I scorn to be ungrateful, I never was, nor ever will be : never did man do me an ill one without rueing the day that he did it either in this world or the next."

Such is the most famous episode of the Fourth Book, the episode of the sheep of Panurge, which ought rather to be called the sheep of Dindenault. Rabelais did not invent it, he took the whole story from an Italian monk, Teofile Folengo, who related it very wittily in Macaronic verse. La Fontaine took it from Rabelais, in his turn, and made of it a story which must seem, I am afraid, rather lifeless compared with its model.

After the adventure with the sheep, the travellers next came to the island of Ennasin, the inhabitants of which have triangular faces ; to the island of Chely, where everybody makes grimaces, and to Pettifogging, which as its name indicates, is the country of pettifoggers, the land of chicanery. An inhabitant of the island explained to Pantagruel how the Catchpolls make their livelihood by being thrashed, so that if they were long without a beating, they would die of hunger, they, their wives and children.

" When a monk," says the author, " Levite, close-fisted usurer or lawyer, owes a grudge to some neighbouring gentleman, he sends to him one of these Catchpolls, who nabs or at least cites him, thumps, abuses and affronts him impudently. By natural instinct and according to his pious instruction ; insomuch that if the gentleman hath got any guts in his brain, and is not more stupid than a Girin frog, he will find himself oblig'd either to apply a foggot-stick or his sword to the rascal's jobbornol, or make him cut a caper out at the window, by way of correction. This done, Catchpoll is rich for four months at least, as if bastinadoes were his real harvest ; for the monk, Levite, usurer or lawyer will reward him roundly, and my gentleman must pay him such swinging damages, that his acres may bleed for't, and he be in danger of miserably rotting within a stone doublet, as if he had struck the King."

This is what Racine has so prettily staged in *Les Plaideurs*.

CHICANNEAU

Mais je ne sais pourquoi, plus je vous envisage,
Et moins je me remets, Monsieur, votre visage.
Je connais force huissiers.

L'INTIMÉ

Informez-vous de moi :
Je m'acquitte assez bien de mon petit emploi.

CHICANNEAU

Soit ! Pour qui venez-vous ?

L'INTIMÉ

Pour une brave dame,
Monsieur, qui vous honore, et de toute son âme
Voudrait que vous vinssiez à ma sommation
Lui faire un petit mot de réparation.

CHICANNEAU

De réparation ? Je n'ai blessé personne.

RABELAIS

Je le crois : vous avez, Monsieur, l'âme trop bonne.

CHICANNEAU

Que demandez-vous donc ?

L'INTIMÉ

           Elle voudrait, Monsieur,
Que, devant des témoins, vous lui fissiez l'honneur
De l'avouer pour sage et point extravagante.

CHICANNEAU

Parbleu ! C'est ma comtesse.

L'INTIMÉ

           Elle est votre servante.

CHICANNEAU

Je suis son serviteur.

L'INTIMÉ

           Vous êtes obligeant,
Monsieur.

CHICANNEAU

      Oui, vous pouvez l'assurer qu'un sergent
Lui doit porter pour moi tout ce qu'elle demande.
Hé quoi donc ? les battus, ma foi, paîront l'amende !
Voyons ce qu'elle chante. Hon . . . " Sixième janvier,
Pour avoir faussement dit qu'il fallait lier,
Étant à ce porté par esprit de chicane,
Haute et puissante dame Yolande Cudasne,
Comtesse de Pimbesche, Orbesche, et cætera,

O   209

Il soit dit que, sur l'heure, il se transportera
Au logis de la dame ; et là, d'une voix claire,
Devant quatre témoins assistés d'un notaire,
Zest ! ledit Hiérome avoûra hautement
Qu'il la tient pour sensée et de bon jugement.
Le Bon." C'est donc le nom de Votre Seigneurie ?

L'INTIMÉ

Pour vous servir. [*A part.*] Il faut payer d'effronterie.

CHICANNEAU

Le Bon ? Jamais exploit ne fut signé Le Bon.
Monsieur Le Bon !

L'INTIMÉ

Monsieur.

CHICANNEAU

Vous êtes un fripon.

L'INTIMÉ

Monsieur, pardonnez-moi, je suis fort honnête homme.

CHICANNEAU

Mais fripon le plus franc qui soit de Caen à Rome.

L'INTIMÉ

Monsieur, je ne suis pas pour vous désavouer :
Vous aurez la bonté de me le bien payer.

CHICANNEAU

Moi, payer ? En soufflets.

RABELAIS

L'INTIMÉ

Vous êtes trop honnête :
Vous me le paîrez bien.

CHICANNEAU

Oh ! tu me romps la tête.
Tiens ! voilà ton paîment.

L'INTIMÉ

Un soufflet ! Écrivons :
" Lequel Hiérome, après plusieurs rébellions,
Aurait atteint, frappé, moi, sergent, à la joue,
Et fait tomber du coup mon chapeau dans la boue."

CHICANNEAU [lui donant un coup de pied]

Ajoute cela !

L'INTIMÉ

Bon ! c'est de l'argent comptant ;
J'en avais bien besoin. " Et, de ce non content,
Aurait avec le pied réitéré." Courage ! . . .
" Outre plus, le susdit serait venu, de rage,
Pour lacérer ledit présent procès-verbal."
Allons, mon cher monsieur, cela ne va pas mal.
Ne vous relâchez point.

CHICANNEAU

Coquin !

L'INTIMÉ

Ne vous déplaise,
Quelques coups de bâton, et je suis à mon aise.

CHICANNEAU [tenant un bâton]

Oui-da ! Je verrai bien s'il est sergent.

RABELAIS

L'INTIMÉ [en posture d'écrire]

Tôt donc,
Frappez. J'ai quatre enfants à nourrir.

CHICANNEAU

Ah ! pardon !
Monsieur, pour un sergent je ne pouvais vous prendre ;
Mais le plus habile homme enfin peut se méprendre.
Je saurai réparer ce soupçon outrageant.
Oui, vous êtes sergent, Monsieur, et très-sergent.
Touchez là : vos pareils sont gens que je révère ;
Et j'ai toujours été nourri par feu mon père
Dans la crainte de Dieu, Monsieur, et des sergents.

L'INTIMÉ

Non, à si bon marché l'on ne bat point les gens.

CHICANNEAU

Monsieur, point de procès !

L'INTIMÉ

Serviteur ! Contumace,
Bâton levé, soufflet, coup de pied. Ah !

CHICANNEAU

De grâce,
Rendez-les-moi plutôt.

L'INTIMÉ

Suffit qu'ils soient reçus :
Je ne les voudrais pas donner pour mille écus.

(Acte II, sc. IV.)

Panurge tells the story of a certain lord of Basché, who could thrash the Catchpolls on the pretext of amusing them. This gentleman, in his turn, related beneath the arbour the story of François Villon, and the sacristan of the Franciscans of St. Maixent. Here is the passage, perhaps the most wonderful, for its style and movement, of the entire prodigious work which we have been studying:

" Master François Villon, in his old age, retired to St. Maixent in Poitou, under the patronage of a good, honest Abbot of the place ; there to make sport for the mob he undertook to get the Passion acted after the way and in the dialect of the country, The parts being distributed, the play having been rehears'd, and the stage prepar'd he told the Mayor and Alderman that the mystery might be ready after Niort Fair, and that there only wanted properties and necessaries, but chiefly clothes fit for the parts.

" Villon, to dress an old clownish father Greybeard, who was to represent God the Father, beg'd of Friar Stephen Tickletoby, Sacristan to the Franciscan Friars of the place, to lend him a cope and stole. Tickletoby refus'd him, alledging that by their provincial statutes, it was rigorously forbidden to give or lend anything to players. Villon reply'd that the statute reached no farther than farces, drolls, anticks, loose and dissolute games, and that he ask'd no more than what he had seen allow'd at Brussels and other places. Tickletoby, notwithstanding, peremptorily bid him provide himself elsewhere if he would and not to hope for anything out of his monastical wardrobe for he certainly would have nothing.

213

" Villon gave an account of this to the players, as of a most abominable action ; adding that God would shortly revenge himself and make an example of Tickletoby.

" The Saturday following he had notice given him, that Tickletoby upon the filly of the convent was gone a mumping to St. Ligarius and would be back about two in the afternoon. Knowing this, he made a cavalcade of his devils of the Passion through the town. They were all rigg'd with wolves, calves, and rams' skins, lac'd and trim'd with sheeps' heads, bulls' feathers and large kitchen tenter-hooks, girt with broad leathern girdles, whereat hang'd dangling huge cow-bells and horse-bells, which made a horrid din. Some held in their claws black sticks full of squibs and crackers ; others had long lighted pieces of wood, upon which at the corner of every street they flung whole handfuls of rosin-dust, that made a terrible fire and smoak.

" Having thus led them about, to the great diversion of the mob, and the dreadful fear of little children, he finally carried them to an entertainment at a summer-house without the gate that leads to St. Ligarius. As they came near the place, he spy'd Tickletoby afar off, coming home from mumping.

" 'A plague on his friarship (said the devils then), the lowsie beggar would not lend a poor cope to the Fatherly Father, let us frighten him.'

" ' Well said,' cry'd Villon ; ' but let us hide our selves till he comes by, and then charge home briskly with your squibs and burning sticks.'

" Tickletoby being come to the place, they all rush'd on a

sudden into the road to meet him, and in a frightful manner threw fire from all sides upon him and his filly foal, ringing and tingling their bells, and howling like so many real devils, hho, hho, hho, hho, brrou, rrou, rrourrs, rrourrs, hoo, hou, hou, hho, hho, hhoi, Friar Stephen, don't we play the Devils rarely?

" The filly was soon scar'd out of her seven senses, and began to start, to bound it, to gallop it, to kick it, to curvet it with double jirks : insomuch that she threw Tickletoby, tho' he held fast by the tree of the pack-saddle with might and main : now his traps and stirrups were of cord, and on the right side, his sandle was so entangled and twisted, that he could not for the heart's blood of him get his foot. Thus he was drag'd about by the filly through the road, she still multiplying her kicks against him and straying for fear, over hedge and ditch ; insomuch that she trepann'd his thick skull so, that his cockle brains were dash'd out near the Osanna, or High Cross. Then his arms fell to pieces, one this way and t'other that way, and even so were his legs serv'd at the same time ; then she made a bloody havock with his puddings and being got to the convent, brought back only his right foot and twisted sandle.

" Villon, seeing that things had succeeded as he intended, said to his devils :

" ' You will act rarely, gentlemen devils, you will act rarely ; I dare engage you'll top your parts. I defie the devils of Saumur, Douay, Montmorillon, Langez, St. Espain, Angers ; nay, by Gad, even those of Poictiers, for all their bragging and vapouring, to match you.' "

This death of the miser Tickletoby, dragged by his filly, makes me think, in spite of myself, of the death of the impious Pentheus, torn to pieces by the Bacchantes. In the Greek tragedy the end of Pentheus is as terrible as the end of Tickletoby is comic in the Pantagruelian story, but the monk of St. Maixent and the king of Thebes were both guilty of an offence against something divine. The one does not recognise a god, the other offends a poet. The punishment of each of them was inevitable, necessary, and in conformity with universal order ; the burlesque of Rabelais equals in grandeur the pathos of Euripides.

Having left the island of the Catchpolls, the fleet of Pantagruel encountered a terrible storm. The sea swelled mountain-high ; the heavens thundered ; the air grew dark ; there was no other light than that of the flashes of lightning ; the ship strained under the assault of the gigantic waves.

Crouching on the deck, Panurge trembles, invokes all the saints and laments :

" O twice and thrice happy those that plant cabbages ! O Destinies, why did you not spin me for a cabbage planter ? O how few are they to whom Jupiter hath been so favourable as to pre-destinate them to plant cabbage ? They have always one foot on the ground and the other not far from it. For as good a reason as the philosopher Pyrrho being in the same danger, and seeing a hog near the shoar, eating some scatter'd oats, declar'd it happy in two respects, first, because it had plenty of oats, and besides that it was on shoar ; hah, for a divine and princely habitation commend me to the cow's floor . . . this wave will sweep us away,

blessed Saviour ! O, my friends ! a little vinegar bous, bous, bous. I am lost for ever. Otto, to, to, I'm drowned ! "

Friar John, who had stripped to his doublet in order to help the sailors, addressed him in passing :

" Odzoons, Panurge the calf, Panurge the whiner, Panurge the brayer, would it not become thee much better to lend us here a helping hand, than to lie lowing like a cow, as thou dost, sitting there like a bald baboon ? "

But Panurge wept and groaned all the more.

" Friar John, my friend, my good father, I am drowning ; I am a dead man. I am drowning : the water is got into my shoes by the collar."

" Come hither and help us (said Friar John) ; in the name of thirty legions of black devils, come, will you come ? "

" Don't let us swear at this time," said Panurge ; " to-morrow as much as you please. Holos, holos, alas, our ship leaks. Above eighteen palefuls of water are got down my gullet. Bous, bous, bous. How damn'd bitter and salt it is ! "

" By the vertue (said Friar John) of the blood, if I hear thee again howling, I'll maul thee worse than any sea-wolf . . . hold fast above ! in truth here is a sad lightning and thundering ; I think that all the devils are got loose, or else Madam Proserpine is in child's labour, all the devils dance a Morrice."

" Oh," said Panurge, " you sin, Friar John. It goes against my heart to tell it you ; for I believe this swearing doth your spleen a great deal of good . . . nevertheless you offend. . . ."

He continues to lament.

" I see neither Heaven nor Earth. Would it were the pleasure of the worthy divine bounty, that I were at this present hour in the close at Seuille, or at Innocent's the Pastry-Cook, over against the painted wine-vault at Chinon, though I were to strip to my doublet, and bake the petty pasties my self . . . "

The storm having subsided and the ship being on the point of entering the harbour, Panurge recovers all his courage and all his assurance :

" Oh, oho ! " quoth Panurge, " all is well, the storm is over. Shall I help you still here ? "

Rabelais is a great comic writer. His only equals are Aristophanes, Molière and Cervantes. His storm is a great scene of human comedy which closes with a touch that is for ever admirable. As for the description of the sea and the sky, it is confused and seems to be based less upon the spectacle of nature than upon literary memories. We must wait until Pierre Loti, or at least Bernardin de St. Pierre, to find in a book a storm that has been felt and seen.

The port where the fleet of Pantagruel put in after the storm is that of the Macréons, whose island, formerly wealthy, busy and populous, is now poor and deserted by the injury of time. There, in a dark forest, amongst ruined temples, obelisks and ancient tombs, the demons and the hero dwell.

An old man relates to the travellers the vicissitudes caused by the life and death of the sublime inhabitants of the forest, and reveals to them, at the same time, the cause of the storm from which they have escaped with such difficulty.

By way of conclusion, he declares his faith in the immortality of the soul :

" I believe that all intellectual souls are exempted from Atropos's scissers. They are all immortal, whether they be of angels, of dæmons, or human."

Then, as he likes to tell stories, he tells the story of the Pilot Thamous, which, familiar as it is, cannot be passed over, because it is too beautiful and inspires a too-insatiable curiosity. It also is taken from the treatise on *Oracles That Have Ceased*. Here it is, in the translation, which Jacques Amyot made of the *Morals* of Plutarch, a few years after the publication of the Fourth Book of *Pantagruel*. The style is pleasant and easy, I shall make no change other than to correct a mistake for, I may say in passing, Amyot did not read and understand his text so well as Rabelais :

" Epitherses was my townsman and schoolmaster, who told me that designing a voyage to Italy, he embark'd himself on a vessel well laden both with goods and passengers. About the evening the vessel was becalm'd about the Isles Echinades. Whereupon their ship drove with the tide till it was carry'd near the Isles of Paxos : when immediately a voice was heard by most of the passengers (who were then awake and taking a cup after supper) calling unto one Thamus, and that with so loud a voice, as made all the company amazed ; which Thamus was a mariner of Egypt, whose name was scarcely known in the ship. He returned no answer to the first calls, but at the third he replyed, *Here ! here ! I am the man.* Then the Voice said aloud to him, *when you are arrived at Palodes, take care to make it known, that the great God Pan is dead.*

Epitherses told us, this Voice did much astonish all that heard it, and caused much arguing, whether this Voice was to be obeyed or slighted. Thamus, for his part, was resolv'd, if the wind permitted, to sayl by the place without saying a word ; but if the wind ceas'd, and there ensu'd a calm, to spake and cry out as loud as he was able what he was enjoyn'd. Being come to the Palodes, there was no wind stirring, and the sea was as smooth as glass. Whereupon Thamus standing on the deck, with his face towards the land, uttered with a loud voice his message, saying, *The Great PAN is dead*. He had not sooner said this, but they heard a dreadful noise, not only of one but of several, who, to their thinking, groan'd, and lamented with a kind of astonishment. And there being many persons in the ship, an account of this was soon spread over Rome, which made Tiberius the Emperor send for Thamus, and seem'd to give such heed to what he told him, that he earnestly inquired who this *PAN* was."

Here is the freer version of Rabelais :

" Epitherses the Father of Æmilian the rhetorician, sailing from Greece to Italy, in a ship freighted with divers goods and passengers, at night the wind fail'd 'em near the Echinades, some islands that lie between the Morea and Tunis, and the vessel was driven near Paxos. When they were got thither, some of the passengers being asleep, others awake, the rest eating and drinking, a voice was heard that call'd aloud Thamous ; which cry surpris'd them all. This same Thamous was their pilot, an Egyptian by birth, but known by name only to some few travellers. The Voice was heard a second time calling Thamous, in a frightful tone ; and none making answer, but trembling and remaining silent, the Voice was heard a third time, more dreadful than before.

" This caus'd Thamous to answer, ' Here am I ; What do'st thou call me for ? What wilt thou have me do ? ' Then the Voice, louder than before, bade him publish, when he should come to Paloda, that the great god Pan was dead.

" Epitherses related, that all the mariners and passengers, having heard this, were extremely amaz'd and frighted ; and that consulting among themselves, whether they had best conceal or divulge what the Voice had enjoyn'd, Thamous said, his advice was, that if they happen'd to have a fair wind, they shou'd proceed, without mentioning a word on't ; but if they chanc'd to be becalm'd, he wou'd publish what he had heard : Now when they were near Paloda they had no wind, neither were they in any current. Thamous then getting up on the top of the ship's forecastle, and casting his eyes on the shore, said that he had been commanded to proclaim, that the great God Pan was dead. The words were hardly out of his mouth, when deep groans, great lamentation, and shrieks, not of one person, but of many together, were heard from the land.

" The news of this (many being present then) was soon spread at Rome ; insomuch that Tiberius, who was then Emperor, sent for this Thamous, and having heard him, gave credit to his words."

Plutarch, like Rabelais, the Alexandrian as well as the humanist, believed that Pan, the great god Pan, was All, the great All ;

πᾶν in Greek means All. It is easy to imagine what mysterious terror was spread by this voice hurled over the sea : " The great god Pan is dead." This etymology, nevertheless, is very false and even absurd. Pan was born with horns, a beard, a snub nose and goat's feet. He dwelt in Arcadia, living in the woods and fields and guarding his flocks ; he invented the pipes on which he made rustic music. This little god sometimes inspired terror in men by his sudden apparition. Such being his appearance and his habits, his name must rather be derived from the verb πάω, which means to pasture, since he pastured sheep, and it is probable that such is its first and real meaning. As for his becoming the symbol of the universe, that is an accident which happened to this demi-man because of a fortuitous resemblance of sounds. Poets very often think in puns and word play, and many men are poets in that respect.

As he did not doubt that the great god Pan was the great All, Pantagruel could not help thinking that this great All is God made man and that the words heard by Thamous announced the death of Jesus Christ.

" I understand it," he said, " of that great Saviour of the faithful, who was shamefully put to death at Jerusalem, by the envy and wickedness of the doctors, priests and monks of the Mosaic Law. He may lawfully be said," the gentle giant added, " to be Pan in the Greek tongue, since he is our All. For all that we are, all that we live, all that we have, all that we hope, is Him, by Him, from Him and in Him ; He is the good Pan, the Great Shepherd, who hath not only a tender love and affection for his

sheep but also for their shepherds. At his death, complaints, sighs, fears and lamentations were spread through the whole fabrick of the universe, whether Heaven, land, sea or Hell."

According to our veracious author, as he spoke in this way, Pantagruel shed tears as large as ostriches' eggs. The interpretation which he gives of Plutarch's story is not entirely his own : it was to be found in Eusebius ; it was abandoned when the critical and historical spirit, breathing over the Christian origins, dissipated the fables. Then the view was that the apocalypse of the Egyptian pilot was a symbol of the death of the gods of antiquity.

" The great god Pan is dead," that means to modern poets and philosophers that the Old World has collapsed and on its ruins a New World rises. The old altars are deserted, a new god is born.

It is thus that Paul Arène, Provençal poet, of the purest and most delicate talent, has interpreted the old myth of Plutarch, in a poem entitled, *Christmas at Sea.*

I think we may well quote it, after Plutarch and Rabelais, as an example of the rejuvenation of an ancient theme and of the eternal vitality of legends. It should be heard from the lips of that consummate artist in the speaking of verse, Sylvian, of the Comédie Française, who recites this poem admirably. I shall quote only the first lines which deal with my subject.

> Lorsque le vieux Thamus, pâle et rasant le bord,
> A la place prescrite eut crié : " Pan est mort ! "
> Le rivage s'émut, et, sur les flots tranquilles,
> Un long gémissement passa, venu des Iles :

On entendit les airs gémir, pleurer des voix,
Comme si, sur les monts sauvages, dans les bois
Impénétrés, les dieux, aux souffles d'Ionie,
Les dieux, près de mourir, disaient leur agonie.
Le soleil se voila de jets de sablè amer :
Un âpre vent fouetta les vagues de la mer,
Et l'on vit, soufflant l'eau de leurs glauques narines,
Les phoques de Protée et ses vaches marines
S'échouer, monstrueux, et pareils à des monts,
Sur l'écueil blanc d'écume et noir de goémons.
Puis, tandis que Thamus, le vieux patron de barque,
Serrait le gouvernail et jurait par la Parque,
Un silence se fit et le flot se calma.
Or, le mousse avait pu grimper en haut du mât.
Et, tenent à deux mains la voilure et l'antenne :
—Père ! s'écria-t-il tout à coup, capitaine !

Père ! un vol de démons ailés et familiers
Vient sur la mer, dans le soleil, et par milliers,
Si près de nous que leur essaim frôle les planches
De la barque ! Je les vois passer, formes blanches.
Ils chantent comme font les oiseaux dans les champs ;
Leur langue est inconnue et je comprends leurs chants.
Ils chantent : Hosanna ! Les entendez-vous, père ?
Ils disent que le monde a fini sa misère,
Et que tout va fleurir. Père, ils disent encore
Que les hommes vont voir un nouvel âge d'or !

Un dieu nous le promet, un enfant dont les langes
N'ont ni dessins brodés à Tyr, ni larges franges
Pourpres, et qui vagit dans la paille et le foin . . .
Quel peut être, pour qu'on l'annonce de si loin,
Cet enfant-dieu, né pauvre, en un pays barbare ?
D'un coup brusque le vieux Thamus tourna la barre :

—Les démons ont dit vrai, mon fils. Depuis le temps
Que Jupiter jaloux foudroya les Titans,
Et que l'Etna mugit, crachant du soufre,
L'homme est abandonné sur terre, l'homme souffre,
Peinant toujours, gelé l'hiver, brûle l'été,
Sans te vaincre jamais, ô maigre pauvreté !
Qu'il vienne, celui qui, detrônant le hasard,
Doit donner à chacun de nous sa juste part
De pain et de bonheur. Plux de maux, plus de jeunes,
Les dieux sont bons parfois, mon fils, quand ils sont jeûnes.

There is the myth of old Thamous interpreted by a modern poet. M. Salomon Reinach, in his *Orpheus,* has recently given a more literal and more exact explanation of it, by connecting it with the festivals of Adonis. Adonis, beloved of Aphrodite, was killed by a wild boar while hunting, and mourned by his mistress. Every year, on the anniversary of his death, the women of Byblos mourned the young god and in their lamentations called him by his sacred name, Thamous, which was never uttered save in these mournful mysteries. This cult and these rites spread all over Greece. While they were going along the coast of Epirus, the Greek passengers on an Egyptian boat, whose pilot's name happened to be Thamous, heard the cry during the night : Θαμοῦς, Θαμοῦς, Θαμοῦς πανμέγας τέθνηκε, that is, Thamous, the very great, is dead. The pilot thought that he was being called and that thus was being announced the death of great Pan, Πᾶν μέγας. That is the end of the legend, at least it ends gracefully in a chorus of weeping women and amongst the lamentations of those taking part in the mysteries.

I have lingered long over the Macréons. But the country, the stories, the ideas, the images—everything has a singular attractiveness and a rare beauty. In the description of this melancholy island and its sacred wood, all is grave, religious, heroic. We can imagine it as something like that island of black pines, bathed by the waters of Corfu, which Boecklin has painted with such grandeur, such sadness, and such mystery.

Pantagruel and his companions continue their journey in search of the Oracle of the Bottle. Scarcely had the island of the Macréons disappeared from view than the Sneaking-island hove in sight. It is a miserable island inhabited by Shrovetide, that is to say, by Lent in person. Rabelais, who in religion never encroaches upon dogma, is a great reformer, on the contrary, in matters of ecclesiastical discipline. He personifies Lent as an odious and ridiculous monster, a fish-eater, a dictator of mustard, foster-father to physicians, a good Catholic, for the rest, and of great piety, weeping three-quarters of the day and never assisting at any weddings.

Rabelais makes Xenomanes describe the anatomy of Shrovetide. The passage is very long, and for a long time it remained unintelligible. It must be admitted that it is difficult to understand a text such as this :

" Shrovetide has membranes like a monk's cowle, a stomach like a belt, the pleura like a crow's bill, nails like a gimlet, etc."

Quite recently a learned physiologist and compatriot of Rabelais, Dr. Ledouble, discovered a meaning in these comparisons. It appears that Master François shows a great knowledge of anatomy. I can well believe it. They are the jokes of a man of science, but they are a bore.

On leaving the Sneaking-island, as they came near the Wild Island, the navigators encountered an enormous whale. As a good humanist, who likes to use Greek and Latin, Rabelais calls it a physetere. Pantagruel harpoons the animal, and the author describes whale-fishing with his customary exactness, like a man who knows the technique of the arts, crafts and industries. People have wondered what symbol is concealed beneath this maritime episode, and whether the opponent of Lent did not wish to kill the canonical fast with this cetaceous monster. This is rather far-fetched. As M. Abel Lefranc remarks, " A fishing incident of this kind was almost obligatory in the course of a journey in North American waters, where every year at this time, the fishermen of the Bay of St. Brieuc, of La Rochelle, of Olonne, of St. Jean de Luz, and Ciboure went to hunt the whale, which was already rare in those parts of the ocean which were closer to Europe."

But, after all, we are at liberty to see in this physetere anything we please. It is one of the great charms of the book which we have been analysing, that it means different things to different minds, according to their curiosity and their genius. The Wild Island is inhabited by Chitterlings. Compared with the island of Shrovetide, it is plenty contrasted with fasting, or perhaps the Calvinists opposed to the Papists. The fact that they are terrible leads one to believe that these Chitterlings are Calvinists. Pan-urge was terrified by them. Friar John, at the head of the cooks, charged them impetuously and ran them through with his spit.

What does that mean ? Is Rabelais so ill disposed towards the Reformers ? Not so long ago he seemed to lean in their direction. The matter must be examined more closely. He did not dislike the Reformers of France ; he execrated the Reformers of Geneva, the demoniac Calvins, who felt no less strongly about him. The Chitterlings, whose massacre and extermination he so joyfully relates, are apparently Chitterlings from Geneva. If they had been from Troyes, he would have pitied them and would not have permitted such carnage.

However, we must beware of attributing a too symbolical meaning to the adventures of Captains Mawl-Chitterling, and Cut-Pudding, and Niphleseth, queen of the Chitterlings, and of the inhabitants of Ruach, who live only on wind, and of the giant, Widenostrils, who fed on windmills, and who choked to death eating a lump of fresh butter at the mouth of a hot oven, by the advice of his physicians.

But when we reach the Island of Popefigs and learn that the inhabitants of this country escaped from the yoke of the Papimen only to fall under that of the feudal lords, we cannot help thinking of the German Church, which Luther snatched from the rapacity of the Roman Pontiffs only to subject it to the authority of the German princes. Here the allusion meets us halfway, with its veil half raised.

The Island of Popefigs, in the Gallic tradition, is most celebrated for its little Devil who could not yet hail and thunder, unless it were on parsley and cabbage, and being very innocent could neither read nor write.

Seeing a labourer in his field, he asked him what he was doing. The poor man replied that he was sowing his field with corn to help him to subsist the next year.

" Ay," said the little devil, " but the ground is none of thine, Mr. Plough-jobber, but mine."

In effect, ever since the inhabitants of Popefig land had offended the Pope, their entire country had been consigned to the devils.

" However," the little devil continued, " to sow corn is not my province ; therefore I will give thee leave to sow the field ; that is to say, provided we share the profit."

" I will," reply'd the farmer.

" I mean," said the devil, " that, of what the land shall bear, two lots shall be made, one of what shall grow above ground, the other of what shall be cover'd with earth ; the right of chusing belongs to me, for I am a devil of noble and ancient race ; thou art a base clown. I therefore chuse what shall lye underground, take thou what shall be above. When dost thou reckon to reap, hah ? "

" About the middle of July," quoth the farmer.

" Well," said the devil, " I'll not fail thee then : in the meantime, slave as thou oughtest. Work, clown, work : I am going to tempt noble nuns, I am more than sure of these."

When the middle of July came, the devil appeared at the cornfield, accompanied by a squadron of little imps. There, meeting the farmer, he said to him : " Well, clod-pate, how hast thou done since I went? Thou and I must now share the concern."

" Ay, Master Devil," quoth the clown, "'tis but reason we should."

Then the farmer and his men began to cut the corn. At the same time, the little imps pulled out the stubble. The farmer thrashed his corn, winnowed it, put it into sacks and went to the market to sell it. The imps did the same and sat down in the market beside the farmer to sell their straw. The farmer sold his corn for a good price and filled an old demi-buskin, which was fastened to his girdle with the money. The devils sold nothing, but, on the contrary, the peasants jeered at them in the open market place. When the market was over, the devils said to the farmer :

" Well, clown, thou hast chous'd me once, 'tis thy fault ; chouse me twice, 'twill be mine."

" Nay, good sir devil," reply'd the farmer, " how can I be said to have chous'd you, since 'twas your worship that chose first. The truth is that by this trick you thought to cheat me, hoping that nothing would spring out of the earth for my share, and that you should find whole underground the corn which I had sow'd . . . but troth, you must e'en go to school yet, you are no conjuror, for aught I see ; for, the corn that was sow'd is dead and rotten, its corruption having caus'd the generation of that which you saw me sell : so you chose the worst, and therefore are curs'd in the Gospel."

" Well, talk no more on't," quoth the devil, " what cans't thou sow our field with for next year ? "

" If a man would make the best on't," answer'd the ploughman, " 'twere fit to sow it with raddish."

" Now," cry'd the devil, " thou talkst like an honest fellow, bumpkin. Well, sow me a good store of raddish, I'll see and keep them safe from storms, and will not hail a bit on them ; but harke'e me, this time, I bespeak for my share what shall be above ground, what's under shall be thine : drudge on, looby, drudge on. I am going to tempt hereticks, their souls are dainty victuals when broil'd in rashers and well powder'd."

When harvest time arrived, the devil went to the radish field with his imps who began to cut and gather the radish-leaves. After him the farmer dug, pulled up the big radishes and put them in bags. Then they all went off together to the market. The farmer sold his radishes very well, the devil sold nothing. What is worse, people publicly jeered at him.

" I see thou hast play'd me a scurvy trick, thou villainous fellow (cry'd the angry devil)."

It is hardly necessary to say that Rabelais did not invent this story. Rabelais took it from popular tradition. La Fontaine took it from Rabelais and put it into verse. Here is the story as the poet wrote it in an excellent style.

> . . . Papefigue se nomme
> L'île et province où les gens autrefois
> Firent la figue au portrait du Saint-Père.
> Punis en sont ; rien chez eux ne prospère :
> Ainsi nous l'a conté maître François.
> L'île fut lors donnée en apanage
> A Lucifer ; c'est sa maison des champs.
> On voit courir par tout cet heritage
> Ses commensaux, rudes et pauvres gens,
> Peuple ayant queue, ayant cornes et griffes,
> Si maints tableaux ne sont point apocryphes.

Advint un jour qu'un de ces beaux messieurs
Vit un manant rusé, des plus trompeurs,
Verser un champ dans l'île dessus dite.
Bien paraissait la terre être maudite,
Car le manant avec peine et sueur
La retournait et faisait son labeur.
Survint un diable à titre de seigneur.
Ce diable était des gens de l'Evangile,
Simple, ignorant, à tromper très facile,
Bon gentilhomme et qui, dans son courroux,
N'avait encore tonné que sur les choux :
Plus ne savait apporter de dommage.
—Vilain, dit-il, vaquer à nul ouvrage,
N'est mon talent : je suis un diable issu
De noble race, et qui n'a jamais su
Se tourmenter ainsi que font les autres.
Tu sais, vilain, que tous ces champs sont nôtres ;
Ils sont à nous dévolus par l'édit.
Qui mit jadis cette île en interdit.
Voux y vivez dessous notre police.
Partant, vilain, je puis avec justice
M'attribuer tout le fruit de ce champ ;
Mais je suis bon, et veux que dans un an
Nous partagions sans noise et sans querelle.
Quel grain veux tu répandre dans ces lieux ?
Le manant dit :—Monseigneur, pour le mieux
Je crois qu'il faut les couvrir de touzelle ;
Car c'est un grain qui vient fort aisément.
—Je ne connais ce grain-là nullement,
Dit le lutin, Comment dis-tu ? . . . Touzelle ? .
Mémoire n'ai d'un grain qui s'appelle
De cette sorte ; or, emplis-en ce lieu ;

Touzelle, soit, Touzelle, de par Dieu !
J'en suis content. Fais donc vite et travaille ;
Manant, travaille ! et travaille, vilain !
Travailler est le fait de la canaille :
Ne t'attends pas que je t'aide un seul brin,
Ni que par moi ton labeur se consomme ;
Je t'ai dit que j'étais gentilhomme,
Ne pour chômer et pour ne rien savoir.
Voici comment ira notre partage :
Deux lots seront, dont l'un c'est à savoir
Ce qui hors terre et dessus l'héritage
Aura poussé, demeurera pour toi ;
L'autre, dans terre, est réservé pour moi.
L'août arrive, la touzelle est sciée,
Et, tout d'un temps, sa racine arrachée
Pour satisfaire au lot du diableteau.
Il y croyait la semence attachée,
Et que l'épi, non plus que le tuyau,
N'était qu'une herbe inutile et sechée.
Le laboureur vous la serra très bien.
L'autre au marché porta son chaume vendre :
On le hua ; pas un n'en offrit rien ;
Le pauvre diable était prêt à se pendre.
Il s'en alla chez son copartageant.
Le drôle avait le touzelle vendue,
Pour le plus sûr, en gerbe et non battue,
Ne manquant pas de bien cacher l'argent.
Bien le cacha. Le diable en fut la dupe.
—Coquin, dit-il, tu m'as joué d'un tour
C'est ton métier. Je suis diable de cour
Qui, comme vous, à tromper ne m'occupe.
Quel grain veux-tu semer pour l'an prochain ?

Le manant dit :—Je crois qu'au lieu de grain
Planter me faut ou navets ou carottes :
Vous en aurez, monseigneur, plaines hottes,
Si mieux n'aimez râves dans la saison.
—Râves, navets, carottes, tout est bon,
Dit le lutin. Mon lot sera hors terre ;
Le tien dedans. Je ne veux point de guerre
Avec que toi, si tu ne m'y contrains.
Je vais tenter quelques jeunes nonnains.
L'auteur ne dit ce qui firent les nonnes.
Le temps venu de recueillir encore,
Le manant prend râves belles et bonnes,
Feuilles sans plus tombent pour tout trésor
Au diableteau qui, l'épaule chargée,
Court au marché. Grande fut la risée ;
Chacun lui dit son mot, cette fois-là.
—Monsieur le diable, où croît cette denrée ?
Où mettrez-vous ce qu'on en donnera ?

With what fidelity La Fontaine, the best linguist of his century, reproduces the forms of language, the turns of phrase, the vocabulary of his model !

However, let us continue our journey in search of the Oracle. After the Island of Popefigs, Pantagruel and his companions reach the Island of Papimany.

" Have you seen him ? " the inhabitants cried at once. " Have you seen him ? "

Seeing that they meant the Pope, Panurge replied that he had seen three of them, and had derived little profit from the sight.

" How ? " cried the Papimen. " Our sacred decretals inform us that there never is more than one living."

" I mean, successively, one after the other," return'd Panurge ; " otherwise I never saw more than one at a time."

Here it is Rabelais who is speaking in the name of that rascal Panurge. In effect, at the time when he was writing the Fourth Book, Rabelais had seen three popes : Clément VII, Paul III, and Julius III.

The entire population of the country, men, women, little children, having come to meet them in a procession, raised their hands to Heaven and cried :

" Oh thrice and four times happy people ! "

Homenas, the Bishop of Papimany, kissed their feet.

This prelate, having invited them to dinner, the repast, rich in capons, hogs, pigeons, leverets, turkeys, etc., was served by young lasses, fair, good conditioned, blonde, soft, comely, dressed in white robes with a double girdle, their heads bare, their hair knotted with tapes and ribbons of violet silk, stuck with roses, gilly-flowers, and marjoram, who invited the guests to drink with neat and gentle courtesies.

In this the good man Homenas was merely following the custom of the Valois, who, instead of the usual service by pages, substituted at their table the service of young and beautiful girls. Homenas, in the midst of this magnificent feast, sang the praises of the sacred decretals, which, he said, if they were obeyed, would effect the happiness of the human race and begin an era of universal happiness.

Q

The decretals, as we know, are the letters in which the Pope, by solving a question submitted to him, gives a solution concerning a particular instance which is applicable to all analogous cases. Sometimes false ones were produced in order to create favourable precedents.

It is not for nothing that Rabelais conducts his readers to a Papiman who is mad upon the subject of decretals. He seizes the opportunity to mock abundantly, and with an acrimoniousness unusual in him, these texts, real or false, upon which the Sovereign Pontiff pretended to establish his rights over peoples and princes. He puts plenty of jokes at the expense of these holy epistles in the mouth of Pantagruel's companions. Ponocrates relates how Jean Chouart of Montpellier took a leaf of decretals to beat his gold and all his pieces were spoiled.

At Mans, said Eudemon, François Cornu, an apothecary, had made paper bags with those decretals which are called extravagantes, that is to say, scattered, and everything he wrapped up in them was immediately poisoned, corrupted and spoiled.

In Paris, said Carpalin, a tailor named Groignet had used some old decretals for patterns : all the clothes cut on these patterns were lost.

The two sisters of Rhizotome, Catherine and Renée, having put some collarettes freshly washed, finely starched and white, in a volume of decretals, took them out again, blacker than a bag of coal.

Homenas, having listened to these malicious remarks, and still many others (for Rabelais is inexhaustible in his thrusts, good and

bad, against the decretals), replied : " I understand you ; this is one of the quirks and little satyres of the new-fangled hereticks."

That is going too far. Rabelais was undoubtedly in favour of the reform of the Church, but he was neither a schismatic nor a heretic. He had not enough faith to sin against the faith. My own belief is that he believed nothing. But here it is not a question of his private thoughts : it is a question of his doctrine. He was with the bishops and prelates of France against the Sorbonne and the monks ; he was a Gallican ; he was a zealous defender of the rights of the Church and of the Crown of France ; he was against the Pope and in favour of the most Christian King. At bottom, his chief reproach against the Roman policy, as expressed in the decretals, was that it usurped the temporal power of the kings ; that it drew the gold of France to Rome. With dogma he has no concern and showed himself to be as accommodating as possible in this connection. He was never concerned in any way about the Mass and the Sacraments. On the contrary, what he had at heart was the interests of the kingdom and its sovereign. We must remember the ancient quarrel between the Kings of France and the Popes. It fills the history of the eldest daughter of the Church. Rabelais was heart and soul for his country, for his prince ; that is his politics, that is his theology.

Having left the island of Papimany, Pantagruel and his companions, on the lonely confines of the Frozen Sea, suddenly heard the sound of voices, the noise of a crowd of people, and distinguished syllables and words ; and these words in the desert of waters caused some surprise and some fright among them.

The pilot reassured them :

" About the beginning of last winter happen'd a great and bloody fight. Then the words and cries of men and women, the neighing of horses, and all other martial din froze in the air : and now the rigour of the winter being over by the succeeding serenity and warmth of the weather, they melt and are heard."

We are approaching the end of the Fourth Book.

Pantagruel stayed at the manor of Messer Gaster, the stomach in person, first master of the arts of the world. An allegorical journey, if ever there was one, and one which supplied an excellent theme to the abundant wisdom of Rabelais. The incomparable author shows us how Messer Gaster is the father of the arts :

" Accordingly, from the beginning he invented the Smith's art and husbandry to manure the ground that it might yield him corn ; he invented arms, and the art of war to defend corn ; physick and astronomy, with other parts of mathematicks, which might be useful to keep corn a great number of years in safety from the injuries of the air, beasts, robbers and purloiners ; he invented water, wind and hand-mills, and a thousand other engines to grind corn, and turn it into meal, leaven to make the dough ferment, and the use of salt to give it a savour, for he knew that nothing bred more diseases than heavy, unleaven'd, unsavoury bread.

" He found a way to get fire to bake it ; hour-glasses, dials and clocks to mark the time of its baking ; and as some countries wanted corn, he contriv'd means to convey some out of one country into another.

" He had the wit to pimp for asses and mares, animals of different species, that they might copulate for the generation of a third, which we call mules, more strong and fit for hard service than the other two. He invented carts and waggons to draw him along with greater ease ; and as seas and rivers hindred his progress, he devis'd boats, gallies and ships (to the astonishment of the elements) to waft him over to barbarous, unknown, and far distant nations, thence to bring, or thither to carry corn."

Ah ! if he were to return to the world to-day, if he were in our midst, what new and marvellous inventions old Master François would have to add to the ancient arts of Messer Gaster ! Steam transportation, the market rates known instantaneously by telegraph all over the globe, the preservation of meat by freezing, chemical manures, intensive cultivation, methodical selection, American vines being used to revive the exhausted old stocks of ancient Europe, the Bacchus of the new world giving life to our Latin Bacchus, and all the other marvels of man whose urgent needs render him ingenious.

After the manor of Messer Gaster, when we have pointed out the island of Chaneph inhabited by hypocrites, holy mountebanks, hermits, sham saints, all of them poor wretches living on the alms given them by travellers, we shall have covered all of the journey of Pantagruel in search of the Oracle of the Bottle, which François Rabelais published in his lifetime.

The good Rabelais has pointed out to us with his gigantic finger : there is the first cause of your energies, of your great social qualities. It is Messer Gaster, the first master of arts in the world, who has taught you the rapid exploitation of the wealth of your soil, inspired your commercial activity, caused your economic and financial progress.

CHAPTER VIII

THE LIFE OF RABELAIS (continued)

THE Sorbonne censored the Fourth Book and publication was stopped by a decree of Parliament, dated 1st March, 1552, stating that, " Whereas the Faculty of Theology has censored a certain evil work, offered for sale under the title of The Fourth Book of Pantagruel, with the King's privilege, the Court orders that the bookseller shall be immediately brought hither and that he shall be forbidden to sell or show the said book within a period of fourteen days : during which time the Court orders the King's Proctor to inform his Majesty aforesaid of the condemnation pronounced upon the said book by the said Faculty of Theology, and to send him a copy thereof to be dealt with at his pleasure."

The printer, Michel Fezandat, having been summoned to court, was forbidden to sell the work for fourteen days on penalty of corporal punishment. After an interval, which cannot be determined, the suspension was withdrawn.

In November 1552, there was a rumour that Rabelais had been thrown into prison and was in chains. The rumour was false. The author of Pantagruel was at liberty, but he was approaching his end. The date and place of his death are unknown. His epitaph, composed by Tahureau, gives us reason to believe that he was surrounded by friends during his last moments and that he joked at their grief.

Colletet says that he died at Paris in a house in the Rue des Jardins, and that he was buried in the cemetery of St. Paul, under a large tree which was still pointed out in the seventeenth century.

At that time, poets and humanists used to like to compose epitaphs on the illustrious dead. Ronsard consecrated an epitaph to Rabelais, in the form of an ode, in which he is chiefly celebrated as a drinker :

> Jamais le soleil ne l'a vu,
> Tant fût-il matin, qu'il n'eût bu,
> Et jamais au soir la nuit noire,
> Tant fût tard, ne l'a vu sans boire.
> Il chantant la grande massue
> Et la jument de Gargantue,
> Le grand Panurge et le pays
> Des Papimanes ébahis,
> Leurs lois, leurs façons, leurs demeures,
> Et frère Jean des Entommeures
> Et d'Epistémon les combats.
> O toi, quiconque sois, qui passes,
> Sur sa fosse répands des tasses,
> Répands du bril et des flacons,
> Des cervelas et des jambons.

At the first glance, our modern delicacy is inclined to find these lines insulting, and we should not have expected that the prince of poets would speak thus of the incomparable master. But on closer observation we see that this epitaph is an imitation of several little poems in the Greek Anthology, consecrated to the memory of Anacreon. In the mind of Ronsard, that is an honour for Rabelais.

Another poet of the Pleiad, Baïf, composed a funeral epigram for Rabelais which is not without grace :

> O Pluton, Rabelais reçoi,
> Afin que toi qui es le roi
> De ceux qui ne rient jamais
> Tu ais un rieur désormais.

But I shall be more pleased to quote a very beautiful epitaph in Latin verse which Pierre Boulanger, who was a doctor and had known Rabelais, composed in honour of the author of Pantagruel. The following is a literal translation :

" Beneath this stone sleeps the most excellent of laughing men. Our descendants will seek out the kind of man he was, for all who lived in his time well know |who he was ; every one knew him, and more than any other, he was dear to all. Perhaps they will believe that he was a buffoon, a clown, who by dint of his jokes earned a good meal. No, no, he was not a buffoon, nor a public clown. But, with his exquisite and penetrating genius, he mocked at the human race, at its insensate desires and the credulity of its hopes. Undisturbed about his fate, he led a happy life ; the winds always blew in his favour. Yet, no more learned man could be found when, forgetting his jokes, he was pleased to talk seriously and to play a serious part. Never did any Senator, with threatening brow and severe and melancholy glance, sit more seriously upon his lofty seat. A large and difficult question had only to be propounded and to require great skill and knowledge for its solution and one would have thought that large subjects were open to him alone and to him only were the secrets of nature revealed. With what eloquence he could adorn whatever he was pleased to say, to the admiration of all whom his biting pleasantries and his usual witticisms had led to believe that this joker was nothing of a scholar ! He knew everything that Greece and Rome had produced, but, like a new Democritus, he laughed at the vain fears and the desires of the common people and of princes, at their frivolous cares and at the anxious labours of this brief life in which is consumed all the time which a benevolent divinity is willing to grant us."

This doctor from Poitiers has succeeded in expressing the mind, the soul, the genius of Rabelais in his beautiful epitaph.

Rabelais, as we have seen, died leaving his *Pantagruel* incomplete. Nine years after his death appeared a fragment of the Fifth and last Book, making sixteen chapters. The entire book was published in 1564 without the name of the bookseller or the place of publication.

It has been denied that Rabelais was its author. Many people, struck by the Calvinist tendencies found in this work, do not recognise the author whom Calvin regarded as an atheist, and who regarded Calvin as demoniac. But the Calvinism of the Fifth Book is practically limited to attacks on monks, and Rabelais always mocked those poor hooded creatures. Like Lenormant, I think I can recognise here and there in these pages the lion's claw.

That is not to say that we are certain of possessing in its entirety the actual text of Rabelais. It is probable that the author had not

put the finishing touches to his work. There were lacunæ, obscurities. The editor explained and completed, as the case required,
and sometimes perhaps when there was no necessity, in order to
make improvements and show his talent. The editors of that
time did not understand their duties as do those of our time. They
did not feel bound to be faithful and tried to embellish the work
which they were issuing. All the posthumous works of the sixteenth
century give evidence of this infidelity. It is not surprising that
such evidence can be found in the Fifth Book, as it has come down
to us. A thing that is, I confess, rather disturbing, is the quatrain
which the anonymous editor placed at the beginning, and which
is as follows :

> Is Rabelais dead ? A Book see yet again !
> His better part with life is still aglow,
> Another of his writings to bestow,
> Which make him live immortal among Men.

So far as I can understand it this means : Rabelais is dead, but
he recovered consciousness in order to present us with this book.
It must be admitted that a pastiche would not be differently
announced. But we must take into account the unskilfulness of a
bad rhymer, and it might mean : Rabelais is not dead, since he
lives again in this book. By prolonging this debate we merely
succeed in accumulating doubts. Let us face the enigmatic work.

THE FIFTH BOOK

CHAPTER IX

THE FIFTH BOOK

THIS posthumous Book relates the continuation and end of the journey of Pantagruel and his companions in search of the Oracle of the Holy Bottle. I shall not examine it in such detail as the others because, while I believe it to be, in the main, the work of Rabelais, we cannot be certain that all of it is his. Furthermore, a considerable part is occupied by allegories, which rendered lifeless so many chapters of the Fourth Book, and which make it dull and dreary, while the tone grows sharper, and the attacks on the hobgoblins and the Furr'd Lawcats become more violent than in anything that the author himself gave to the public.

The travellers first land on Ringing Island, where bells are heard perpetually. Rabelais could not tolerate the sound of bells, and the dark picture of this country would seem to be authentically his. The Island is inhabited by caged birds of clerical origin as their names indicate : clerghawks, monkhawks, priesthawks, abbothawks, bishhawks, cardinhawks, one popehawk, who is a species by himself, clergkites, nunkites, priestkites, abbesskites, bishkites, cardinkites, popekites. These birds are not indigenous to the Island, but come from outside. Some were sent there while young by their mothers, who could not bear to have them at home. The majority came from Breadless Day, which is very long. This amounts to saying that the cruel selfishness of parents and the poverty of large families people convents.

It was here that Panurge told the story of the Horse and the Ass. It is worthy of Rabelais, but I must refer to the text those readers who are not frightened by the greater freedom of the old tongue.

The travellers next arrived at the Island of Tools. The trees there bear tools and arms instead of fruit : pickaxes, hoes, scythes, sickles, spades, trowels, hatchets, bill-hooks, saws, adzes, shears, pincers, daggers and poniards. When a tool or an arm is required, the tree is shaken and these iron fruits fall, fitting into the handles and scabbards growing below. Each reader will interpret this myth according to taste.

Then we are taken to the Island of Sharping, that is, to the Island of Deceit, of Mockery. There, amongst other peculiarities, are square rocks about which greater destruction, greater losses in lives and property had occurred than about all the Syrtes, Syllas, Charybdes, Sirens and gulfs in the universe. These square rocks are dice. Here, like a good Catholic preacher, Rabelais is protesting against games of chance.

On the Island of Sharping we encounter people of a type which is not extinct : dealers in faked antiques. One of them sold the Pantagruelists a piece of the shell of the two eggs laid by Leda. At the same time, relic-showmen, for a consideration, allowed them to touch a feather from the wings of the Archangel Gabriel.

The Pantagruelian ships then put in at the Island of Condemnation, the seat of the criminal courts. The judges who administer it are the Furr'd Law-cats. They have the hair and claws of cats. This is the author's description of them :

" They hang all, burn all, draw all, quarter all, behead all, murder all, imprison all, ruin all, and waste all. For among them Vice is call'd Virtue ; Wickedness, Piety ; Treason, Loyalty ; Robbery, Justice ; Plunder is their motto. Their wickedness is no more known in the world than the Cabala of the Jews, and therefore 'tis not detested, chastis'd, and punish'd, as 'tis fit it shou'd be. But shou'd all their villainy be once displayed in its true colours, and expos'd to the people, there never was, is, nor will be any spokesman so sweet-mouth'd, whose fine colloguing tongue could save 'em ; nor any laws so rigorous and Draconic, that could punish 'em as they deserve ; nor yet any magistrate so powerful as to hinder their being burnt alive in their coney-boroughs."

The Island of Apedefers, where they next disembark, is the Island of Ignoramuses. The Apedefers are occupied solely in putting into wine-presses houses, meadows, fields, in order to squeeze money out of them, only part of which went to the King. The rest disappeared.

Next we come to the Island of For-ward Folks. Our ancestors doubtless enjoyed, as they might a picture by Breughel, these descriptions of fat people who, after gorging, burst their skins with a horrible noise. Nowadays we like them only out of friendship for the past and as an archæological fantasy.

Having steered forward (the pun is in the text and is none the better on that account), we reach the realm of Quintessence, where the inhabitants are ingenious and subtle. Some make Blackamoors white by rubbing their bellies with the bottom of a pannier. Others plough their fields with a yoke of foxes. Others cut fire with a knife, others keep water in a sieve. There are those who measure the hop of a flea and those who guard the moon from the wolves.

However, these clever people could give no news of the Oracle to the Pantagruelians, who continued their journey and landed on the Island of Odes, where the ways walk. On this Island the roads move of themselves and walk like animals.

The inhabitants ask :

" Whither do's that way go ? "

They answer :

" To the parish, the city, the river."

Just as everywhere else, but in Odes the reply is literal. The travellers take the right road and, without further effort or fatigue, are taken to their destination.

From this it has been concluded that Rabelais foresaw the escalator at the Exhibition in 1900. But, obviously, the author is joking, and playing upon the current expression, that a road goes from such-and-such a place to such-and-such a place.

What is more worthy of notice in this chapter, is the following passage :

" Reflecting on the different manner of going of these moving ways, Seleucus became of the opinion in this Island that the earth turns round about its poles, and not the heavens, whatever we may think to the contrary, as when we are on the River Loire, we think the trees on the bank move. However, they do not move, but we do, by the floating down of the boat."

The system of Seleucus is that which Copernicus expounded in 1543. Rabelais declares that the earth turns on its poles ; in his time this was novel and daring. More than a century later Pascal was not so well informed, and up to the end of the eighteenth century in France the handbooks of cosmography for use in schools taught the system of Ptolemy, giving that of Copernicus as a pure hypothesis. Even to-day, in the twentieth century, we cannot assume that the asinine herd, the mob, is so well informed in such matters. In France quite recently a misunderstood proposition of the great mathematician Poincaré was sufficient for a crowd of literate ignoramuses (the species flourishes) to situate the earth at the centre of the world, a great subject of human pride. However, let us continue the journey.

After leaving the Island of Odes, we arrive at the Island of Sandals, where there is a monastery of very humble monks who call themselves the Semiquaver Friars, because they incessantly trill psalms. On seeing these monks, Friar John exclaimed :

" Now I know that this is our very Antipodes. In Germany they pull down monasteries and unfrockifie the monks ; here they act clean contrary to others, setting new ones up."

This might well seem to be a favourable allusion to Luther's Reformation. In all his writings Rabelais never fails to point out that monks are unfortunate, useless and injurious. He makes great fun of them but, as a matter of fact, he does not hate them, save when they behave like hobgoblins, cruelly persecute those who study Greek, and want to have people burned because of their learning and intelligence. When he accuses the poor monks of being too fond of the kitchen, he does it more in good humour than in anger. It must be remembered that, of all the characters in his universal comedy, the person whom he has endowed with the most courage, kindness, and active virtue is a monk, and not a renegade monk, a defrocked monk, but a real monk, " a right monk," as he says, " if ever there was any since the monking world monked a monkerie." When he founds a social institution into which he puts all his intelligence and all his heart, it is still an abbey, an abbey where the rules are in conformity with nature, where people love life, where they think less about heaven than about this world, but an abbey none the less, and a conventual dwelling.

The good Pantagruelists' last port of call is the Land of Satin, where the trees and flowers are of velvet and damask, and the animals and birds are of tapestry. They do not eat, sing or bite.

On this island the travellers saw a little old hunchback, deformed and monstrous, whose name was Hear-say. His mouth was slit up to his ears, and in his mouth were seven tongues, each of them cleft into seven parts. All seven spoke together. He had as many ears on his head and the rest of his body as Argus had eyes.

" About him," the author adds, " stood an innumerable number of men and women, gaping, list'ning, and hearing very intensely. . . . Among 'em I observed a very handsome bodied man, who held then a map of the world, and with little aphorisms compendiously explain'd everything to 'em ; so that those men of happy memories grew learned in a trice and would most fluently talk with you of a world of prodigious things ; the hundredth part of which would take up a man's whole life to be fully known, of the Pyramids, of the Nile, of Babylon, of the Troglodytes, the Pygmies, the Cannibals, of all the devils : every individual word of it by hear-say. There I saw Herodotus, Pliny, Solinus, Berosus, Philostratus, Mela, Strabo, and God knows how many other antiquaries, Albert the Great, Paulus Jovius, Jemmy Cartier, Marco Paulo, and forty cart-loads of other modern historians, scribbling the Lord knows what, and all by hear-say."

This passage offers food for thought. Rabelais, if indeed the text is entirely his (for in this Fifth Book every detail is suspect), places Jacques Cartier, the King's pilot, amongst the writers of fables. This is rather in contradiction with the system which makes the Pantagruelian voyages a species of literary variation on a geographical theme of the St. Malo explorer. Rabelais seems to say that everything in Jacques Cartier's stories is not true. But what is most unusual, to any one who knows the spirit of the Renaissance, is to see a humanist, a Hellenist, a Latinist, like Rabelais, throw doubts upon the historical authority of Philostratus, Strabo, Herodotus, and Pliny ; to hear a learned—and very learned—person, like Rabelais, making fun of the illustrious ancients, and alleging that they talk by hearsay, like a Marco Polo, a Paulus Jovius, or any other modern. This is so contrary to the usual attitude of the scholars of the period, it is so peculiar, that it justifies the suspicion that Master François was a great sceptic, who believed in nothing in the world save our pitiful human lot, which is helped by compassion and softened by irony. To doubt the stories of Herodotus in 1540 ! Why, our excellent Rollin still believed them under Louis XIV !

After this last stop at the Island of Lies, Pantagruel and his companions finally reached the end of their journey. He came to Lantern Land, the description of which is taken from the *True History*, so abundantly exploited in the Fourth Book. That is a good sign. In these imitations of Lucian we seem to recognise our Rabelais and we are less doubtful of having the key of the temple and hearing the words of the Oracle. Lantern Land is inhabited by living lanterns. The Queen is a lantern dressed in rock crystal, wrought damask-wise and beset with large diamonds. The lanterns of the royal blood are clad in gypseous alabaster, the rest in horn, paper and oil-cloth. One of them is earthen and shaped like a pot. It is the lantern of Epictetus which, according to Lucian, was sold to a collector for three thousand drachmas.

The Pantagruelists dine with the Queen, and it would seem as if it were a philosophical banquet, that these lanterns and torches represent wisdom and virtue. When the banquet was finished, the Queen gave each guest his choice of a lantern to light his way home. Here it is Rabelais who speaks, and who but Rabelais could have said what follows ?

" We selected and chose the friend of the great Messer Pierre Lamy, whom I had formerly known. Unmistakably she also recognised me, and she appeared to us more divine, more sprightly, more learned, more wise, more eloquent, more kindly, more gracious, and more suited to conduct us than any other that was in the company. Very humbly thanking the Royal Lady, we were accompanied as far as our ship by seven young jigging torches, the clear Diana shining brightly."

Who but Rabelais could have written these exquisite lines ? Who could have recalled in this learned allegory the forty-year-old memory of the young monk who shared at the Abbey of Fontenay the studies and perils of Friar François, and who consulted the Virgilian lotteries in order to find out whether he should fear the hobgoblins ? Who but Rabelais could thus have paid the tribute of memory to the friend of his young years ?

Now we have come to the Oracle of the Holy Bottle, which is on an island quite close to Lantern Land, where Pantagruel and his companions are conducted by a wise lantern. First they pass through a large vineyard filled with all sorts of vines, bearing leaves, flowers and fruits all the year round. The learned lantern orders each of them to eat three grapes, to put vine leaves in his shoes, and to take a green branch in his left hand. At the end of the vineyard stood an ancient arch, ornamented with the trophies of the drinker, which led to an arbour consisting of vine branches loaded with grapes, under which the travellers went.

" Jupiter's priestess," said Pantagruel, " would not have walked under this arbour."

" There was a mystical reason," answered the most perspicacious lantern, " for had she gone under it, the wine, or the grapes of which 'tis made, had been over her head, and then she would have seem'd overtopt and master'd by wine. Which implies that priests, and all persons who devote themselves to the contemplation of divine things, ought to keep their minds sedate and calm, and avoid whatever might disturb and discompose their tranquillity ; which nothing is more apt to do than drunkenness. You also could not come into the Holy Bottle's presence, after you have gone through the arch, did not the noble priestess, Bacbuc, first see your shoes full of vine-leaves ; which action is diametrically opposite to the other, and signifies that you despise wine and tread it under foot."

They went underground through a vault on which was painted a dance of women and satyrs, like the painted cellar at Chinon, the foremost city in the world—which sounds like authentic Rabelais. At the foot of the stairway they came to a portal of jasper of Doric order, on which was written in letters of gold : ἐν οἴνῳ ἀλήθεια (*In vino veritas*). The massive gates were of bronze, with carved reliefs, in which we may see an allusion to the gates of the baptistry of the beautiful San Giovanni in Florence, which Michaelangelo declared worthy to be placed at the entrance

to Paradise, and which Rabelais admired while Friar Bernard
Lardon of Amiens was looking for a cook-shop.

The gates opened. The visitors beheld two tablets of Indian
bronze, of a bluish colour, bearing these two inscriptions :

Ducunt volentem fata, nolentem trahunt, which the author translates :
" Fate leads the willing and the unwilling draws," And this
sentence from the Greek : " All things tend to their end."

The temple which they entered was paved in mosaics, representing vine-leaves, lizards and snails, which the author describes
as one who has seen Roman mosaics : on the roof and walls they
saw, also in mosaic, the victories of Bacchus in India, and old
Silenus accompanied by rustic youths, horned like kids, cruel as
lions, perpetually dancing the Cordax. The description of these
pictures betrays an admirer of the works of antiquity, and especially a reader of Philostratus and Lucian. The number of figures,
which is both exact and enormous, sixty-nine thousand, two hundred and twenty-seven, in one case, and eighty-five thousand, one
hundred and thirty-three, in the other, is quite in accordance
with the statistical procedure of Master François. The lamp,
which illuminated the temple as the sun would have done, had a
body ornamented with a frieze representing a children's battle.
The oil and wick burned perpetually, without ever being renewed.

While the travellers were admiring these wonders, Bacbuc, the
priestess of the Holy Bottle, and her attendants, came towards
them, her face joyful and smiling, led them to a fountain surrounded by columns and topped by a dome which rose in the
middle of the temple, and, handing them cups and goblets,

graciously invited them to drink. Each drinker found that the water of this fountain tasted like whatever wine he fancied, Beaune, Grave, gracious and sparkling, wine of Mireveaux, colder than ice ; as their fancies changed the water changed its taste.

Then the priestess clothed Panurge in the habit of the neophytes admitted to the mysteries and, after he had sung some verses by way of incantation, she threw a powder into the fountain which caused it to boil and hum like a beehive. Then this word was heard :

TRINC

Bacbus took Panurge gently by the arm, saying : " Friend, offer your thanks to indulgent heaven, as reason requires ; you have soon had the word of the Goddess Bottle, and the kindest, most favourable and certain word of an answer that I ever yet heard her give, since I officiate here at her most sacred oracle."

Having spoken thus, the priestess took a huge book covered in silver, plunged it into the fountain and said :

" The philosophers, preachers and doctors of your world feed you up with fine words and cant at the ears : now, here we really incorporate our precepts at the mouth. Therefore, I'll not say to you, read this chapter, see this gloss ; no, I say to you, taste me this fine chapter, swallow me this rare gloss. Formerly an ancient prophet of the Jewish nation eat a book, and became a clerk even to the very teeth ; now will I have you to drink one, that you may be a clerk to your very liver. Here, open your mandibules."

" Panurge gaping as wide as his jaws could stretch, Bacbuc took the silver book, at least we took it for a real book, for it look'd just for the world like a breviary," but it was a venerated, true and natural bottle, filled with Falernian wine of which she made Panurge swallow every drop.

" This," quoth Panurge, " was a notable chapter, a most authentic gloss ! Is this all that the Trismegistian Bottle's word means ? "

" Nothing more," returned Bacbuc, " for trinc is a panophean word, that is, a word understood, us'd and celebrated by all nations, and signifies Drink.

" Here we hold not that laughing but drinking is the distinguishing character of man. I don't say drinking, taking the word singly and absolutely in the strictest sense ; no, beasts then might put in for a share ; I mean drinking cool, delicious wine. For you must know, my beloved, that by wine we become divine ; neither can there be a surer argument, or a less deceitful divination ; wine, οἶνος in Greek, means strength, power, for 'tis in its power to fill the soul with all truth, learning and philosophy. If you observe what is written in Ionian letters on the temple-gate, you may have understood that truth is in wine. The Goddess Bottle therefore directs you to that divine liquor, be your self the expounder of your undertaking."

Thus spake Bacbuc.

" 'Tis impossible," said Pantagruel, " to speak more to the purpose than does this true priest, Wine, then."

" Let us trinc," said Panurge.

What is this wine drawn from the holy fountain, which gives strength and power to the mind ? The author does not say, but he allows us to guess. It is not the juice of the grape, in the strict and literal sense ; it is knowledge which, in an upright soul, teaches real duties and gives happiness, at least so far as the latter is attainable in this world. There is no longer any question of Panurge's getting married, and whether his wife will deceive him. The good Pantagruel and his learned company did not take so long a journey in order to find the answer to a riddle which, after all, concerned only Panurge himself. It was about the whole of humanity that the Pantagruelists went to consult the Oracle of the Holy Bottle, and the Oracle replied : trinc, drink your fill at the fountains of knowledge. To know, in order to love, is the secret of life. Avoid the hypocrites, the ignorant, the cruel : free yourselves from vain terrors ; study man and the universe ; learn to know the laws of the physical and moral world, so that you may obey them and them alone ; drink, drink knowledge ; drink truth ; drink love.

CHAPTER X

CONCLUSION

MADAME ROLAND, when condemned by a bloody tribunal, appealed on the scaffold to impartial posterity—the happy illusion of an innocent victim. Posterity consists of human beings, and is never impartial, basing its unanimous consent upon ignorance and indifference. Sometimes posterity has an epic and legendary sense which magnifies and simplifies. It never has any historic sense nor any perception of the truth.

Tradition effects strange metamorphoses, causing the heroes whom it sweeps along to lead a posthumous existence very different from the life they lived in flesh and blood. Rabelais is a case in point. He was popular because of his undeserved reputation as an intrepid drinker, and tradition composed a biography of him wholly dissimilar from that of which I have tried to present the solid elements. It may not be without interest, after we have seen the real Rabelais, to indicate some of the traits of the legendary Rabelais. Therefore, selecting two or three wretched fables, which are to be found in all the old biographies of the author, I shall relate them as briefly as possible, beginning with one of the most fabulous, which is concerned with the last stay of Master François in Montpellier.

While Rabelais was professing medicine, according to the legend, Chancellor du Prat rendered a decree abolishing the

privileges of the Faculty at Montpellier. The masters had recourse
to this colleague whose mind they esteemed. They deputed him
to go to court and have the decree revoked which affected
them. On his arrival in Paris Rabelais presented himself at
the Chancellor's house and, not having been received, he
marched up and down in front of the door in a green robe
and wearing a long, grey beard. Everybody stopped to look at
him. To those who questioned him he replied that he was a
flayer of calves and that those who wished to be the first to
be flayed must hurry. The Chancellor was at table when they
reported to him the remarks of this eccentric person. He
ordered him to be brought in, and Rabelais harangued him
with such learning and eloquence that the Chancellor promised
to re-establish and confirm the privileges of the University of
Montpellier.

It is hardly necessary to insist upon the improbability of such a
story.

In the old lives of the author there is also an incident which
recalls the episode of Sancho Panza's doctor on the Island of
Barataria.

Rabelais, Guillaume du Bellay's physician, being present at
one of that gentleman's dinners, struck with his rod a dish containing a fine fish, and declared that it was indigestible. Whereupon the servants carried away the fish intact to the kitchen,
where Master François hastened to devour it. When Seigneur
Guillaume, discovering his doctor at table, asked him why he
was eating a dish which he had declared to be bad for the stomach,

Rabelais replied : " I did not mean that the fish was indigestible but merely the dish which contained it."

Thus our forebears tried to render the life of Rabelais Rabelaisian.

Although it is insignificant and incongruous, the famous little story must be told which has given rise to the phrase : " Rabelais' quarter of an hour," since the phrase has passed into the language. It is as follows :

On his return from Rome our author happened to be in hostelry at Lyons, badly dressed, and without money to pay for his lodging and his journey to Paris, where business awaited him. In these circumstances he took some ashes from the fireplace and put them in little bags, on which he wrote : " Poison to kill the King " ; " Poison to kill the Duc d'Orléans." Then he left them very conspicuously about his room. The landlady found them there and, greatly terrified, went to the King's lieutenant who promptly sent the man with the bags to Paris. When he was brought before the King he greatly amused the latter by telling him the story of his expedient.

It is strange that such a story could have seemed credible.

Once upon a time it was held that the statement was authentic which Rabelais made, when dying, to the page sent by Cardinal du Bellay to inquire about the patient's health : " Tell Monsignor the state in which you see me. I am going away in search of a great perhaps. He is in the magpie's nest. Tell him not to leave it. Drop the curtain, the farce is over." This is much more literary than the rest and is partly imitated from Suetonius. But it is equally untrue.

Rabelais became popular only through the three of four anecdotes which I have quoted. His writings never reached the ignorant masses, and it is an actual fact, although scarcely credible, that the broadsides and the volumes in the Bibliothéque Bleue, which spread the portrait and life of Gargantua throughout the French countryside, show none of his traits as described by Rabelais. They are derived from popular stories earlier than his. Panurge and Friar John are unknown to them. Despite what has been said of it, *Pantagruel* is a work written solely for the lettered ; Pantagruelism is a philosophy accessible only to the *élite* of rare minds ; it is almost an esoteric doctrine, hidden and secret. Prominent amongst these rare minds in the sixteenth century, is Cardinal du Perron, who described *Pantagruel* as the book *par excellence*, the true Bible, and consigned to the servants' pantry those of his guests who confessed to not having read it.

Montaigne mentions Rabelais once in his *Essays*. I shall quote the passage, although it has little intrinsic value, because everything in Montaigne is of interest :

" An over obstinate continuation and plodding contention doth dazle, dul, and weary the same. My sight is thereby confounded and diminished—— If one booke seeme tedious unto me, I take another, which I follow not with any earnestness, except it be at such houres as I am idle, or that I am weary with doing nothing. I am not greatly affected to new bookes, because ancient authors are in my judgement more full and pithy, nor am I much addicted to Greeke bookes, forasmuch as my understanding can not well rid his worke with a childish and apprentise intelligence. Amongst

moderne bookes meerly pleasant, I esteeme Bocace, his
Decameron, Rabelais, and the kisses of John the second (if they
may be placed under this title) worth the paines-taking to reade
them. As for Amadis and such like trash of writings, they had
never the credit so much as to allure my youth to delight in them."

Thus Montaigne ranks *Pantagruel* amongst the works of mere
entertainment which amuse him. This opinion, it seems to me,
is irresponsible and frivolous, to say the least ; a lapse on the part
of the genius who must be placed with Rabelais in the first rank
of sixteenth century writers. What a contrast between the son of
Touraine, solid, massive, compact, four square, rough, colourful,
and the supple Gascon, drifting, and variable ! Montaigne is
assuredly an agreeable and profitable companion, but he is
difficult to grasp ; he slips away, he escapes. Only the professors
are certain that they understand him, because it is their profession
to understand everything. I read him constantly, I like him, I
admire him, but I am not sure that I know him well. His mind
changes from one phrase to another, sometimes in the middle of
a phrase, and it need not be a very long one either. If it is true
that he has portrayed himself in his *Essays*, he has given an image
of himself more broken than the reflection of the moon upon the
sea. I have departed a little from my subject, but I could not pass
over the great name of Montaigne in silence.

This Rabelais, whom Montaigne pronounced frivolous, was
esteemed for his judgment and teaching above all the writers of
his time by Estienne Pasquier, a grave jurist, a profound historian,
and a wise philosopher.

279

In his *Recherches* he says : " By reason of the humour which he brought to light, jesting at everything, he made himself without an equal. For my own part, I will frankly confess that I have so playful a mind as never to be tired of reading him, nor did I ever read him without finding food for laughter and my own profit as well."

Estienne Pasquier is not the only grave magistrate of his time who was pleased and edified by Rabelais. President de Thou, the great historian, praises Rabelais for having written with the freedom of Democritus and with joyful buffoonery a most ingenious work in which, under fictitious names, he introduces every order of the State and society.

Jacques de Thou did not, any more than Estienne Pasquier, fall into the error of Montaigne who saw in Rabelais only a buffoon. Nevertheless, when he wrote some Latin verses about the incomparable author, conforming to popular tradition, he made of him a merry toper. The drunkenness of this Silenus of Chinon was material for classic verse. It was in 1598 that Jacques de Thou composed the verses to which I refer, in the following circumstances. Having gone that year to Chinon, he stopped at the house of Rabelais' father, which had become a hostelry. At the request of one of his travelling companions, he wrote some verses on this subject, making the shade of Rabelais speak of his satisfaction at the change. It is a pleasant little poem, of which I shall quote a French translation, made at the beginning of the eighteenth century :

RABELAIS

J'ai passé tout mon temps à rire :
Mes écrits libres en font foi.
Ils sont si plaisants qu'à les lire,
On rira même malgré soi.

La raison sérieuse ennuie
Et rend amers nos plus beaux jours.
Que peut-on faire de la vie,
Sans rire et plaisanter toujours ?

Aussi Bacchus, Dieu de la Joie,
Qui régla toujours mon destin,
Jusqu'en l'autre monde m'envoie,
De quoi dissiper mon chagrin.

Car de ma maison paternelle
Il vient de faire un cabaret
Où le plaisir se renouvelle
Entre le blanc et le clairet.

Les jours de fête on s'y régale,
On y rit du soir au matin.
Dans le salon et dans la salle,
Tout Chinon se trouve en festin.

Là, chacun dit sa chasonette ;
Là, le plus sage est le plus fou,
Et danse au son de la musette
Les plus gais branles du Poitou.

La cave s'y trouve placée
Où fut jadis mon cabinet.
On m'y porte plus sa pensée
Qu'aux douceurs d'un vin frais et net.

Que si Pluton, que rien ne tente,
Voulait se payer de raison
Et permettre à mon ombre errante
De faire un tour à ma maison,

Quelque prix que j'en puisse attendre,
Ce serait mon premier souhait,
De la louer ou de la vendre
Pour l'usage que l'on en fait.

Thus, for the Muses, for the Latin Muse of de Thou, as for the French Muse of Ronsard, Rabelais is a drunkard. The Muses are liars ; but they know how to win credit and to have their fables believed.

Amongst the Pantagruelists of the seventeenth century may be mentioned Bernier, the Gassendist philosopher, the friend of Ninon de Lenclos and Madame de la Sablière ; the scholar Huet, Bishop of Avranches ; Ménage ; Madame de Sévigné ; La Fontaine ; Racine ; Molière ; Fontenelle—a rather fine list, it must be admitted. As for La Bruyère, his opinion of our author is well known : " Where he is bad, he far exceeds the worst, that is what charms the vulgar ; where he is good, he achieves the exquisite and the excellent ; he is fit for the consumption of the most delicate." Of course, *Pantagruel* was a dish for the most delicate, for La Fontaine, Molière, for La Bruyère himself. So far as charming the vulgar is concerned, if by the vulgar he means people who have neither intelligence nor education nor refined knowledge, how could Rabelais have done it at the time when La Bruyère was writing, about 1688, since his language by that time was comprehensible only to the lettered ? To the peasant, the porter, the shop assistant, the tradesman, it was Greek.

Voltaire came late to Rabelais, but when he began to like him, he became madly enthusiastic and learned him by heart. The eighteenth century might be offended in its delicacy at times by Rabelais, but it could not but enjoy the philosophy of the Curé of Meudon, who then had rather successful imitators, like the Abbé Dulaurens.

In 1791 Ginguené, poet and publicist, published a book entitled, *On the Authority of Rabelais in the Present Revolution and in the Civil Constitution of the Clergy,* in which our author is considered as a philosopher, as a politician, and rather dragged by force into modern ideas. Rabelais, who mocked prophets and soothsayers, must have laughed in the Elysian Fields at the commentators who made him predict the French Revolution. However, it is only fair to say that great thinkers see far ahead, prepare the future and set the task for the statesmen who accomplish it, while wearing blinkers, or sometimes blindfolded, like horses in a riding school. Of course, I do not refer to any existing European statesmen.

In the nineteenth century, criticism was well informed, very alert and, on the whole, very supple, skilful in understanding the feelings, manners, characters and language of the past, and it was very favourable to Rabelais, recognised his genius, consecrated his glory. But, as it is difficult, perhaps impossible, to get away from one's own period, even at a time of evocation, restitutions, reconstructions, at a time when Michelet had made history a resurrection ; as all of us seek and see only ourselves in others, as we cannot help attributing our feelings to the people of former times, the general tendency of the critics, great and small, of 1830 and 1850 was to romanticise the author of *Pantagruel*, and to incline him, if not to melancholy—that was too obviously impossible —at least to gravity, to meditative profundity, and if one were in the least tinged with liberalism and free thought, to identify him with an independent philosophy which was not of his time nor in his character. This is noticeable in Michelet, in Henri Martin, in Eugène Noël. Sainte-Beuve, with his customary subtlety, corrected this error and restored his independence and his free humour to the giant of the sixteenth century.

Lamartine has said many harsh things about Rabelais. Victor Hugo speaks very well of him. Neither of them had read him, but each of them had a species of intuition. Lamartine divined in him a man quite different from himself, a genius quite opposed to his own. On the contrary, Victor Hugo imagined that there was some relationship, some resemblance between the creator of Gargantua and the creator of Quasimodo. Hence the judgments which they pronounced. Each of them, while talking of Rabelais, was thinking of himself. Guizot, as we have seen, devoted a lengthy and substantial study to the pedagogy of Rabelais. There is no aspect from which our author was not considered during the nineteenth and twentieth centuries. We have had excellent works upon Rabelais the doctor, Rabelais the botanist, Rabelais the humanist, Rabelais the jurist, Rabelais the architect. Amongst the most modern works on this great man I shall mention the interesting analyses of Jean Fleury, and Paul Stapfer's excellent literary study, the notes of Rathery, of Moland, the work of Marty-Lavaux, and the invaluable articles in the *Revue des Etudes Rabelaisiennes*, edited with such zeal and knowledge by M. Lefranc of the Collège de France.

Now we have reached the end of our task, which your kind forbearance has rendered easy and pleasant. We have made a tour around the giant, and, like the pilgrims in the tale, approached them without fear. Happy am I if I have been able to commend him to you as being as good and lovable as he is great and imposing. It will be an honour to me to have celebrated the French genius before Latins called, in the New World, to a most magnificent destiny. And I take my leave happy and proud of my task if I have been able to contribute, even with so trivial an offering, towards the tightening of the bonds of sympathy which link the spirit of the Argentine to the spirit of France.